Cultural Policy, Innovation and the Creative Economy

Morag Shiach • Tarek Virani
Editors

Cultural Policy, Innovation and the Creative Economy

Creative Collaborations in Arts and Humanities Research

Editors
Morag Shiach
Queen Mary University of London
London, United Kingdom

Tarek Virani
Queen Mary University of London
London, United Kingdom

ISBN 978-1-349-95111-6   ISBN 978-1-349-95112-3 (eBook)
DOI 10.1057/978-1-349-95112-3

Library of Congress Control Number: 2016956415

© The Editor(s) (if applicable) and The Author(s) 2017
The author(s) has/have asserted their right(s) to be identified as the author(s) of this work in accordance with the Copyright, Designs and Patents Act 1988.
This work is subject to copyright. All rights are solely and exclusively licensed by the Publisher, whether the whole or part of the material is concerned, specifically the rights of translation, reprinting, reuse of illustrations, recitation, broadcasting, reproduction on microfilms or in any other physical way, and transmission or information storage and retrieval, electronic adaptation, computer software, or by similar or dissimilar methodology now known or hereafter developed.
The use of general descriptive names, registered names, trademarks, service marks, etc. in this publication does not imply, even in the absence of a specific statement, that such names are exempt from the relevant protective laws and regulations and therefore free for general use.
The publisher, the authors and the editors are safe to assume that the advice and information in this book are believed to be true and accurate at the date of publication. Neither the publisher nor the authors or the editors give a warranty, express or implied, with respect to the material contained herein or for any errors or omissions that may have been made.

Printed on acid-free paper

This Palgrave Macmillan imprint is published by Springer Nature
The registered company is Macmillan Publishers Ltd.
The registered company address is: The Campus, 4 Crinan Street, London, N1 9XW, United Kingdom

Acknowledgements

The research underpinning this book was made possible by funding from the Arts and Humanities Research Council (AHRC) [grant number AH/J005142/1].

The editors would like to acknowledge the many contributions from all team members on the Creativeworks London project to enabling and supporting the work done within the Creative Voucher scheme. The Culture Capital Exchange, as Creativeworks London's knowledge exchange delivery partner, played a key role in the success of this scheme, for which we thank them particularly.

Our sincere thanks go to Jana Riedel, the Creativeworks London Hub Manager, who in addition to her many and varied responsibilities on the project also found time to support key aspects of the editorial work necessary for this volume. We could not have done it without her.

Finally, we are grateful to Rob Waters for his contributions to the final stages of preparation of the volume.

CONTENTS

Introduction 1
Morag Shiach and Tarek Virani

Cultural Policy, Collaboration and Knowledge Exchange 17
Morag Shiach and Tarek Virani

Bringing the Past into the Present: Mobilising Historical
Research Through Creative and Digital Collaboration 31
John Price

Creating Archival Value in a Changing Mediascape:
The "World in a Cube" Project 45
Ian Christie, Wendy Earle, Eleni Liarou, Karen Merkel,
and Akim Mogaji

Consumer as Producer; Value Mechanics in Digital
Transformation Design Process, Practice and Outcomes 61
Karen Cham

Goldsmiths Digital: Research and Innovation in the Creative
Economy 83
Mick Grierson

Getting Inside the Creative Voucher: The Platform-7
Experience 97
Andy Pratt and John McKiernan

Devising Bespoke Art and Design Interventions for a
Dialysis Community 115
Rachel Louis and Luise Vormittag

The BeatWoven Project 133
Noam Shemtov

At Home with Collaboration: Building and Sustaining a
Successful University–Museum Partnership 147
Alastair Owens, Eleanor John, and Alison Blunt

Connections—Movements—Treasures: Unlocking the Potential
of the June Givanni Pan African Cinema Archive 163
Emma Sandon and June Givanni

Process as Outcome: Research Across Borders 179
Caspar Melville

Social Art Map: Reflections on a Creative Collaboration 189
Emily Druiff and Sophie Hope

Making Friends: Childhood, the Cultural Economy and
Creative Collaboration Through Technology 201
Tessa Whitehouse and Emilie Giles

Outside the Voucher: Evaluating the Creative Voucher
Scheme 217
Andy Pratt, Helen Matheson-Pollock, and Tarek Virani

Creative Collaborations: The Role of Networks, Power and Policy 231
Roberta Comunian

Bibliography 245

Index 257

Contributors

Alison Blunt is Professor of Geography at Queen Mary University of London and Co-Director of the Centre for Studies of Home, a joint venture between Queen Mary and the Geffrye Museum of the Home. Her interests span geographies of home, empire, migration and diaspora, including research on imperial domesticity in British India, Anglo-Indian women and the spatial politics of home, and the city as home for people living in diaspora. Alison is Principal Investigator for three AHRC Collaborative Doctoral Award extended programmes: "The Child in the World: Empire, Diaspora and Global Citizenship" (with the V&A [Victoria and Albert Museum] Museum of Childhood), "Home-Work: Connections and Transitions in London from the Seventeenth Century to the Present," and "Home and Religion: Space, Practice and Community in London from the Seventeenth Century to the Present" (both with the Geffrye Museum of the Home).

Karen Cham is a critical design practitioner who works with technology. With a background in experimental electronic arts, she made her first website and touchscreen in 1994, and is an expert in design methods for complex digital products, services, business models and strategies. She is Professor of Digital Transformation Design, a digital-first, design-led, user-centred industrial method for engineering transformation of complex, evolving human-centred systems. Her research concerns narrowing the "semantic gap" in the user experience (UX) by developing emotional engagement methodologies. Current research and design is in nudge mechanics, neuronavigation and neurotransformation.

Ian Christie is Professor of Film and Media History at Birkbeck College, University of London, with a special interest in London films and contemporary archival practice, from his role as a founder of the London's Screen Archives network. As the academic director of the "World in a Cube" project, he worked closely with the film historian Eleni Liarou, who acted as project officer, and Wendy Earle, Birkbeck's Impacts and Knowledge Exchange Manager. Karen Merkel and Akim Mogaji, partners in New Media Networks, made the initial contacts with Tate & Lyle and facilitated much of the research process.

Roberta Comunian is Lecturer in Creative and Cultural Industries at the Department of Culture, Media and Creative Industries at King's College London. Her work focuses on the relationship between arts, cultural regeneration projects, and the cultural and creative industries. She has recently worked on the connections between higher education and the creative economy via an AHRC-funded research network. She has published extensively on the relationship between higher education and the creative economy and on the career opportunities and patterns of creative graduates in the UK.

Emily Druiff is Executive Director of Peckham Platform, and her belief in the power of social arts practice to make contemporary art more relevant to people's everyday lives is what drives the curatorial vision for the organisation. In 2010, she oversaw the capital build and opening of Peckham Space, under the umbrella of University of the Arts London. She has an MA in Curating from Goldsmiths and a BA in Fine Arts from Camberwell College of Arts. She has worked independently as a curator and tutor across Europe, with projects funded by Arts Council, British Council, ARS Electronica and the Prague Biennale, and also co-founded artist-run spaces, contributing to the rich understanding of place, community and cultural activity in Peckham.

Emilie Giles is an artist, producer and educator, with her work spanning creative technology, crafting and pervasive gaming. She is Head of Outreach and Participation at Codasign, an education company that teaches people how to be creative with open-source tools in museums and art galleries. Emilie is also a research student at The Open University, exploring how e-textiles can be used as interactive tools for blind and visually impaired people. She teaches at the University of Westminster as a visiting lecturer, specialising in physical computing for design and media arts.

June Givanni is a film curator, archivist and consultant in African and African diaspora cinema. June is a leader in this sector, where she has worked for over three decades. She has worked with the British Film Institute, where she ran the African and Caribbean Film Unit and published the Black Film Bulletin with Gaylene Gould, and edited the book *Symbolic Narratives/African Cinema*. At the Toronto International Film Festival, she programmed *Planet Africa*, and is known as an expert in the field of Pan-African cinema generally on four continents. June continues programming at international festivals and is currently developing the June Givanni Pan African Cinema Archive (www.junegivannifilmarchive.com) based on collections from her years of working in this field.

Mick Grierson is Director of Creative Computing at Goldsmiths. Grierson co-founded the Goldsmiths Embodied Audiovisual Interaction Group (EAVI) with Marco Gillies and Atau Tanaka. He is involved in a range of research in Creative Computing, including sound, graphics, interaction and accessibility. Grierson runs Goldsmiths Digital, a consultancy that develops core technology and product prototypes for commercial organisations. He led the world's first Massive Open Online Course (MOOC) in Creative Coding, which was also the first MOOC by any English university. Over 150,000 people enrolled. He also contributes to the Coursera specialisation in Responsive Web Development.

Sophie Hope 's practice-based research investigates the uncertain relationships between art and society. Her current projects include hosting dinners about art and politics in the year 1984, exploring physical relationships to immaterial labour and mapping understandings of socially engaged art. She works full time at Birkbeck, University of London, in the Film, Media and Cultural Studies Department, where she completed her PhD: *Participating in the Wrong Way? Practice-Based Research into the Relationships Between Cultural Democracy and Commissioning Art to Effect Social Change*.

Eleanor John is Director of Collections, Learning and Engagement at the Geffrye Museum of the Home and Co-Director of the Centre for Studies of Home, a joint venture between the Geffrye Museum and Queen Mary University of London. She manages the exhibition programme at the Geffrye, producing a wide range of exhibitions engaging with home. Her research interests concentrate on the homes of London's middling sorts in the seventeenth and eighteenth centuries.

Rachel Louis is a creative producer who supports relationships between artists and communities, to inspire creativity and engagement in those who may not traditionally access the arts, in spaces where art would not normally be encountered. Rachel develops projects which place an emphasis on the shared creative process. She designs dynamic projects to engage wider audiences, creating opportunities to explore, perform, exhibit, curate and commission. Rachel's mission is to get more people to experience and be inspired by the arts by actively taking part in creative opportunities in the places where they live. London born, Rachel lives in Bergen, Norway.

Helen Matheson-Pollock was the Evaluation and Dissemination Officer at Creativeworks London from 2015 to 2016. She has a PhD in Renaissance Studies from University College London and has published on early modern women and political engagement.

John McKiernan is a producer for *Platform 7 Events*, an abstract live art events network, creating innovative, provocative and thought-provoking interventions discussing social issues in the public realm.

Caspar Melville is a lecturer in the School of Arts and convenor of the MA in Global Creative & Cultural Industries at the School of Oriental and African Studies (SOAS), University of London. He has worked as a music journalist for numerous publications, including *Blues & Soul* and *Touch* magazine, served as executive editor for the political debate website openDemocracy.net and for seven years served as the editor of *New Humanist* magazine and Chief Executive of the Rationalist Association. His first book, *Taking Offence*, was published in 2009.

Alastair Owens is Professor of Historical Geography at Queen Mary University of London. His research focuses on the material cultures of Victorian domesticity and the social history of investment and wealth holding in late nineteenth- and early twentieth-century Britain. He is currently working on a book about families, inheritance and "wealth fare" in Britain, 1850–1930. Collaboration with organisations outside of academia is a key feature of Alastair's research and he is currently involved in funded partnerships with the Bank of England, Geffrye Museum of the Home, Ragged School Museum and the V&A Museum of Childhood. He also co-edits the *Journal of Victorian Culture*.

Andy Pratt is Professor of Cultural Economy and Director of the Centre for Culture and the Creative Industries at City, University of London. Andy specialises in the analysis of the cultural industries globally. This research has three strands. The first focuses on the social and economic dynamics of clustering and knowledge exchange. The second strand concerns the definition and measurement of employment in the cultural, or creative, industries. The third concerns urban and national cultural policy and evaluation. Andy has worked as a consultant or advisor for national and urban cultural and creative industry policy makers, and the European Union (EU), United Nations Educational, Scientific and Cultural Organization (UNESCO), United Nations Conference on Trade and Development (UNCTAD), and World Intellectual Property Organization (WIPO) and the British Council.

John Price is Lecturer in Modern British History at Goldsmiths, University of London, and Research Officer at the University of Roehampton. John has published widely on the topic of civilian heroism, including *Heroes of Postman's Park: Heroic Self-Sacrifice in Victorian London* (2015) and *Everyday Heroism: Victorian Constructions of the Heroic Civilian* (2014). His other research interests include the history of social movements and popular protest, the history of London, and learning and teaching practices in higher education. John is a Senior Fellow of the Higher Education Academy, a Fellow of the Royal Historical Society and the Chairman of the Friends of the Watts Memorial.

Emma Sandon lectures in film and television at Birkbeck, University of London. Her research publications are on British colonial film and photography, early British television history and South African film history. She was on the core management team of the Colonial Film: Moving Images of the British Empire project, http://www.colonialfilm.org.uk, and is on the steering group of the Women's Film and Television History Network (UK), https://womensfilmandtelevisionhistory.wordpress.com. She is an Honorary Research Fellow of the Archive and Public Culture Research Initiative at the University of Cape Town and a research associate to the Chair of Social Change at the University of Johannesburg.

Noam Shemtov is Senior Lecturer in Intellectual Property and Technology Law at the Centre for Commercial Law Studies (CCLS) at Queen Mary University of London. His interest areas include intellectual property (IP) and the creative industries, IP and digitisation, and open-source software. He is a visiting academic in universities in Spain, France and the Netherlands, where he lectures on IP in his areas of interest. Noam is a qualified solicitor both in the UK and in Israel.

Morag Shiach is Director of Creativeworks London, and also Professor of Cultural History in the School of English and Drama at Queen Mary University of London. Her research expertise is in the cultural history of modernism, cultural representations of labour, theorisations of "popular culture," and knowledge exchange and the creative economy.

Tarek Virani has been a postdoctoral research assistant on the Place/Work/Knowledge research strand of Creativeworks London since 2012. He has a PhD in Human Geography/Cultural and Creative Industries, and has published extensively on creative innovation clusters and on relations between universities and the creative industries.

Luise Vormittag is a London-based artist, designer, illustrator and educator with a particular emphasis on participatory and collaborative approaches. She has completed a number of projects in health-care environments working with patient and community groups. From 2002 to 2014 she practised under the name Container in various collaborative constellations, completing a broad range of commissions for national and international clients. She now works as a lecturer at Central Saint Martins on the Graphic Communication Design Programme and is studying towards a PhD at the London College of Communication.

Tessa Whitehouse is Lecturer in Eighteenth-Century Literature at Queen Mary University of London. She is the author of *The Textual Culture of English Protestant Dissent 1720–1800* (Oxford University Press, 2015) as well as of articles and chapters on publishing history, transatlantic friendships and religious literature. She directs the Queen Mary Centre for Religion and Literature in English, is a founding member of the Digital Initiatives Network, convenes the "Concepts and Practices of Friendship" research network, and has contributed to the BBC Radio 4 series "500 Years of Friendship" (2014). In 2015 she collaborated on the award-winning Ragged School Museum exhibition "Ragged Children, Mended Lives?"

List of Figures

Fig. 1 "What have we here?" (Professor Ian Christie from Birkbeck, Akim Mogaji from New Media Networks together with researcher, Frances Bull, at the Tate & Lyle Refinery in Silvertown, East London, beginning work on the World in a Cube) 47
Fig. 1 Process flow diagram that differentiates co-design for a user completion model (2013) 76
Fig. 1 Selina's Bangladeshi fish curry recipe card 127
Fig. 1 An example of a fabric design created by Nadia-Anne Ricketts, proprietor and designer of BeatWoven, based on Tchaikovsky's Nutcracker (Tchaikovsky's work is no longer protected by copyright, whose term of protection is 70 years after the author of the work died, and therefore does not pose a problem.) 137
Fig. 1 Period room "intervention," part of "Swept under the Carpet: Servants in London Households, 1600–2000," Geffrye Museum of the Home, 15 March to 4 September 2016 (Credit: © Geffrye Museum of the Home) 156

List of Tables

Table 1	Creative Voucher rounds aligned to Ideas Pools themes	4
Table 2	The eleven stages in the Creative Voucher process	6
Table 1	Example of variation in voucher types	22
Table 1	Insights from interview with Ann Granger	118
Table 2	Common complaints by patients	118
Table 3	Project ideas	122
Table 1	Centre for Studies of Home: main activities	151
Table 2	Centre for Studies of Home–funded projects, 2011–16	153
Table 3	Case study	155
Table 1	Participants in the "Making Friends" Idea Forum	206
Table 1	Proportion of attendees, to applicants, to awards	224

Introduction

Morag Shiach and Tarek Virani

This volume of essays draws on the work and the research findings of Creativeworks London.[1] Creativeworks London is a Knowledge Exchange Hub for the creative and cultural economy, whose aims are to build new and productive relationships between arts and humanities researchers and the creative economy in London, and to generate research findings that will have a major impact on that economy. Between 2012 and 2016, Creativeworks London received £4 million of funding from the UK's Arts and Humanities Research Council (AHRC), and was thus able to develop a number of innovative funding schemes to promote collaboration between academic researchers and small- and medium-sized enterprises (SMEs). Through a range of funding schemes it was able to support co-created research that addressed diverse research questions and contributed directly to the business needs of a range of companies within the creative economy in London, and led to a number of collaborative projects between creative SMEs and academics.

Regarding its structure, Creativeworks London is a partnership of twenty-one universities and independent research institutions and twenty-two organisations in the creative and cultural economy, including its

M. Shiach (✉) • Tarek Virani
Queen Mary University of London, London, UK

© The Author(s) 2017
M. Shiach, Tarek Virani (eds.), *Cultural Policy, Innovation and the Creative Economy*, DOI 10.1057/978-1-349-95112-3_1

knowledge exchange delivery partner, The Culture Capital Exchange. Creativeworks London has focused its research on three main areas, based on the needs of London's creative economy and the expertise of its research leads: Andy Pratt (City, University of London); Barry Ife (Guildhall School of Music and Drama); John Sloboda (Guildhall School of Music and Drama); Mark Plumbley (University of Surrey); and Geraint Wiggins (Queen Mary University of London). Its research has thus focused on the cultural geographies of innovation, the changing nature of London's audiences, and modes of innovation within the digital economy. These three research areas, which have led to an exciting range of books, articles, working papers, films, and other forms of dissemination, have also crucially informed one key element of Creativeworks London funding for collaborative research: its Creative Voucher scheme.

The Creative Voucher scheme was an innovation voucher scheme designed to facilitate the building of research partnerships between academics and SMEs, based on models of co-creation and knowledge exchange. As will be discussed in much more detail in the chapter "Cultural Policy, Collaboration and Knowledge Exchange", there is significant policy interest in the impacts of voucher schemes, especially in Europe, that are designed to support growth within the creative economy, particularly through co-created and collaborative research with universities. Creative Vouchers were awarded over seven different rounds between 2012 and 2014, and were closely linked to one of the three research areas outlined above. Participants involved in a project seeking support through a creative voucher could apply for up to £15,000 in funding with a maximum of £10,000 going to the academic institution and £5000 to the SME. Creativeworks London supported fifty-one Creative Voucher projects in total between 2012 and 2014,[2] and this volume of essays builds on what was learned by academics and by SMEs and creative entrepreneurs as a result of participating in thirteen of these projects.

The research methodologies employed within these partnerships are varied; and the outcomes also range, for example, from new business models to new technologies, different modes of audience engagement, or more accessible archives. Not all of the collaborations discussed in this book were in a straightforward sense "successful," but all have generated significant insights into the conditions that enable or constrain effective collaborations between arts and humanities researchers and SMEs in the creative economy. The aim of this volume is to provide insights into how collaborative research can happen on the ground: who is involved; how is the research relationship curated; what are the barriers to productive collaboration; and what does success look like for each partner?

There are a number of recent studies of knowledge exchange in relation to the creative economy that raise issues relevant to this volume, such as James Leach and Lee Wilson's, *Subversion, Conversion, Development* (2014), and Jay Mitra and John Edmondson's *Entrepreneurship and Knowledge Exchange* (2015).[3] The first of these examines specific cases where forms of knowledge and cross-cultural encounters are shaping technology use and development. While creative and digital technologies are also important for many of the projects discussed in this volume, it deliberately covers a much broader range of case studies in terms of the different sectors of the creative economy that are discussed. Similarly, although entrepreneurship is an important focus within this volume of essays, it is more concerned with the possibilities of collaborative research between universities and the creative industries than with the educational mission of universities discussed by Mitra and Edmondson.

As will be explored in the chapter "Cultural Policy, Collaboration and Knowledge Exchange" later in this book, there is also a considerable existing literature examining the design and impact of innovation voucher schemes of various sorts. For example, Hasan Bakhshi et al.'s, *Creative Credits* (2013) is one of a significant number of policy reports addressing the impact of specific innovation voucher schemes, which have been of particular interest to policy makers and funders.[4] The design and implementation of Creativeworks London's Creative Voucher scheme were certainly influenced by schemes such as NESTA's creative credits, but Creativeworks London also developed a distinctive approach based on various forms of curation of and close support for the collaborative research relationships it built.[5] The importance of such curation and support emerges clearly across the chapters that follow.

The curation process for the Creative Voucher scheme hinged importantly on what were termed "Ideas Pools." These events brought together around 100 researchers and creative industry companies and cultural entrepreneurs. Creativeworks London's knowledge exchange delivery partner, The Culture Capital Exchange organised these Ideas Pools in collaboration with Creativeworks London researchers, where both drew on their already developed networks of creative SMEs and academics. Ideas Pools were designed to identify the key business challenges associated with seven specific themes (see Table 1) and also to share ideas and approaches developed by researchers that were relevant

Table 1 Creative Voucher rounds aligned to Ideas Pools themes

Voucher round	Theme and description	Date of Ideas Pools and location (vouchers awarded nine weeks after Ideas Pools)
Round One	Mobile Culture: The Creative Industries are highly mobile and rely on mobility of people, projects, ideas, and products. They also increasingly utilise mobile technologies and apps as part of core business so much so that it is becoming the new norm. With this come fresh opportunities, challenges, needs, and responsibilities.	November 30, 2012. Birkbeck University. London.
Round Two	Co-Creation: As audiences and consumers look for more creative and personally meaningful ways to interact with culture, and to bring their own creativity to bear in the course of their experiences new challenges are thrown up for creative businesses. What effect is the move towards "mass customisation" having on your business? Are you able to meet the expectation of your customers for increased input and communication? What is the impact on your internal creative process? How can you exploit this desire for increased involvement with the creative process to bring you closer to your audience and develop new business models?	December 11, 2012. The Abbey Centre, London.
Round Three	Localities: The aim of this particular Ideas Pool is to pin down exactly how "place matters," why it matters, for whom, and in what circumstances, in the field of the creative economy. There is a growing body of research on the creative industries that acknowledges the relationship between place and creativity. The focus is almost entirely on creativity as a collective or social process and largely concentrates on creativity as a product of interactions within clusters of creative firms.	March 7, 2013. Rich Mix, Shoreditch, London.
Round Four	Open Round: The Open Call is open to those who have ideas for collaborative research projects that have not so far fitted into any specific theme covered by the Creative Vouchers competition so far.	May 29, 2013. Rich Mix, Shoreditch, London.

(*continued*)

Table 1 (continued)

Voucher round	Theme and description	Date of Ideas Pools and location (vouchers awarded nine weeks after Ideas Pools)
Round Five	Archives: Ideas Pools involve thinking about archives in the twenty-first century, including: the increasing digitising of cultural assets to create archives; the potential to link archives to consumers and other interested parties; digital curation in its widest sense; archives preservation; informal or hidden/unrecognised archives; and archives as assets.	October 7, 2013. St Bride Foundation. Fleet Street, London.
Round Six	Demonstrating Value: A brief look at current initiatives makes it apparent that the Arts and Creative Industries are currently exploring major changes in the way we think about value: How can we capture "value"? What would you like to be able to measure that you currently cannot? How can we develop what we do to more strongly provide the value we seek? How can we demonstrate that our work does meet the values that we espouse?	January 23, 2014. Rich Mix, Shoreditch, London.
Round Seven	Networks: Is networking "organic" to cultural and creative industries? Are creative entrepreneurs by their nature established and proficient networkers? Where are the gaps in the networks and what kinds of organisations could be involved in such networks to mutual benefit? Are networks place- or space-based or digital and what works? How do SMEs network now? What kinds of networks help you (the SME) do what you do? How do networks help SMEs change or grow?	May 28, 2014. St Bride Foundation, Fleet Street, London.

to these challenges. Developing the themes was a vital first step since it meant that "bridge-building" and "brokering" could begin by aligning broader concerns for academics and SMEs around these specific areas—in whatever way they were understood by both parties. All awardees surveyed by the Creativeworks London evaluation team at the end of the scheme indicated that they found the Ideas Pools an essential and valuable part of the Creative Voucher process because of the collaborations forged, both with their project partners but also with others with whom they might consider working in future.

The involvement of Creativeworks London's postdoctoral researchers in Ideas Pools and subsequent roundtables and workshops was also praised during the post-project evaluations as encouraging engaged discussion that linked the specific projects undertaken to the wider research questions being explored. The Creative Voucher scheme as a whole had generated 191 outputs by April 2016, including new processes, apps, prototypes, software, research reports, and journal articles. Business impacts include new business models and new design approaches. Social and environmental impacts of the Creative Voucher scheme have included enhancing democratic citizenship, improving health and well-being through arts interventions, and articulating alternative models of cultural value. The essays in this volume have been chosen to reflect this diversity of approach, outcome, and impact as well as to illustrate the different modes of collaboration that were enabled by the Creative Voucher scheme.

The design and implementation of each round within the Creative Voucher scheme was broken down into eleven stages, and the whole cycle for each Voucher round lasted nearly a year. All steps in this process were designed to make the process as "light touch" as possible, while enabling rigorous evaluation of the importance, feasibility, and potential impact of the collaborative research being funded. See Table 2 for the eleven stages in the Creative Voucher process.[6]

Table 2 The eleven stages in the Creative Voucher process

Stage 1	Announcement/Call for Creative Voucher Round (week 1)
Stage 2	Ideas Pool with TCCE/Research Leads/PDRAs & Notice Boards for SMEs and Academics (week 8)
Stage 3	Application Workshop (including session on Collaboration) (week 12)
Stage 4	Draft application feedback (week 13–15)
Stage 5	Application awarded by panel (week 17)
Stage 6	Feedback to non-successful applications (week 18)
Stage 7	Signature of Contract (including IP Agreement) (week 19–20)
Stage 8	QMUL payment of 50 % of SME award (week 19–20)
Stage 9	Project Delivery (week 20–36/44; based on 4–6 months' delivery)
Stage 10	Final report (week 37/45)
Stage 11	QMUL payment of final grant awards to SME and HEI (week 38–39/46–47)

In commissioning this current volume of essays, our thinking has been significantly shaped by the ideas and arguments in Cathy Brickwood et al.'s *(Un)Common Ground: Creative Encounters Across Sectors and Disciplines*.[7] This 2007 volume also emerged from a specific moment of encounter between researchers from a range of disciplinary backgrounds and contexts, thinking through the theoretical and practical issues related to collaboration, creativity, and cultural policy. Brickwood articulates an important word of caution and challenge in the Preface to *(Un)Common Ground*, noting:

> The explosive growth, not just in interdisciplinary practice but in creative collaborations across whole *sectors* including business, art, design, the public sector and academia, requires collaborative practice to become less ad hoc and more strategically informed.[8]

In assembling the essays in this current volume, we have been keen to rise to this challenge and to offer connected insights into the mechanisms of collaboration beyond ad hoc encounters, and also to explore the affective elements of collaboration that might enable or constrain successful outcomes. Understanding of these dynamics within the detail of specific collaborations is essential to the development of a more strategic approach to university and industry collaborations.

The diversity of the collaborations explored in this book is striking; with many researchers finding themselves working with partners from sectors of the creative economy that may have seemed quite remote to them and with SMEs finding partners in academic disciplines whose methods initially might have seemed unfamiliar. This echoes the findings in *(Un)Common Ground,* as David Garcia argues in the "Introduction" that rather than a search for "common ground" being necessary to underpin productive collaborations: "Rather, many of the most creative encounters were in fact founded on a willingness, even a desire, to occupy *uncommon ground.*"[9] Creativeworks London had a specific aim of reaching out to a wide range of academic disciplines within the arts and humanities, and it was inherent in this ambition that both the researchers and SMEs that were funded needed to be willing to move beyond comfortable common ground, and work in new ways with new partners.

Finally, the ideas explored in *(Un)Common Ground* have also led to our commitment to including reflection on the more uncomfortable aspects of collaboration in some essays within this volume. As Anne Galloway argues in the final and fascinating essay in *(Un)Common Ground*, "Seams and Scars, or How to Locate Accountability in Collaborative work" the finished outputs of a creative collaboration need to be seen in relation to the preceding phases where co-creation was not obvious, where different perspectives were not able to meet, and where damage and pain may have resulted. Galloway writes of seams and scars as different forms of veiling or covering these uncomfortable aspects of collaboration, as marking "the places where different subjects and objects were separated and connected."[10] In assembling the essays in this volume we have been keen to let the seams and scars show, recognising, as is more fully discussed by Roberta Comunian in the chapter "Creative Collaborations: The Role of Networks, Power and Policy", the ethical issues involved in doing so.

In the chapter "Cultural Policy, Collaboration and Knowledge Exchange", Morag Shiach and Tarek Virani (Queen Mary, University of London) set out the policy context and landscape under which the Creative Voucher scheme was developed as well as describing the significant differences between this scheme and others that have been classed under the rubric of "innovation voucher schemes." Shiach and Virani usefully point out that while voucher schemes have been around since the early to mid-1990s and their specific raison d'être has not always been uniform, their ease of implementation and their "nudging" of two sectors of the economy together—sectors that usually do not have ease-of-access to each other—are potentially their most attractive qualities. Not least because, as others have pointed out, co-creation and collaborative journeys need a starting point, or a catalytic spark which gives individuals and organisations "permission" to collaborate, while making it worth their while fiscally.

In the chapter "Bringing the Past into the Present: Mobilising Historical Research Through Creative and Digital Collaboration", John Price (Goldsmiths, University of London) explores the transformative potential of providing targeted information and enhancing experiences through interactive interpretation delivered via mobile devices. It is about how this collaboration uses mobile devices to bring the Watts Memorial to Heroic Self-Sacrifice in Postman's Park (a small park nested within the City of London) to life. This voucher collaboration came together under the theme "mobile culture" which has been increasingly recognised across the arts and humanities, particularly in relation to social and cultural history, memory, heritage, and identity. Furthermore, the wealth of technological research and development being undertaken clearly represents an important opportunity for collaborations between the creative digital industries and arts and humanities researchers and academics. This chapter documents one such collaboration and illustrates how these partnerships can revolutionise public engagement with research, transform dissemination and impact beyond traditional academic channels, and deliver a wealth of new knowledge, experience and skills to all those involved.

In the chapter "Creating Archival Value in a Changing Mediascape: The 'World in a Cube' Project", Ian Christie et al. (Birkbeck) detail a pioneering, three-way collaboration between: the social entrepreneur New Media Networks, Tate & Lyle Sugars, and Birkbeck, University of London. This collaboration points towards the potential for developing new archival resources, and understanding the multiple roles of film in twentieth-century industry. This voucher collaboration also came together under the theme of "mobile culture." The project team took an "action research" approach which allowed them to explore and evaluate effective ways to reach contributors through live participation and digital exhibition and distribution. They explored how live and digital experiences can create access to an archival collection, contribute new interpretations through public discussion, and generate opportunities for people to use their cultural products (the films) creatively.

In the following chapter "Consumer as Producer; Value Mechanics in Digital Transformation Design Process, Practice and Outcomes", Karen Cham (University of Brighton) aims to explore the potential for interaction between high-end fashion accessory designers and their customers in the design process as part of a prototype product customisation platform and the possibilities afforded by integrating "user generate content" (UGC) into the design process. However, this collaboration seemed to—as the author states in the chapter—"dissolve into a shifting miasma of competing perspectives on the perceived value of the cultural capital of the process and project itself." This important chapter explores how competing views, different incentive structures, and lack of translation in collaborative processes can have damaging consequences for all parties involved. It exposes the substantial clashes between "mass market commercial demands" and "high-end design." This collaboration came under the theme of "co-creation" which looked at the blurred boundaries between consumption, customisation, production, and creative collaboration.

In "Goldsmiths Digital: Research and Innovation in the Creative Economy", Mick Grierson (Goldsmiths) discusses his setting up of Goldsmiths Digital—"a research-led practice initiative to provide consultancy and contract research services to the Creative Economy sector, the primary outputs of which would be software and hardware prototypes" and some of the inherent successes as well as trials and tribulations of working within the constructs of the higher education complex. He provides a case study of his Creative Voucher collaboration discussing the goal of creating a "brand awareness remix app" to support the release of an album by The Fish Police—a band fronted by autistic rock star, Dean Rodney, who works closely with Heart n Soul, the Deptford-based disability arts charity. This collaboration also came under the co-creation theme.

"Getting Inside the Creative Voucher: The Platform-7 Experience", sees Andy Pratt (City, University of London) and John McKiernan (Platform 7/Creative Publics) detail their use of a Creative Voucher collaboration to reflect on "the very experience of using a creative voucher" through an event called "Silent Cacophony" curated and created by an organisation called Platform 7. They employ a perspective, through reflection, on the process rather than the outcomes. In this chapter they interrogate the process of "knowledge exchange" and its link to a "final product or process" while at the same time also interrogating the notion (or lack thereof) of locality—the theme under which this voucher was awarded. The argument, quoted from the authors, "is that the other processes (intended and unintended) that surround (or constitute) the voucher need to be included in what we might call the 'voucher experience.'" Importantly, the authors combine voucher policy, knowledge exchange policy, and their collaborative journey to provide a robust and critical rethinking of what collaboration in this arena must at times negotiate with.

In "Devising Bespoke Art and Design Interventions for a Dialysis Community", Rachel Louis (Vital Arts) and Luise Vormittag (Central Saint Martins/UAL) discuss the transformation of a micro-locality—in this case the Renal Dialysis Unit at the Royal London Hospital in Whitechapel, East London. The chapter details the many steps necessary for the creation of a dialysis cookbook in order to transform the experience of those undergoing treatment. Specifically this collaboration allowed the authors to explore ways of improving this micro-locality through activities and design interventions that engage and enrich patients' experience of being in hospital, creating a positive environment and a sense of place and community. This collaboration also came under the locality theme.

In "The BeatWoven Project", Noam Shemtov (Queen Mary University of London) discusses the issue of copyright for a company called

BeatWoven which translates music into woven textiles. This collaboration came under the "Open Round" where Creativeworks London did not announce a specific theme. As Shemtov explains "the process at issue concerns a textile designer who is utilising another person's work in his/her transformative creation process, while generating his/her own original creative expression." This chapter explores in a rounded way the issue at hand and asks whether or not our current copyright laws are equipped to deal with the ever quickening pace of change regarding digitisation and copyright.

In "At Home with Collaboration: Building and Sustaining a Successful University–Museum Partnership", Alastair Owens et al. (Queen Mary University of London) discuss the partnership between a university (Queen Mary University of London) and a museum (The Geffrye Museum of the Home), in their chosen collaborative project on "archives." They state that while "universities and museums do have many things in common, it is also the differences and the complementarities of their aims, missions and reach that provide opportunities for strong and mutually beneficial partnerships." This chapter describes their partnership, reflecting on the nature of collaboration, as well as considering the benefits and challenges of universities and museums working together.

"Connections—Movements—Treasures: Unlocking the Potential of the June Givanni Pan African Cinema Archive" examines the collaboration between June Givanni, independent archive curator, and Emma Sandon (Birkbeck). The collaboration was funded not only by a creative voucher but also through Creativeworks London's follow-on funding scheme, BOOST. It has explored and enhanced the potential of the *June Givanni Pan-African Cinema Archive* (JGPACA) to function as a publically available and sustainable resource. JGPACA was able to orchestrate a series of artistic events that showcased the archive, demonstrating its unique cultural and historical value, and to create a business plan and model for its long-term sustainability. This project also came under the archives theme.

In "Process as Outcome: Research Across Borders", Caspar Melville (School of Oriental and African Studies—SOAS) discusses his collaboration with Carthage Music. This collaboration revolved around global music copyright laws and issues where a specialist music publisher representing many repertoires from outside the Western world, especially West African music, needed a better understanding of how copyright could be made to work better for them and their catalogue of artists. This chapter narrates this collaboration which came under the "demonstrating value" theme.

In the following chapter "Social Art Map: Reflections on a Creative Collaboration", Emily Druiff (Peckham Platform) and Sophie Hope (Birkbeck College) respond to a set of questions about their collaborative work on the Social Art Map. The pair reflect on their motives for collaborating, their experiences of the process, and challenges it raised for them as a commissioner and director of an arts organisation and a researcher in a university. As an example of "creative collaboration" they also explore the meaning and relevance of bridging the gap between research and practice in a political context, which promotes the "creative economy." This collaboration came under the "networks" theme.

"Making Friends: Childhood, the Cultural Economy and Creative Collaboration Through Technology" describes a pilot project developed in collaboration between Tessa Whitehouse (Queen Mary University of London) and Emilie Giles (Codasign). It explored historically informed research questions about childhood friendships and technology through hands-on electronics-based creative activities with children. The project, entitled "Making Friends," is now an exciting and ongoing collaboration between humanities researchers, creative technologists, children, and museums, the aim of which is to create open spaces for idea-sharing and activity development which were informed by the research. The children participated in three workshops and a presentation afternoon while the adults were invited to two sessions that were called "Idea Forum" workshops.

A broad analysis is staged in "Outside the Voucher: Evaluating the Creative Voucher Scheme", where Andy Pratt, Helen Matheson-Pollock, and Tarek Virani (Queen Mary University of London) elaborate on the complexities of implanting and then delivering and evaluating Creativeworks London's Creative Voucher scheme. They describe what made the project difficult, and the fact that while innovation voucher schemes are in the policy instrument mainstream, "creative" vouchers were something untried and untested at the start of the Creativeworks London project in 2012. To understand the real value and impacts achieved, an evaluation framework encompassing a diverse range of impact types needed to be developed. This chapter describes some of the evaluation tools used to understand these impacts as well as some lessons learned regarding how to evaluate knowledge exchange initiatives in the arts and humanities.

Finally, in the chapter "Creative Collaborations: The Role of Networks, Power and Policy", Roberta Comunian (King's College London) reflects on the emergence of creative collaboration between higher education and the creative economy with particular emphasis on the role of networks, power, and policy in their establishment and development. While many authors argue for the value of an organic, grassroots development of creative collaborations and networks, recently a lot of investment and attention have been placed by policy (both higher education and economic development policy) to the value of creating and expanding a range of mechanisms of interaction and collaboration across universities and the creative economy for the benefit of participation, cultural development, and the economy. The chapter explores these dynamics and their importance to future developments in this field.

In summary, the diversity of the collaborations explored in this book is key to its contribution to important policy and research questions. Private and public funders of regeneration and development, investors in the creative economy, and national and international research funders, have all recognised the importance of the role the creative economy currently plays in enabling economic growth and regeneration, engaging communities and supporting citizenship, and ensuring that cities are not only smart but also liveable spaces. They have also recognised the role that universities and other research organisations can play in enabling this, as long as appropriate ecosystems to build and sustain such partnerships can be created. This volume captures the fine-grained detail and the complexity of a range of partnerships that have enabled innovative and co-created research, with benefits for researchers, SMEs, and creative entrepreneurs. It digs beneath generic assumptions about what motivates different partners in such collaborations, to uncover the diversity of the creative encounters necessary to drive innovation.

The work this book explores was enabled by Creativeworks London, whose aims are to build new and productive relationships between art and humanities researchers and the creative economy in London, and to generate research findings that have a major impact on that economy. Across the volume, contributors demonstrate how disciplinary contexts shape their collaborations, and how innovation vouchers can be used to address diverse business needs and produce significant impacts for businesses and for researchers. The different chapters are designed to showcase the range and diversity of work that can emerge in co-created research between universities and SMEs in the creative economy, and in so doing also to highlight important characteristics of the collaborative projects undertaken in this context. As readers will notice many of the chapters are purposefully reflective in order to allow the "story" of collaboration to come through. This story takes many different forms across the various projects, but the central narrative desire for innovation, new ideas, and new ways of working is compelling.

Notes

1. Further information about Creativeworks London can be found at http://www.creativeworkslondon.org.uk/.
2. Fuller discussion of the Creativeworks London's Creative Voucher scheme can be found in Helen Matheson-Pollock, *Creativeworks London: A Knowledge Exchange Hub for the Creative Economy 2012-2016* (London: CWL, 2016), http://www.creativeworkslondon.org.uk/cw-news/creativeworks-london-evaluation-report-a-knowledge-exchange-hub-for-the-creative-economy/.
3. James Leach and Lee Wilson, *Subversion, Conversion, Development: Cross-Cultural Knowledge Exchange and the Politics of Design (Infrastructures)* (Boston: MIT Press, 2014); Jay Mitra and John Edmondson, *Entrepreneurship and Knowledge Exchange* (London: Routledge, 2015).
4. Hasan Bakhshi, John Edwards, Stephen Roper, Judy Scully, Duncan Shaw, Lorraine Morley and Nicola Rathbone, *Creative Credits: A Randomized Controlled Industrial Policy Experiment* (London: Nesta, 2013).
5. See Tarek Virani, "Do voucher schemes matter in the long run? A brief comparison of Nesta's Creative Credits and Creativeworks London's Creative Voucher schemes" (Creativeworks London Working Paper No. 10, Creativeworks London/Queen Mary, University of London, 2015), https://qmro.qmul.ac.uk/xmlui/bitstream/handle/123456789/6693/Working%20Paper%2010.pdf?sequence=2.
6. See Morag Shiach, Jana Riedel and Jasmina Bolfek-Radovani, "Fusing and Creating: A Comparative Analysis of the Knowledge Exchange Methodologies Underpinning Creativeworks London's Creative Vouchers and London Creative and Digital Fusion's Collaborative Awards" (Creativeworks London Working Paper No. 25, Creativeworks London/Queen Mary, University of

London, 2014), https://qmro.qmul.ac.uk/xmlui/bitstream/handle/123456789/11413/Shiach%20Fusing%20and%20Creating%202014%20Published.pdf?sequence=1.
7. Cathy Brickwood, Bronac Ferran, David Garcia, and Tim Putnam, eds., *(Un)Common Ground: Creative Encounters Across Sectors and Disciplines* (Amsterdam: BIS Publishing, 2007).
8. Cathy Brickwood, "Preface," in ibid., 6.
9. David Garcia, "Introduction," in *(Un)Common Ground*, 9.
10. Anne Galloway, "Seams and Scars, or How to Locate Accountability in Collaborative work," in *(Un)Common Ground*, 153.

Cultural Policy, Collaboration and Knowledge Exchange

Morag Shiach and Tarek Virani

The essays in this volume all emerge from projects that were developed within and funded by Creativeworks London's Creative Voucher scheme, which has been a central element of its research and knowledge exchange activities undertaken over the past four years (2012–2016). This scheme enabled SMEs in London's creative sector to develop short-term, collaborative research and development activities with Creativeworks London's academic partners and independent research organisations (IROs).[1] The scheme was primarily designed to foster university-industry collaborations for small amounts of money, expedited and implemented in a quick and easy manner. It is a variant of "innovation voucher schemes"—which will be described in more detail later—and follows the same trajectory and logic. From 2012 to 2014 Creativeworks London awarded 51 vouchers aimed at fostering collaborations between creative SMEs and higher education institutions (HEIs) and IROs in London.[2] The diversity of the potential impacts of the Creative Voucher scheme was understood from the outset, and even at the point of applying to the Arts and Humanities Research Council for funding in 2011 the case was made that:

M. Shiach (✉) • Tarek Virani
Queen Mary University of London, London, UK

© The Author(s) 2017
M. Shiach, Tarek Virani (eds.), *Cultural Policy, Innovation and the Creative Economy*, DOI 10.1057/978-1-349-95112-3_2

> Our KE brokerage will [take place] through schemes such as Creative Vouchers (modelled on NESTA's creative credits) that allow SMEs access to HEI expertise as a taster for further interactions, including access to collaborative research opportunities, skills and space, new forms of mentorship and creative lab time.[3]

There is significant cultural policy interest in the impacts of what have been termed generally "innovation voucher schemes." These schemes are designed to boost innovation and support growth within primarily the SME sector and particularly through co-created and collaborative research with knowledge providers like universities. Such schemes touch on models for university/business engagement; the idea of the university as an "anchor institution"; and also on the potential impact of small levels of investment on growth and innovation. Similarly, and especially in the UK, there has been significant policy interest in extending the reach and activity of the creative and cultural industries (CCI) by focusing on the creative SME—voucher schemes have been a way to realise and marry these policy ambitions. One of the first voucher schemes to target the creative sector specifically was NESTA's "Creative Credits" scheme.[4]

Creativeworks London originally suggested that its voucher scheme would resemble NESTA's Creative Credits, which were designed to be "a new model for supporting innovation and growth within small to medium enterprises (SMEs) through knowledge transfer from creative businesses."[5] NESTA's scheme was piloted in the Manchester City Region in 2009–10, and was based on the idea that SMEs might be "nudged" towards enhanced innovation through working with creative companies of various sorts.[6] Both the Economic and Social Research Council (ESRC) and the AHRC were partners on the Creative Credits project, suggesting that they believed it would also have a beneficial impact on the research base in arts, humanities and social sciences. The Creative Credits scheme built on insights within a 2008 NESTA Report into the ways that the creative industries support and enhance innovation across the wider economy.[7] This being said, while Creativeworks London's scheme initially modelled itself on NESTA's there were significant differences between them.

This chapter will thus explore the extent to which this stated affiliation to NESTA's Creative Credits scheme actually played out in the scheme's final design and implementation, and will argue that there are important policy implications that emerge from the ways in which the methodology was refined between the 2011 funding bid and the award of the final round of Creative Vouchers in 2014. This chapter will first lay out the policy landscape regarding innovation voucher schemes and then will discuss how Creativeworks London's Creative Voucher scheme differed from NESTA's Creative Credits and the possible policy ramifications of this for the creative sector.

Innovation voucher schemes, and their many variants, have become very popular "innovation policy instruments" in Europe in the last 20 or so years. Their raison d'être is quite straightforward—and is built on the insight that SMEs may have limited exposure to public knowledge providers and research organisations (like HEIs) and may also see these institutions as either irrelevant to their business activities or simply out of reach.[8] Knowledge providers (a term that covers a range of innovation and research-based organisations, including universities) on the other hand are more familiar with, and also more used to working with, public agencies and larger companies as opposed to SMEs. Thus the general aim of many voucher programmes is to build new relationships between SMEs and knowledge providers to stimulate knowledge transfer/exchange and to act as a "catalyst" for the formation of collaborative relationships based on innovation and competitiveness.[9]

The basic premise behind innovation vouchers is that they represent a "light touch" intervention where scrutiny and accountability need not necessarily be as extensive (or cumbersome) as may be necessary with other types of policy instruments. Behind this approach is a general consensus that SMEs (and enterprise in general) move at such a fast pace that any intervention that is too cumbersome, for example by requiring lengthy administrative processes and/or bureaucratic systems such as traditional business loan applications and the like, could have detrimental effects on their speed of potential growth. This, it is argued, could hinder their competitive advantage, especially within certain sectors of the economy where the rate of innovation and change is faster paced. Thus, innovation vouchers exist to move innovation along by providing a light nudge towards accessing knowledge providers that may be able to help SMEs in one capacity or another, thereby furthering policy that aims at growing and maintaining the SME sector.

Since the first voucher scheme was implemented in 1997, in the Limburg region of The Netherlands, there has been an explosion of voucher schemes, primarily across Europe. There has been a partial process of standardisation in the aims and implementation of such schemes in

Europe; as is evidenced by the Riga Declaration.[10] This being said there now exists a number of different types or versions of innovation vouchers, aimed at SMEs, that are all designed to "nudge" innovation through some sort of collaboration or the fostering of an organisational relationship. Most of these schemes are modelled on the original Dutch scheme and are aimed at catalysing innovation in some capacity but they vary in a number of ways such as: their specific aims, whether they are sector specific or not, the voucher amount, their operational duration and whether or not an evaluation is conducted (see Table 1). Moreover, the mechanisms that underpin how the voucher might be used can vary dramatically. For instance some vouchers require the SME to co-fund part of the voucher, some only select successful voucher recipients after the collaboration is finalised, some only fund new collaborations and some are on a first-come first-served basis. Generally, these vouchers allow SMEs from different sectors of the economy to purchase services from public knowledge providers such as HEIs (higher education institutions) or R&D (research and development) organisations in order to promote collaboration and stimulate the creation of small-scale innovations at firm level. Importantly, there is a growing critical literature addressing their effectiveness.[11]

The policy motives behind the development of such voucher schemes have been varied, but as Tarek Virani has argued elsewhere, innovation voucher schemes are attractive particularly because of "their ease of implementation and their role in facilitating knowledge exchange for relatively small sums."[12] Examples of such voucher schemes that refer explicitly to the role of knowledge providers in promoting growth and encouraging innovation also include a scheme run recently by Innovate UK ("an innovation voucher provides funding so that your business can work with an expert for the first time, gaining new knowledge to help your business innovate, develop and grow"[13]) as well as one run by the Audiovisual and Design Industries Innovation Scheme in Catalonia, which provided companies with up to €4000 "to work directly with a service provider" to support innovation.[14] The metaphor used here, of "providing knowledge," is one that the essays in this volume implicitly challenge, exploring as they do a much greater degree of co-creation and collaboration in the generation of knowledge through a voucher-supported series of projects.

Another important contemporary example of an innovation voucher scheme, whose methodology and outputs are relevant to this volume, is the Fusion Collaborative Awards scheme (FCA). This scheme was run as part of London Creative and Digital Fusion, a project led by the University of Lancaster and funded by the European Regional Development Fund between 2012 and 2014. Creativeworks London was also a partner in this project, and had particular responsibility for running the Fusion Collaborative Awards. The Fusion Collaborative Awards:

> Gave selected firms access to innovation vouchers, with which they could purchase support from a range of expert providers. The programme delivered 37 collaborations between SMEs and universities, enabling companies to create new jobs, processes and products that are leading their businesses into growth and sustainability.[15]

As its name suggests, the methodologies deployed within the London Creative and Digital Fusion programme built explicitly on recent research into the importance of "fusing" creative and digital expertise within the creative economy, represented for example in the Brighton Fuse report published in 2013.[16] The Fusion programme was designed to, "address co-ordination failures, which inhibit greater and faster innovation across and within sectors."[17] The methodology developed for FCAs was distinct from the approach developed within the Creative Voucher scheme of Creativeworks London, though the schemes did run in parallel. The FCA scheme drew on other innovation schemes discussed in this chapter, but also on the approaches developed through Knowledge Transfer Partnerships:

> The FCA model included an element of brokering and expert diagnosis characteristic of KTPs (typically lacking in innovation voucher models) in order to set companies' expectations from the outset and prepare inexperienced companies for collaboration with universities ... Each FCA would be procured from across a bank of selected partners or "Knowledge Base Providers" on a case-by-case basis and in full accordance with ERDF regulations.[18]

It is interesting to see the oscillation here between the idea of "knowledge provision" and the richer sense of partnership and collaboration with which the FCA scheme also engaged.

From these examples we can discern the extent to which innovation voucher schemes generally have become important innovation policy tools. And recently there have been more examples of innovation voucher schemes aimed at prompting innovation specifically in the creative and cultural industries (CCI). These schemes have myriad names, similar to the national innovation voucher schemes listed in Table 1, such as: Creative

Table 1 Example of variation in voucher types

Country and voucher name	Voucher amount (euros)	Sector specific	Evaluation method	Aim of voucher
Austria (Innovation voucher)	5000	No	Collection of baseline data and application data	Stimulating knowledge transfer between SME and knowledge providers
Belgium (Wallonia Technology Voucher)	Up to 5000	No	Application data, final report and telephone survey	Improvement of technological capacity of SMEs
Cyprus (Innovation Voucher)	5000	No	No evaluation	To promote the importance of innovation to SMEs
Denmark (Knowledge Voucher and small innovation projects)	Up to 14,000	Yes	Annual financial report	Increase research and development access for SMEs
Germany (Innovation vouchers for SMEs)	2500–20,000	Yes	No official evaluation	SMEs to access research and development (R&D)
Hungary (INNOSESK Innovation Voucher)	12,000–120,000	Yes	No evaluation	Strengthen knowledge transfer between SMEs and innovation strategy
Netherlands (Innovation Voucher)	3500–7500	No	Application form baseline data, telephone survey for voucher winners and voucher losers (Makeshift RCT)	SMEs to public and semi-public research institutions: universities, polytechnics and the Netherlands Organisation for Applied Scientific Research TNO

(*continued*)

Table 1 (continued)

Country and voucher name	Voucher amount (euros)	Sector specific	Evaluation method	Aim of voucher
Portugal (SME Skills Support System vouchers)	Up to 25,000	No	No evaluation	The goals of this measure are threefold: (1) to encourage SMEs to use external problem-solving services to improve their innovation performance, (2) to contribute towards the sustainability of R&D and innovation consultancy organisations, and (3) to promote cooperation and dialogue between SME and science, technology and innovation infrastructures and service firms
UK (NESTA Creative Credits)	4000GBP plus 1000GBP from SME	Yes	Randomised Controlled Trial, Longitudinal Data Collection, Use of Mixed Methods (Quant Survey/ Qual Interviews)	Designed to encourage SMEs to innovate in partnership with creative service providers

Credits, creative vouchers or creative innovation awards. Essentially, they are innovation vouchers and follow the same trajectory of logic as the original Dutch scheme, albeit their designs and rationale differ in a number of important ways. In 2010, as discussed above, NESTA—an important independent charity in the UK's creative economy and innovation policy arenas—implemented and evaluated their influential pilot Creative Credit scheme. The scheme was primarily a business to business (B2B) venture and was a way to bridge SMEs outside of the CCI with firms from within the creative sector in the Greater Manchester area. The logic behind this particular scheme came from an earlier report by NESTA demonstrating that businesses who bought in creative services were (all other things being equal) significantly more likely to innovate than other companies that had not benefited from this kind of expertise. Seeking to build on this knowledge, NESTA focused on creating a scheme that would "nudge" a wide range of SMEs to access relevant expertise from a range of creative companies.

Under the Creative Credits scheme, SMEs wishing to access support from a creative business were directed towards an online resource known as the "Creative Gallery," where a range of suppliers showcased their services, and the cost of accessing these services was partly met by a £4000 voucher (although SMEs were also required to contribute at least £1000 to the overall cost). The scheme was described by NESTA as innovative because "it seeks knowledge from new sources—creative businesses."[19] This was contrasted with earlier innovation voucher schemes, which had worked on a model of "knowledge transfer" from institutions such as universities and had focused primarily on technical and scientific forms of knowledge.

The NESTA scheme was designed to be light touch, easy for all parties involved to access, and rapid, and these have also been very important features of Creativeworks London's voucher schemes. However, there was no direct brokerage of relationships between SMEs and creative businesses within the Creative Credits scheme; vouchers were "awarded at random";[20] and reporting requirements following the project were also minimal. In these respects the NESTA scheme differs significantly from the Creativeworks London Creative Voucher scheme, which developed a range of techniques to curate relationships between researchers and SMEs; had a clear process for evaluating bids from different research partnerships; and undertook detailed evaluations based on interviews and end-of-project reports. These factors have enhanced the quality of the collaborative partnerships funded, as well as their impact and sustainability.

The Creative Credits scheme eventually supported 150 projects over two years. Of the 300 creative businesses that offered their services on the Creative Gallery, a total of 79 were eventually selected to participate in a project. The main creative services offered by these businesses were advertising, PR, design, web design, and film and video expertise. These services were not offered as collaborative research opportunities, but rather as a form of consultancy. Initially, the NESTA scheme was judged to have demonstrated significant outcomes: "participant SMEs are already reporting that their Creative Credits project had increased the innovative strengths of the business."[21] However, a subsequent evaluation of the impact of these Creative Credits, published in 2013, came to a rather different conclusion. This evaluation used "randomization to establish the scheme's additional impact, but also link(ed) that to longitudinal data collection ... to assess the longer term effectiveness of different policy tools."[22] Whereas initial reports in the six months following the completion of the creative projects had indicated that SMEs assigned credits were significantly more likely than others to have introduced product and process innovations, 12 months after the completion of the Creative Credits project: "there was no longer a statistically significant difference between the treatment and control groups in the proportion of firms innovating, nor in their sales growth."[23]

The lack of long-term impact is a significant weakness of the NESTA scheme, and is something that CWL has sought to address through innovative brokerage, sustained engagement and mutually beneficial forms of collaborative research. In the light of this, the role of the innovation broker (and/or knowledge intermediary) was a pivotal component of Creativeworks London's aim to ensure long-term impact. It is important to note that the Creative Credit scheme did not have any brokerage capacity. The innovation broker (markedly different from the "knowledge" broker) is someone who plays three roles. According to the literature, they are agents of knowledge orchestration (including aspects like: organising meet and greets, bringing people together and providing a platform for dialogue), they enact mediation/arbitration (including conflict resolution, problem handling), and they are sense-makers (including acting as "translator" and expectations manager). These three aspects are vital to the brokerage of, particularly, innovation networks.[24] This essentially means that an experienced third party needs to be involved with the collaboration from the outset. Research on Creativeworks London's voucher scheme has shown that brokerage and/or intermediation at different stages of the collaboration, including before the collaboration has even begun, is important to the success of the collaboration.[25] This points to the fact that the scheme included a number of levels of brokerage, most of which occurred before an application for a voucher was even submitted. These included: (1) the process of network building in order to see what partnerships are available that may be open to collaborations; (2) developing the relationship between the SME and academic; (3) developing the application through an application workshop; (4) actually working up an application; (5) and finally submitting that application. If successful, the project was granted a voucher where another set of brokerage activities took place in the form of roundtables, showcasing events and regular meetings. Brokerage and intermediation were critical throughout the entire process, especially for the collaborations that were new and/or had never worked on projects like this in the past. Interestingly, it was found that the collaborators who had an existing partnership before the voucher and/or had the most levels of brokerage were the ones who were most likely to continue their partnership. Thus the potential for long-term effects were designed into the process by the very notion of implementing a robust brokerage element to the voucher scheme.

Thus while it is clearly true that the Creative Credits scheme was part of the initial thinking for Creativeworks London, the Creative Voucher scheme was eventually delivered by departing from its methodology in significant ways. The impact of these differences can be seen in the ways in which partnerships were formed and sustained within Creativeworks London, and detailed in the following chapters of this volume.

This being said, innovation voucher schemes have a huge amount of variability. Being sector specific does not guarantee that standardisation has been achieved, as is evidenced by the various vouchers aimed at the CCI across the UK and Europe. Although the logic behind their raison d'être is consistent, there are very large variances in their implementation and in their stated aims, in the amounts that the vouchers are worth, as well as in the sectors and actors targeted. The point is that this makes actual comparison studies difficult but also indicates that voucher schemes cannot guarantee long-term effects unless the desire for long-term effects is designed into the process. Creativeworks London's voucher scheme was put together in order to establish sustainable working relationships—or at least a working model for facilitating these relationships—between SMEs and HEIs in the creative sector. For NESTA, this was not a central element of the design of their scheme—instead they were more concerned with nudging innovative capacities of SMEs, looking primarily at behavioural additionality. Thus, long-term effectiveness is, in effect, defined and approached differently by various schemes. Moreover, NESTA's scheme approached the issue of long-term effects from a different perspective looking specifically at long-term "impact" and "additionality" with regard to, primarily, sales growth, whereas the Creative Voucher scheme measured long-term effects through the number of partnerships that have continued to collaborate with each other after the voucher had reached its conclusion. What may be needed is a streamlining of what is meant by the very notion of long-term effectiveness that speaks to policy as well as stakeholders in this area.

Lastly, the policy landscape for higher education funding in the UK in recent years has been informed by the aspirations of both the Department for Business, Innovation and Skills (BIS) and the Higher Education Funding Council of England (HEFCE) to promote the role of universities as "anchor institutions"[26] within a regional economy, offering facilities and expertise that are made available to SMEs through a range of collaborative models built largely on the porosity of boundaries between universities and the creative economy. This model departs from the previously more familiar innovation models based on commercialisation of IP, and as David Docherty has noted in relation to another universities and business collaboration, Brighton Fuse: "there is also a fundamental divergence between the types of innovation taking place in the cluster and the use of intellectual property rights like patents, trademarks or design rights. Only one percent of our respondents applied for a patent in 2010 and none registered a design."[27] The essays that follow will thus explore the range of models of value, business benefit, and growth that have emerged from the collaborative research supported by Creative Vouchers, based on collaborations between universities and businesses, in which IP plays a relatively small part.

Notes

1. Information available at http://www.creativeworkslondon.org.uk/about/
2. Tarek Virani, "Mechanisms of Collaboration Between Creative Small, Medium and Micro-Sized Enterprises and Higher Education Institutions: Reflections on the Creativeworks London Creative Voucher Scheme" (Creativeworks London Working Paper No. 4, Creativeworks London/Queen Mary, University of London, 2014), https://qmro.qmul.ac.uk/xmlui/bitstream/handle/123456789/6542/PWK-Working-Paper-4-SEO.pdf?sequence=2.
3. Proposal from Queen Mary University of London to the AHRC to lead a KE Hub for the Creative Economy (Creativeworks London), July 2011, 6.
4. The National Endowment for Science Technology and the Arts (NESTA) was established in 1998 as a public body designed to

promote creativity and innovation. In 2012 it became an independent charity and adopted "Nesta" as its official name.
5. *A Guide to Creative Credits* (London: NESTA, 2011), 3.
6. The importance of "nudging" as theorised within both behavioural economics and psychology has become a prominent concern in the UK following the publication of Richard H. Thaler and Cass R. Sunstein's *Nudge: Improving Decisions about Health, Wealth and Happiness* (New Haven: Yale University Press, 2008), and also the establishment of the Behavioural Insights Team (or "Nudge Unit") within the UK Cabinet Office in 2010 (later to be part-owned by Nesta).
7. Hasan Bakhshi, Eric McVittie, and James Simmie, *Creating Innovation: Do the Creative Industries Support Innovation in the Wider Economy?* (London: NESTA, 2008).
8. See OECD Innovation Policy Platform, "Innovation Vouchers" (2010), http://www.oecd.org/innovation/policyplatform/48135973.pdf.
9. See Maarten Cornet, Björn Vroomen, and Marc van der Steeg, "Do Innovation Vouchers Help SMEs to Cross the Bridge towards Science?" (CPB Discussion Paper No. 58, CPB Netherlands Bureau for Economic Policy Analysis, 2006), http://www.cpb.nl/sites/default/files/publicaties/download/do-innovation-vouchers-help-smes-cross-bridge-towards-science.pdf.
10. See "Realising the Full Potential of Innovation Voucher Programs: The Riga Declaration" (European Commission Enterprise and Industry, 2010), http://hytetra.eu/d/news/Riga_declaration.pdf.
11. See Virani, "Mechanisms of Collaboration"; Ian Miles and Paul Cunningham, *Smart Innovation: Supporting the Monitoring and Evaluation of Innovation Programmes* (Brussels: European Commission, 2006); Johan Bruneel, Pablo d'Este, and Ammon Salter, "Investigating the Factors that Diminish the Barriers to University–Industry Collaboration," *Research Policy* 39, no. 7 (2010): 858–68.
12. Virani, "Mechanisms of Collaboration," 3.
13. For a description of the Innovate UK innovation voucher scheme see http://vouchers.innovateuk.org.
14. For details of this scheme and its impacts see www.eclaplatform.eu/wp-content/uploads/2013/11/FAD-INS-Final-evaluation.pdf.

15. Cathy Garner, Jasmina Bolfek-Radovani, Helen Fogg, Jana Riedel, Phil Ternouth, Gerard Briscoe, Mariza Dima, Morag Shiach, Tarek Virani, London Creative and Digital Fusion Team, "London Creative and Digital Fusion" (London Fusion, 2014), 31, http://www.creativeworkslondon.org.uk/wp-content/uploads/2015/04/Fusion_digital_Edition_V4.pdf.
16. Jonathan Sapsed and Paul Nightingale, "The Brighton Fuse" (2013), http://www.brightonfuse.com/wp-content/uploads/2013/10/The-Brighton-Fuse-Final-Report.pdf.
17. Application by Lancaster University to the London ERDF Programme 2007–13 to fund London Creative and Digital Fusion, August 2011, 13.
18. See Morag Shiach, Jana Riedel and Jasmina Bolfek-Radovani, "Fusing and Creating: A Comparative Analysis of the Knowledge Exchange Methodologies Underpinning Creativeworks London's Creative Vouchers and London Creative and Digital Fusion's Collaborative Awards" (Creativeworks London Working Paper No. 25, Creativeworks London/Queen Mary, University of London, 2014), 18–19, https://qmro.qmul.ac.uk/xmlui/bitstream/handle/123456789/11413/Shiach%20Fusing%20and%20Creating%202014%20Published.pdf?sequence=1.
19. *A Guide to Creative Credits*, 6.
20. Ibid.
21. Ibid, 8.
22. Hasan Bakhshi, John Edwards, Stephen Roper, Judy Scully, Duncan Shaw, Lorraine Morley and Nicola Rathbone, *Creative Credits: A Randomized Controlled Industrial Policy Experiment* (London: Nesta, 2013), 6.
23. Ibid, 7.
24. Doug Henton and Jessie Oettinger, "Innovation Brokers," in *The Oxford Handbook to Local Competitiveness*, eds. David B. Audretsch, Albert N. Link and Mary Lindenstein Walshok (Oxford: Oxford University Press, 2015), 306–319.
25. See Tarek Virani and Andy C. Pratt. "Intermediaries and the Knowledge Exchange Process," in *Higher Education and the Creative Economy: Beyond the Campus*, eds. Roberta Comunian and Abigail Gilmore (Abingdon: Routledge, 2016), 41.
26. It is interesting in this context to note that the Higher Education Funding Council for England announced in September 2014 three

new dedicated calls for bids to their Catalyst Fund, focusing on universities as "anchor institutions", on supporting technical education and on innovative knowledge exchange.
27. Sapsed and Nightingale, "The Brighton Fuse," 33.

Bringing the Past into the Present: Mobilising Historical Research Through Creative and Digital Collaboration

John Price

I first encountered the Watts Memorial to Heroic Self-Sacrifice during a lunch break nearly twenty-five years ago when I wandered into Postman's Park, a small municipal garden near the Museum of London.[1] Like many visitors, I stumbled across the Victorian monument with no prior knowledge of how or why it was created but that did not diminish my fascination with it. I was absolutely captivated by the fifty or so ceramic memorial plaques fixed to a long stretch of wall and protected beneath a sturdy wooden shelter; each tablet providing a short narrative regarding an otherwise ordinary individual from the distant past who had lost their own life while attempting to save another. A small statuette in the centre indicated that the monument had been created by the Victorian artist George Frederic Watts and the date 1899 was carved into the wooden lintel at the front of the shelter; other than that, there was no further information. As I ate my lunch, I read and absorbed the fascinating stories but left the park that day with many more questions than answers, particularly about the people who were commemorated.

Fast-forward to 2012, and in the intervening years I had been lucky enough to pursue my interest in the monument, publish a detailed study of its origins and development, and amass a wealth of historical research

J. Price (✉)
University of Roehampton, London, UK

© The Author(s) 2017
M. Shiach, Tarek Virani (eds.), *Cultural Policy, Innovation and the Creative Economy*, DOI 10.1057/978-1-349-95112-3_3

about each and every person commemorated.² Publishing this research in a book was always the ultimate plan, but there was a parallel sense that what was also needed was a way to deliver information in situ and directly to visitors, particularly those unexpectedly encountering the monument for the first time. The memorial is grade-two listed so installing interpretation boards was not an option and, even if it had been, there was no practical way to deliver the required quantity of detailed information, so it seemed like an unfeasible proposition. Inspiration struck when, on a visit to the park with some friends, we began talking about the sudden increase in mobile apps and their potential value for delivering detailed information about places while actually visiting them. "Imagine if you had a Postman's Park app" mused my friend, "that told you all about everyone on the memorial and then you could access it when you were visiting if you had questions that needed answering." It seemed an ideal solution, but my personal knowledge of the technology and the industry was virtually non-existent, so I pushed the idea to the back of my mind as something of a pipe dream.

However, thanks to the Creativeworks London (CWL) Creative Voucher Scheme the dream actually became a reality.³ Through a series of networking events in the autumn of 2012, CWL facilitated meetings between academics and potential creative economy partners, providing time and space for constructive and meaningful conversations to take place.⁴ Through the first of these network meetings, I made contact with Gary Gregson and Mark Olleson, co-founders of Prossimo Ventures Ltd and specialists in User Experience Realisation for digital media, audio and mobile applications.⁵ Working with Gary and Mark, a tangible and practical project emerged combining their expertise with my research to create a mobile app about the memorial. The app would solve the problem of invasive interpretation materials by utilising image recognition technology, meaning that all a user would need to do would be to open the app and point the camera of the smartphone or tablet computer at a particular memorial plaque in order to access the information about that person.

As Gary, Mark and I worked together to hone our CWL application, we were pleased and encouraged to discover that we were certainly not lone pioneers. The transformative potential of providing targeted information and enhancing experiences through interactive interpretation delivered via mobile devices was rapidly being recognised across the arts and humanities, particularly in relation to social and cultural history, memory, heritage and identity. One example was the collaboration between Pervasive Intelligence Ltd and the University of Surrey to develop Visit-AR, a mobile app template for use on two-dimensional artworks in indoor gallery spaces.[6] Other examples being developed around the same time, and more in keeping with our Watts Memorial app, included the Welford Road Cemetery app, a result of collaboration between the AHRC-funded Digital Building Heritage Group at De Montfort University and The Friends of Welford Road Cemetery, and the Future Cemetery Project, a collaboration between Arnos Vale Cemetery, the University of Bath, the production agency Calling the Shots and web designers Clear Design UK.[7] The wealth of technological research and development being undertaken clearly represented an important step in the growth of collaborations between the creative digital industries and arts and humanities researchers.[8] It was exciting to realise that our own success in those areas could contain great potential for revolutionising public engagement with research and transforming dissemination and impact beyond traditional academic channels.

Our application to the CWL Voucher Scheme was successful and, for us, one of the major benefits was the relatively straightforward application process and the quick turnaround in decision making. Research academics are used to lengthy and protracted funding applications and so time and resources to undertake them are often built in to the broader structure of the academic year and supported by a research office or enterprise team. For small and medium enterprises (SMEs) time is very much of the essence and it could be impractical and problematic to commit time and resources to projects for which a decision on funding might take up to a year to be finalised. Recognising these issues for SMEs and designing the Creative Voucher Scheme, with its more practical workshop-orientated approach and streamlined application process, was undoubtedly one of the strengths of Creativeworks London from our perspective.

Thus, work began in February 2013 with a series of meetings between Gary, Mark and me, focused on establishing technical and schematic foundations for the app itself. This was one key area, from my perspective, that demonstrates the enormous value and power of collaborations between academics and creative industries. Although I work on digital humanities projects, have experience of creating and implementing websites, and would consider myself to be reasonably IT literate, the technological expertise required for the app was far beyond my capabilities; but it was well within Gary and Mark's. For example, one of the key and defining features of the app is the image recognition facility which allows visitors to the monument to simply point the camera of their mobile device at any of the fifty-four tablets and the app will recognise which tablet it is and deliver the relevant content.[9] It was initially envisaged that this function could be achieved through the use of existing "off the shelf" technology, but when this proved unworkable and too costly Gary and Mark had the experience and expertise to work around the problems and successfully redesign the way in which the image recognition system worked.[10]

Furthermore, whereas it had occurred to me to check that there was some sort of mobile signal coverage in Postman's Park, Gary and Mark knew that, to work effectively, the image recognition and other processes in the app would require a certain amount of speed and bandwidth from that signal, something which they were able to measure and ascertain. My understanding of mobile technology was also limited; I had given little thought to the range of different devices and operating systems on the market or to the specifications required for using the app, from basic things such as needing a rear-facing camera through to more technical issues such as how the CPU or memory of a device might impact its ability to run advanced functions effectively. Investigations into market penetration and benchmark specifications determined our final platforms as devices capable of running iOS 6.0 and above and those running Android 3.0 and above. At the time it was decided that Windows mobile device market penetration was insufficient to warrant the additional time and costs needed to implement the app for that platform. As an alternative for Windows users, a web-based application was created which can be accessed on a mobile device via a standard web browser and which delivers the same content as the mobile app, albeit without the image recognition function.[11] This also makes it possible for anyone, anywhere in the world, who can access the Internet to explore the history and heroism of those commemorated in Postman's Park if they are unable to visit the site in person or in advance of a planned visit. It would have been simply impossible for me to have realised these technical and technological aspects of the project without working in close partnership with Gary and Mark, but this type of cooperation does highlight one particular issue which could prevent or hamper collaboration.

Collaborations between academics and SMEs in the creative industries are not dissimilar to interdisciplinary projects within academia alone and both share the same potential pitfalls. With interdisciplinarity, it is vital that the academics not only understand and appreciate the nuances and peculiarities of other disciplines, but also that they recognise and respect the knowledge, experience and expertise that their partner academics have accumulated in that discipline.[12] It is all well and good to share the tools of one another's trades, but it must be remembered that others may not initially find those tools as familiar or straightforward to use and they may require additional tuition or time for familiarisation. Successful interdisciplinarity in academia relies upon all parties in the process being able to communicate their knowledge, experience and expertise to their partners in ways that will be understood and which, crucially, maintain mutual respect for each other and it is no different in collaborations between academics and creative SMEs.

In terms of knowledge and practice there is, undoubtedly, a world of difference between User Experience Realisation for digital applications and academic history. However, I would suggest that one of the fundamental strengths underpinning the success of our project was the respectful manner in which both partners sought to understand and appreciate the needs and requirements of the other and also to genuinely seek to accommodate those needs and requirements where at all possible. So, for example, from my perspective I had a vast quantity of accumulated research on multiple facets of every person commemorated on the Watts Memorial and Gary and Mark were initially sceptical about the density of the material and the need to include all of it in the app. Through discussion, I was able to explain how revealing the lives of people commemorated was an intrinsic part of understanding the heroics of their death, but I also came to appreciate how the mobile app platform required a very different approach to delivering content and that lengthy portions of thick narrative would not be suitable. Between the three of us and employing both technical expertise and scholarly narrative adaptation, we designed the app so that users creatively and interactively generate their own narrative of the event by accessing and assembling short portions of text from different perspectives all of which then build a complete picture. This collaborative solution delivered the interactive and engaged user experience that Gary and Mark knew the app required, while still maintaining both the quantity and the integrity of the historical research, something which was absolutely central for me.

Gary and Mark are also experts in User Experience Realisation and this, in particular, was an area to which I had given little consideration and which I had little understanding or appreciation of. I initially viewed the app as primarily a mechanism for delivering information to people visiting the park; historical information about the memorial itself and the people commemorated. Other than the fact that they were visiting the memorial, and therefore presumably interested in it and its history, I had not given a great deal of thought to the specifics of the audience for the app or to how it might contribute to their experience of visiting the park. I had, though, over many years spent an enormous amount of time in the park, talking to people about the memorial but also just watching and listening to visitors as they engaged and interacted with it. From my knowledge and several targeted research visits of their own, Gary and Mark were able to draw up a series of representative persona profiles of visitors. These included overseas and British tourists, local residents, local workers, Londoners more generally, walking tours and school parties. From these profiles it was possible to design the app based upon the plausible needs of users and in regard to factors such as language, age, mobility, available time and technical expertise. Gary and Mark were also much more attuned to the need for the app to be entertaining and stimulating as well as informative and educational, something which I was alert to but which I initially regarded as secondary to the provision of information. Again, though, through collaborative discussions we found a suitable middle ground whereby more illustrations, images and maps were incorporated but they were chosen or designed with regard to preserving historical legitimacy and scholarly integrity.

Work on the app continued over the summer of 2013, with each of us progressing independently on our various tasks, but still meeting frequently to discuss issues and undertake testing of prototypes. This ability for us to work independently was also a product of the successful collaboration and primarily the manner in which the database underpinning the app had been conceived and designed by both parties. From the outset, Gary, Mark and I were all keen that I should have independent access to the database; something which took a good amount of trust on their part and acquisition of knowledge and skills on mine. Given the relatively limited resources of the project and the short time span for completion, independent access was important so that I could initially populate the database with my research material, leaving Gary and Mark free to develop the image recognition and other aspects of the app. It was also important, though, because my research on the memorial was (and still is) ongoing and I wanted to be able to add and amend the content of the app beyond the lifespan of the CWL project and without having to trouble Gary and Mark who would, as a growing SME, be committed to other clients. We all worked together to design a database in which I could easily and quickly accommodate my current research material but which I could also, with a small amount of straightforward technical training from Gary and Mark, adapt myself to allow for new research in the future. Once again, thanks to Gary and Mark's technical knowledge and wiliness to accommodate their academic partner, database software was chosen on the basis that it was straightforward for me to use while still delivering the tools they required.[13] Collaboration was invaluable for everyone involved as each party was able to bring different insights into how problems might be solved and how information could be managed.

During meetings and discussions with Mark and Gary it was interesting for me to learn more about why they were so keen to be involved with academic research projects such as this. As a relatively new company, they were, of course, eager to showcase their range of skills and services to potential clients and they recognised that the Watts Memorial and acts of everyday heroism were fascinating and engaging topics, with potential to attract a wide audience and, thus, publicity and exposure for their work. Beyond being a portfolio example of their capabilities, they also viewed the app project as valuable experience for identifying the advantages and disadvantages of developing projects with academic partners and how those might guide them when seeking and establishing collaborations in the future. For example, our partnership highlighted the need to establish good and agreed specifications at the outset, which enabled independent progress to be made by both parties and also to ensure that everyone's needs were met as closely as possible. It also demonstrated the need, from the SME's perspective, for partnerships with academics to be formed around "real" projects, with tangible and realistic outcomes and outputs that can be delivered within a reasonable and achievable timetable, rather than simply good ideas which still need lengthy development before implementation. Gary and Mark also expressed some frustration that highly valuable and adaptable academic research often tended to be shaped and collated in formats solely from an academic perspective and for academic purposes, rather than considering how it might also be shaped to make it more readily available and open to industry.

This was something which, in the early stages of project development, we hoped and planned to address through an additional (and ambitious) technical goal. Beyond delivering the app itself, the wider vision was to develop and implement a comprehensive Application Programming Interface (API) that would facilitate the reuse of the data within a Web Services Description Language (WSDL) definition and create an RDF ontology to bind together the project's datasets (e.g., people, places, images, interpretations) as a series of resources represented by established conceptual models.[14] The expectation was to then expose the historical research data as Linked Data via SPARQL queries conforming to the defined ontology and facilitated by use of the D2RQ Platform.[15] Essentially, this would have made all the historical data fully visible and available to external partners in a recognised format that would have facilitated data-linking and thus ensured that the research underpinning the app could be constructively mined and reused in different ways by a range of different users. Undertaking and achieving this would have given Gary and Mark valuable insights into the practicalities of shaping academic material for external partners and an example case study of why such approaches were desirable and profitable. It would also have been extremely exciting and valuable to me in terms of long-term subject-orientated consequences for research on heroism and the heroic. The establishment of an ontology based on the range of incidents on the Watts Memorial, with the potential to then feed in research material from other sources, would have provided significant opportunities for interdisciplinary and cross-comparative analyses of a wide range of seemingly different conceptions of heroism, assisting researchers to address questions about variable or contested constructions.[16]

Regrettably, although the CWL Voucher Scheme offered a generous grant in relation to small projects, we were unable to stretch the funding beyond the essential tasks required to complete and launch the app within a suitable timescale, which was always the prime objective. Thus, the ambitious plans to develop an RDF ontology were put on hold and, for the app, a RESTful API was implemented instead. This concession illustrates perhaps the most challenging element of the project, for both parties, which was delivering it on time and within budget. Both of these objectives were achieved, but both required the commitment of significantly more time and resources than the funding allowed for. This was, ultimately, something that both parties had foreseen and were prepared for so it was not a major issue. We both anticipated that the lessons we would learn from the collaborative process and the excellence and success of the end product would represent highly valuable and satisfactory returns on the additional time invested and this was very much the case. We would also like to have developed more of the mapping elements, included some audio visual material, and experimented with Augmented Reality to digitally overlay new tablets into spaces on the memorial. These would, though, have been embellishments rather than part of the original project proposal and their absence in no way undermines the finished product which fully delivers on all its original commitments.

The *Everyday Heroes of Postman's Park* mobile app was launched in October 2013, marking the successful completion of our CWL Creative Voucher-funded collaboration. Almost immediately, the app began attracting attention from the public, the media and the academic community. In its first year, the app was downloaded just over 800 times and throughout 2015 the landing page for accessing the app received an average of around 250 visitors a month. In March 2014, the app was exhibited at the Arts and Humanities Research Council's *Creative Economy Showcase* event and appeared as a feature article in the accompanying publication.[17] In June 2014 the app was selected, out of 230 entries, as a finalist in the National Co-ordinating Centre for Public Engagement's *Engage* Competition and there have been feature articles on it in magazines including the Christmas 2013 edition of *Family History*.[18] The app also, to some extent, helped to support the publication of my book *Heroes of Postman's Park: Victorian Self-Sacrifice in Victorian London* which extends and elaborates upon the research contained in the app and places it into a wider historical and academic context.[19] The book and the app reciprocally promote and support one another; working in tandem to provide an authoritative, comprehensive and widely accessible history of the Watts Memorial and all those currently commemorated upon it.

There can be no doubt that the creative collaboration between Gary, Mark and I that was established and supported by the Creativeworks London scheme was anything but a resounding success. The project was completed on time, on budget and delivered everything that was expected and detailed in the original proposal. For Prossimo Ventures, the app provided a showcase for the extensive skills and capabilities of its two founders and, on a more tangible business level, a follow-up contract for further work of a similar nature for the University of Roehampton. Experientially, Gary and Mark also had the opportunity to work closely with an academic partner, which not only provided them with valuable historical research content for their product, but more profoundly with insights into the wider potential offered by historical research material and academics with open minds and flexible approaches to collaborative ventures with creative partners. The clever and calculated way in which the funding grants were tailored and administered by CWL encouraged and stimulated short-term projects, with limited, realistic and achievable goals but long-term outcomes beyond the timescale and remit of the project itself; something which was ideally suited to this particular collaboration and meant that we could work together intensively to achieve our aims and then move on to other projects.

For me, the impact of the project continues to reach far beyond the app itself and my research and teaching have both been heavily shaped and influenced by the experience, knowledge and skills it fostered. One of the most valuable things I learned through working with Prossimo and co-creating the app is the need for academics to be able to adapt their research, teaching, writing and publishing to suit a range of modern and ever-changing outputs, including platforms such as apps, blogs and other social media. This, in turn, led me to think about the changing nature of work and employment, especially in relation to the undergraduate history students that I teach. In a 2008 study, John Palfrey and Urs Gasser discussed the Western concept of "digital natives"; people who were born after 1980 and into a world where networked digital technologies are the norm. "These kids are different," they tell us, "they study, work, write, and interact with each other in ways that are very different from the ways that you did growing up."[20] In contrast to the older generation of "digital immigrants," the natives have lived much of their life without consciously distinguishing between their online and offline identities; they tend to multitask, to express themselves through digital media, to employ technology to create new knowledge and art forms, and "for these young people, new digital technologies…are primary mediators of human-to-human connections."[21] This generation have also been nicknamed "Knowmads," a term coined by John Moravec to describe a new type of worker "a creative, imaginative and innovative person who can work with almost anybody, anytime and anywhere…"[22]

I believe it is vitally important that university educators, such as myself, understand and accommodate this new generation, because they are the students filling our lecture theatres, attending our seminars and expecting the education we deliver to qualify them for a world where "[i]ndustrial society is giving way to knowledge and innovation work."[23] They are, essentially, people who may well go forward to work in the creative industries that have so much to offer in terms of partnerships and collaborations with academia. It would seem, though, that the education sector has been particularly slow and to some extent stoically stubborn to fully incorporate new technology into its professional practice, a view summed up by Professor Steve Wheeler who has asserted that "inflexible delivery of teaching, outmoded assessment methods and siloed curricula do little to support the development of the Knowmad society."[24] Working on the app project and being exposed to just a small degree of the creative and technological developments and opportunities on offer has led me to investigate and implement different strategies in my teaching and assessment of students. For example, in 2014, I introduced student blogging as an assessed assignment in two of the undergraduate history modules that I teach. As Julia Davies and Guy Merchant have highlighted, "Blogs are now a well-established and widely recognised form of digital communication and this alone suggests that they should be taken seriously in educational settings."[25] Despite this, at the current time the blog platform remains a comparatively underused tool in UK universities. My experience with them suggests that blogs are relatively straightforward to implement, for example, as a form of assessment, and they substantially repay the effort by providing a very engaging and interactive method of stimulating and assessing learning, while at the same time helping to equip students with a set of new and highly valuable transferable skills suited to a "Knowmad" society.

Set into the context of external drivers such as employability, transferable skills, inclusion, diversified assessment, and the changing nature of work and the workplace, it is clear that student blogging in educational settings has huge potential for delivering a relevant and valuable range of skills and ways of thinking. Furthermore, the increasing use of blogging and other technologies, including apps, wikis, podcasts and vlogs (video blogs) also has implications within my own academic discipline of history. The Quality Assurance Agency benchmarks for the subject, although progressive, still suggest a rather conservative and suspicious attitude towards assignments other than essays and something of a privileging, or even fetishisation, of lengthy pieces of formally structured written coursework.[26] Meanwhile, historical research is increasingly being presented to public audiences in ways that contrast with that approach; the BBC's *History of the World in 100 Objects* being just one prime example; employing objects, podcasts, radio programmes, websites and short articles as its means of dissemination and engagement.[27] There are also a number of history projects benefitting from the emergence of "citizen science" as a methodology for collecting, collating and analysing historical evidence.[28] As my own collaborative experience revealed to me, apps and interactive resources for mobile devices are also on the increase, but they require entirely different approaches to writing historical content that history undergraduates (and to some extent academics) are simply not being widely exposed to or encouraged to produce within universities. The teaching, learning and dissemination of historical research needs to reflect the wider and more profound impact that digital technology is having on the way that information is created and shared; something which I came to see very clearly through my collaborative experience.

Finally, the app project has had an impact upon my research on the Watts Memorial to Heroic Self Sacrifice in Postman's Park. While revisiting some archive documents as a result of researching for the app, I realised, for the first time, that G.F. Watts, the creator of the memorial, had actually documented his complete vision for the monument and listed the names of all the people who he wished to commemorate on the 120 tablets he had originally planned for his memorial wall. Realising this has led me to begin researching the sixty or so additional individuals who should have been commemorated but who are currently missing from the monument. Once this research is complete, all the additional material on those individuals and the incidents in which they perished, will be incorporated in the app database and also published in a follow-up volume entitled, *The Forgotten Heroes of Postman's Park*. Also, as a result of the publicity generated by the app and the book, I have founded *The Friends of the Watts Memorial*, an organisation for anyone who wants to help support, protect and preserve the monument.[29] Ultimately, in the long term, the plan is to commission and install the missing ceramic tablets so as to finally complete the Watts Memorial as its creator intended; in some ways, the ultimate collaboration for me but one that will also involve a high degree of partnership with the general public and a range of creative industries outside of academia. Thanks to my previous experience of creating the app, that is something I am very much looking forward to and I am certain it will help to ensure that the Watts Memorial continues to delight and enchant visitors for many years to come.

Notes

1. For information on Postman's Park see http://www.cityoflondon.gov.uk/things-to-do/green-spaces/city-gardens/Pages/park-gardens.aspx.
2. John Price, *Postman's Park: G. F. Watts's Memorial to Heroic Self-Sacrifice* (Compton: Watts Gallery, 2008).
3. See http://www.creativeworkslondon.org.uk/creative-voucher-scheme/.
4. See Tarek Virani, "Mechanisms of Collaboration Between Creative Small, Medium and Micro-Sized Enterprises and Higher Education Institutions: Reflections on the Creativeworks London Creative Voucher Scheme" (Creativeworks London Working Paper No. 4, Creativeworks London/Queen Mary, University of London, 2014), https://qmro.qmul.ac.uk/xmlui/bitstream/handle/123456789/6542/PWK-Working-Paper-4-SEO.pdf?sequence=2.
5. See http://www.prossimo-ventures.co.uk/.
6. See http://www.pervasive-intelligence.co.uk/projects.
7. See https://itunes.apple.com/gb/app/welford-road-cemetery-trail/id803193039?mt=8; http://futurecemetery.org/.
8. Also exemplified by the "All in Hand: Mobile Technology and Museums" seminar at the British Museum on 28 November 2013, http://bit.ly/1jsALyQ, and the "Social Networking for Historians" symposium at the Institute of Historical Research (IHR) on 8 February 2014, http://events.history.ac.uk/event/show/12501.
9. The "Everyday Heroes of Postman's Park" mobile app can be downloaded from http://www.postmanspark.org.uk.
10. This was accomplished using the OpenCV library, http://opencv.org/.
11. The web interface can be accessed at http://www.everydayheroism.org.uk/.
12. For more on interdisciplinarity see Joe Moran, *Interdisciplinarity: The New Critical Idiom*, 2nd ed. (London: Routledge, 2010).
13. See http://www.microsoft.com/web/webmatrix/.
14. Web Services Description Language (WSDL), http://www.w3.org/TR/wsdl.
15. See http://d2rq.org/.

16. For the importance of this see, Max Jones, "What Should Historians Do with Heroes?" *History Compass* 5, no. 2 (2007): 439–54, and John Price, *Everyday Heroism: Victorian Constructions of the Heroic Civilian* (London: Bloomsbury, 2014); for an example of a comparative dataset see, Craig P. Barclay, "Heroes of Peace: The Royal Humane Society and the Award of Medals in Britain, 1774–1914" (PhD diss., University of York, 2009).
17. See http://www.ahrc.ac.uk/documents/publications/the-creative-economy-showcase/.
18. See https://www.publicengagement.ac.uk/work-with-us/engage-competition-2016/engage-competition-2014/.
19. John Price, *Heroes of Postman's Park: Heroic Self-Sacrifice in Victorian London* (Stroud: The History Press, 2015).
20. John Palfrey and Urs Gasser, *Born Digital: Understanding the First Generation of Digital Natives*, 2nd ed. (New York: Basic Books, 2013), 2.
21. Ibid., 4.
22. John W. Moravec, ed., *Knowmad Society* (Minneapolis: Education Futures, 2013), 18.
23. Ibid.
24. Steve Wheeler, *Learning with 'E's: Educational Theory and Practice in the Digital Age* (Bancyfelin: Crown House, 2015), 11; see also Ken Robinson, "How Schools Kill Creativity," *TED Talks* (2006), http://www.ted.com/talks/ken_robinson_says_schools_kill_creativity.
25. Guy Merchant and Julia Davies, *Web 2.0 for Schools: Learning and Social Participation* (New York: Peter Lang, 2009), 34.
26. Quality Assurance Agency, "Subject Benchmark Statement, History" (The Quality Assurance Agency for Higher Education, 2014), http://www.qaa.ac.uk/en/Publications/Documents/SBS-consultation-history.pdf.
27. British Broadcasting Corporation, "History of the World in 100 Objects" (2010), http://www.bbc.co.uk/ahistoryoftheworld.
28. For examples see https://www.zooniverse.org.
29. Details available at http://www.wattsmemorial.org.uk.

Creating Archival Value in a Changing Mediascape: The "World in a Cube" Project

Ian Christie, Wendy Earle, Eleni Liarou, Karen Merkel, and Akim Mogaji

Like many of the most exciting research projects, it began with a chance discovery. Karen Markel, a partner in New Media Networks, was visiting Tate & Lyle's London Refinery as part of an Away Day for a charity:

> At the end of the day, a small group of us was given a tour of the large site. We stood by the pontoons on the Thames watching container ships landing the unrefined cane, diggers moving the "sugar mountains" around, computers running the refining machines, and thousands of boxes of sugar rolling back into containers. Walking through the small "museum" created for a visit from the Queen some decades earlier, we saw the many black and white photographs on display and I asked, "were there any films?" To my surprise, I was taken into a small windowless storeroom, with shelves from floor to ceiling containing all kinds of documents, objects such as small statues and medals, samples of every kind of packaging that had been used to transport the refined sugar, and "the film collection." The original cans were safe inside hundreds of fading, soft card boxes, and just waiting to be viewed by someone with interest. It was like being in the middle of a film moment, of the kind that just doesn't happen—but it did.

I. Christie (✉) • W. Earle • E. Liarou • K. Merkel • A. Mogaji
Birkbeck, London, UK

New Media Networks asked the company for a licence to explore this collection for educational purposes, which was granted three months later. Wendy Earle, Impacts and Knowledge Exchange Manager at Birkbeck, University of London and Karen Merkel began drafting an application to Creativeworks London (CWL). At this point, Eleni Liarou, a former Birkbeck research student with a special interest in historic London film, had joined the team, and when the CWL voucher was granted, we began our exploration of the collection, with much excitement and a degree of support and interest from Tate & Lyle (T&L).[1]

Film historians might be reminded of the momentous discovery in 1994 of a cache of early films made by the Blackburn partnership of Sagar Mitchell and James Kenyon between 1897 and 1909. These had been packed tightly into milk churns in Bradford, and their survival, followed by an extended programme of restoration, research and popular diffusion in print and on television and DVD, opened up extraordinary new perspectives on early British filmmaking and viewing.[2] Mitchell & Kenyon's "factory gate" filming, followed by town hall shows where ordinary people could see themselves on screen, revealed an interactive phase of film activity, before the emergence of commodified entertainment cinema.

The Tate & Lyle collection seemed unlikely to have such a transformative impact, with any equivalent wide public appeal. But on the basis of early inspection, it offered different opportunities, as well as immediate challenges. There were clearly issues of industrial change, of global trade and of community in play here, which might be mobilised and linked with existing research interests.[3] The funding and timescale of the CWL project also dictated a different approach, aiming above all to demonstrate the potential "use value" of such a collection to a variety of audiences. By a combination of screenings for differentiated audiences, recorded discussions and involvement of young filmmakers in "creative repurposing," our *World in a Cube* project amounts to a blueprint for a dynamic research methodology, with potentially valuable lessons for others seeking support to research archival film (Fig. 1).

Varieties of "Documentary"

The term "documentary" has been used so indiscriminately for many different kinds of non-fiction or non-entertainment films that it has become virtually useless as a category.[4] To make sense of a body of work such

Fig. 1 "What have we here ?" (Professor Ian Christie from Birkbeck, Akim Mogaji from New Media Networks together with researcher, Frances Bull, at the Tate & Lyle Refinery in Silvertown, East London, beginning work on the World in a Cube)

as the T&L collection, we need to sidestep broad labels and consider some of the varied uses to which film has been put. Quite apart from its entertainment value, at the beginning of the twentieth century the new medium offered progressive companies a new way of promoting their products. Not only could it "remediate" conventional advertising images in a novel manner, but film made possible a new way of portraying both process and interaction. One of the Lumières' first franchise holders, Ludwig Stollwerck, was primarily in the confectionary business in Cologne.[5] And some of the oldest advertising films that have survived, for Vinolia soap and Peek Frean biscuits, show these products being manufactured, packed and despatched.[6] In effect, they illustrated a combination of tradition, quality and modernity, although only a few examples of the many advertising films created during cinema's early decades have been preserved.[7]

Britain has what may be a uniquely celebrated relationship with advertising or promotional film, as a result of the concentration on this form in the 1930s. State agencies such as the Empire Marketing Board and the General Post Office established film units largely due to vigorous lobbying by John Grierson, and many commercial bodies followed suit. Among Grierson's models was the work of the Soviet avant-garde, largely devoted to celebrating the achievements of the Soviet regime, in films such as Dziga Vertov's *One Sixth of the World* (1926, for the Soviet external trade agency) or Viktor Turin's *TurkSib* (1929, marking completion of the Turkestan-Siberia railway link).[8] The result was that most of Britain's avant-garde filmmakers in this decade learned and practised their craft by making public information or advertising films.[9] This trend would inform wartime filmmaking, and continue after the war, as many inventive and ambitious filmmakers alternated between public service sponsorship and commercial commissions. Most of the directors who comprised British cinema's "new wave" of the early 1960s had received their training in this sector, traditionally, if inadequately, known as "documentary" or "sponsored."[10]

This history is worth summarising because it has often been ignored, as if acknowledgement of advertising or sponsorship work would tarnish the status of filmmakers otherwise regarded as artists in the same sense as literary writers or painters selling their output to collectors. Only in recent years have television advertising and music promotion been considered acceptable forms of commercial subsidy for filmmakers of significant cultural reputation.

The issue, however, is not merely one of cultural status. It also concerns the social and indeed commercial role of films in relation to industry throughout the last century. Commissioning and circulating films of many kinds was an important activity for many companies. But what little research there has been tends to focus on consumer advertising, rather than the many other communication functions that film has played. Training, and documenting company activities and achievements were just two of these; the latter especially important for a commodities company with a worldwide reach. In the case of Tate & Lyle, there was also an important public information and political function, to promote the case for imported cane sugar within the European economy, which tended to favour beet sugar grown in Europe. And what else might we find, if we had the rare opportunity to explore a commercial company's film collection?

T&L, created in 1921 from the merger of two historic companies engaged in sugar production and refining for centuries, is one of Britain's oldest established commodities companies.[11] Long based at a massive Thames-side refinery complex, it has deep roots in the histories of East

London and Britain's imperial trade. Yet until very recently, the modern company barely realised it had a film collection. When Karen Merkel of NMN realised the potential significance of this, she was already in discussion with Birkbeck about a cultural regeneration project in East London, focused on the creation of a digital heritage site for the Royal Commonwealth Society, which would also create access to the extensive archives based in the Queen Elizabeth Olympic Park. With a new campus due to open in Stratford, Birkbeck was envisaged as the principal education partner, potentially creating courses based on public engagement with various East London-related film collections. However, the T&L collection offered an unexpectedly specific opportunity to test this larger ambition.

World in a Cube might be compared to "rescue archaeology." All that could be done within the available funding and timespan was a pilot probe, to reveal what the collection might contain—and to whom it might be of interest. Yet the constraints have arguably been beneficial, forcing those involved to focus on achieving visible results, rather than merely speculating on possible courses of action and waiting for potential academic interest or research funding. The history of research on collections of non-fiction film—indeed on historic film collections per se—is far from encouraging, and strongly suggests that a more measured approach might have achieved little. But *World in a Cube* offers a working model of a new dynamic approach to collection research, which may lead to future detailed work on the T&L films in relation to the company that produced them; and may also offer the outline of a methodology for such work in other contexts.

The Collection—So Far

What's particularly valuable about the T&L collection is that it appears to include many kinds of film material pertaining to the company over a number of decades. On the basis of what has so far been inspected, this might be tentatively divided into three main categories:

- "outward-facing" films, showing the company's basic work and ethos, presumably aimed at general audiences, including potentially those it is trying to influence;
- internal films recording company achievements, presumably intended for showing at company-organised events;

- "functional" films, covering technical aspects of processing its products. One of these, however, appears to be a film intended for staff development use. *Attitudes* offers a range of opinions and vignettes of workplace behaviour, which suggest that it might be a "starter" film for HR or staff development use.

This, however, can only be a tentative taxonomy, since the full extent of the collection remains unknown. Most of the films are on 16 mm and remain at the refinery. Viewing and working with them has involved a limited programme of videoing off-screen and digitisation, which amounts to no more than sampling.

Producing a full inventory of the physical collection is certainly an essential prerequisite to further preservation and research activity. But securing the resources for this involves making some estimate of what it might subsequently yield. Is it, in crude terms, "a major find," or what might be expected from the accumulation of redundant company records? So far, no supporting paper records have been located, which makes contextualisation of the films an "archaeological" process.

A Provisional Sample

Constrained by limited time and finance, a selection of material to digitise had to be made quickly. Six films were chosen for work with the focus groups and four were offered for the remix project. These spanned a period from the 1950s to the early 1980s, featuring places and events all over the world, as well as the T&L refinery on the Thames in East London.

British Refined *(1960)*[12]

An industrial process film that follows the sugar product from harvesting to distribution and sale. Starting in Jamaica, West Indies, where cane sugar is grown and harvested, we move to London, to the T&L refinery for the refining process. The sugar is cut into cubes, packaged and sold on worldwide, with the West African market shown here in some detail. A freighter sails first from London to Ghana; and part of the sugar cargo is unloaded at Accra, to be sold at the market of Kumasi, in Ashanti. The next stop is Lagos, Nigeria, where the T&L sugar cubes are sold at the local market. From here, the sugar continues its journey, travelling to the market of Kano, ancient trading city of Nigeria.

Attitudes *(c. 1972–76?)*[13]

A training or "trigger" film about human relationships in industry. Workers at the London refinery, and at other industries within the larger T&L group in Toronto and New Orleans, talk about how professional hierarchies within the workplace create a "them and us" situation.

Simunye—The Third Mill *(Probably Early 1980s)*[14]

Taking its name from an irrigation and sugar production project carried out in the Kingdom of Swaziland, Southern Africa, from the mid-1970s to 1980, the film explains the company's involvement in this project, and shows its relationship with local authorities and the Royal Swaziland Sugar Corporation.

PA E. Strauss Honoured by Senior Members of Tate and Lyle Nig Ltd *(c. 1973–74)*

This film documents the retirement party for Mr Strauss, Managing Director of Tate and Lyle Nigeria Ltd, and the process of handing the directorship of the company over to the newly appointed Nigerian Managing Director.

A Family Affair *(1959)*[15]

A brief history of cane sugar production and the role of Tate & Lyle in this history through the story of a West Indian sugar worker and his young son, who is fascinated by a rocket he's seen in a picture. After an accident, in which the boy falls off a tree and hurts his shoulder, he is taken to hospital for treatment by a white doctor, who is also responsible for looking after the sugar plantations in the area. Meanwhile, at the Tate & Lyle factory in Kingston, a manager organises buying a toy rocket for the injured boy.

A *Nationwide* report on Tate & Lyle made for the BBC's flagship evening magazine programme in 1977, stressed how this old-established company is "moving with the times." Featuring Saxon Tate, Chairman of the company's Executive Committee, John Lyle, Chairman, and Colin Lyle, it characterises Tate & Lyle's business practices, particularly the company's "battle" to defend cane sugar in the face of the European Common Market's preference for beet sugar.

A Dynamic Research Methodology

We wanted to develop both community and creative opportunities for public engagement with these films, to harness expertise, but also to show the films to those for whom they might have personal meaning and significance.[16] This involved two main strategies: running a series of focus groups, and offering a selection of the films in digitised form for young filmmakers to produce a creative response in "remix" form. An advisory group was created, bringing together historians specialising in London, a company representative, and a range of BFI staff with experience in archiving and education. The three focus groups were intended to unlock memories of individuals and communities, to *use* film as a "trigger" for a public discussion about working-class life in London and in the company's operational territories; about histories of migration, mainly within a Commonwealth framework; and about the changing experience of trade and industry.

History Focus Group

Much of the discussion focused on the production history of the films, with *Attitudes* generating the most interest. It was noted that the film is quite sophisticated in its message, composition and imagery and rather untypical of industrial films. The political context for the film was discussed; it was suggested that the issues it raises should be understood within the context of the UK's entry to the EU and the Equal Opportunities legislation introduced in the 1970s. More specific to T&L's history, the film was considered to fit in with the company's ideas of industrial democracy, by having "authentic" voices openly questioning paternalism in the workplace. Despite its international scope (it looks into work relationships in industries in the UK, USA and Canada), it was criticised for its lack of reference to work practices and relationships in other parts of the world, such as Africa or Afro-Caribbean countries or any of the places where sugar is grown.

Voices, Places and Social Change

Comparison was made between the "silent" East End workforce shown in *British Refined* and the East End voices heard in *Attitudes*. It was pointed out that by the time *Attitudes* was made there was a retreat from representations of a "faceless workforce." When seen together, these two films—*British Refined* and *Attitudes*—produced up to fifteen years apart, serve as an index of industrial and social change, visually and orally capturing the momentous changes that took place in British society in the post-war years.

Referring to the representation of West Indian workers in films such as *British Refined*, it was noted that the employment of black workers at T&L remains a somewhat hidden story, and suggested that there should be more questioning of what is usually presented as the "refined" (that is, white) history of the company and its communities in the East End.

Post-Colonial Histories: National and Transnational

British Refined, Simunye—The Third Mill, The Retirement of Mr Strauss: for some participants the imagery in these films, particularly *British Refined*, evoked the colonial origins of sugar production, and its troublesome history of connection with the transatlantic slave trade. At the same time, there was a recognition that the history of sugar is also one of employment and economic development.

More personal memories were also recorded: work experiences, cultural differences in the consumption of sugar (for example, white cubes in Africa, brown sugar in the Caribbean), and the implications of the product's differential pricing in different parts of the world. One participant reflected:

> As someone of African descent and born in the Caribbean, watching [*British Refined*] reminded me very much of some of my apprenticeship days...I was an apprentice fitter...But I also remember that for the housewife in the Caribbean, they had to pay more for the sugar than the housewife in England and the sugar was produced in the Caribbean and that's interesting because, if investment was made so that the sugar could be refined there, everyone would have bought it cheaper and it would have produced work etc. So those are the things that I'm still trying to make sense of...[17]

Discussion of *Simunye—The Third Mill* prompted reflection on the parallels that could be drawn between past and present in terms of corporate control over natural resources, international business trades and the destruction of environment.

Community Focus Group[18]

Responses to the films from this group, which included some former T&L workers and local residents, were varied. Among the themes that emerge from the participants' responses and the discussion referring to changing industrial relations as shown in *Attitudes*, one comment was:

> The shock is that it was the 70s but things have moved on. The jobs that people have done are completely different, but in some respects the attitudes haven't changed, they're embedded—why we come to work is the same reason. Most people come to work for the money, they wouldn't do it otherwise. Kids these days wouldn't dream of working in a factory, they don't expect to be bored.

Another referred to the place of the refinery in the changing industrial landscape of East London:

> I was fairly convinced that the actions of the LDDC and the arrival of the new "Isle of Dogs as in Canary Wharf" had expunged all industry from the river, I knew that T&L was on the river and at Silvertown, but was flabbergasted to see the scale of the operation—the ship, gantry, cranes in a scene that was resonant of years gone by—I was amazed and also stunned by the gigantic scale of everything—including the international reach of T&L—it is massive, suddenly I realised I was probably seeing about 2% of the operation.

A former employee commented:

> We had no interest in where the sugar came from, we loved the firm, it was very generous—all our meals were free; you were only interested in the final product. OK, we knew sugar was produced in the West Indies but that was about it because we used to play cricket with the West Indians.

For others, the West Indian and African locations in *British Refined* provoked reflections on change:

> I was surprised that the sugar was shipped on to Ghana—that was extraordinary. The first film was in the West Indies where all gets put together... the road that my mum lived on (my parents are from Jamaica), that road is still the same with the sugar cane growing, but there's no factory anymore. There's a whole population of young people who now go to Florida to cut the sugar cane but it's the same journey...

T&L provided regular employment. In 1936 they expanded into the West Indies and took their industrial approaches with them, and their paternalism at the time. The countries wanted a "trade benefit." It wasn't a question of old-style exploitation, it was an industrial process that existed here. Whether it worked or not, it's a different question.

And comments on the changing nature of the sugar industry:

The sugar industry has been dependent on aid. The people have moved to where the sugar industry is now. The sugar industry is reduced in places such as Jamaica and St. Kitts.
The process of sugar refining is strange and complicated. Every market wants a different end product for sugar—it's much easier and cheaper to transport it raw and then produce the final product at the point of sale.

Carrying out this research in partnership with the company not only allowed one screening to take place within the refinery, surrounded by historic artefacts, but also made possible a tour, which provoked strong responses to the visible scale of the operation. The mountains of sugar, and the variety of its colours and textures, made a powerful impact on some participants, as well as the realisation that the way in which the sugar comes into London hasn't changed; the sugar is loaded on and off the bulk carrier ships on the river.

One object which perhaps best signifies the historical themes of benevolence and paternalism in a post-imperial world, and which attracted several focus group participants' attention, was a T&L sugar advert. For some it was a familiar image that triggered memories of distant homelands, for others it was a visually arresting piece of history. The advert features in the film *British Refined*—placed amidst the packets of T&L sugar in the markets of Kumasi and Kano, as well as on cars and in the streets. After all its travels, the advert now "lives" in the T&L museum, occupying its own space and history amidst other historical artefacts of the company.

The Retirement of Mr Strauss provided one small example, within the culture of this company, of what can now be seen as the more general process of the "shedding of empire":

A poignant handing over of the British manager to the Nigerians. That was a time of great optimism in Nigeria in the 1960s-70s. But what's happened since then?

The 1960s–70s "handover process." Britain presented itself paternalistically but with benevolence, a dominant theme throughout. It's quite an interesting historical moment that is reflected there…

British Refined begins and ends with images of black workers, in Jamaica and in West Africa, which evoke a tradition of portraying workers in the third world as "exotic"—somehow happier in their manual labour than equivalent workers in the First World.

Those stereotypes of "gleaming Africans"…how they were represented as exotic creatures in ways that the more unfortunate encyclopaedias of the 1950s would have done, particularly the men who were cutting the cane, but especially those who were rowing canoes [in Ghana] with their gleaming backs etc. This was not "British" behaviour, just not "how it's done."

A film historian looking beyond Britain might observe how this theme of portraying the exoticism of tropical labour was evoked—and indeed mocked—at the end of Raul Ruiz's film *Great Events and Ordinary People* (1979), as a reproach to the whole Griersonian tradition of documentary.[19] Today, it also prompts reflection on the disappearance of physical labour in Britain:

There's no real manual labour aspiration these days. We don't tend to show work heroically any more… [in the films] all that work and all those workers are shown fairly heroically. And I just wonder what that shift is about, what our attitude to work is now.

The aspiration is not to do physical work any more. The industrial world doesn't exist in this part of Europe. Living in Britain, de-industrialisation separates us from our history even. Increasingly, it's a minority experience.

Living Experience

The focus groups aimed to unlock memories of individuals and communities, to use this small sample of films as "triggers" for a public discussion about working-class life, histories of migration and Commonwealth, trade and industry. The themes that emerged indicated how such films might enable people with varying interests and skills to interpret and creatively "repurpose" the T&L films. Showing them in their original 16 mm format in the refinery to a cross-section of T&L staff provided a "time travel" experience that clearly helped prompted memories and discussion.

But we wanted to do more. Today's digital environment offers so many opportunities for access and engagement, creating visibility for this unique collection is both an opportunity and a challenge. Rather than merely publish them online, or in DVD format, what if we could interest young aspiring filmmakers to work with them, as "raw material," to unlock potential which those involved with them as documents might not perceive? Through contacts with universities and art schools, we offered four of the films in a "remix competition." The task was to produce a film or audio/visual sequence of up to five minutes inspired by material from the Tate & Lyle film archive, for which there would be cash prizes and the chance to have work more widely seen.[20]

The results were encouraging, attracting a sizeable audience of emerging filmmakers interested to view and discuss the films. Participants saw the potential for "lyrical" interpretation of imagery that had previously been essentially functional; or for treating it satirically, as the components of a potential disaster movie. Above all, they showed that such material, seemingly overdetermined by its original purpose and context, could in fact be seen quite differently, much as avant-garde filmmakers of the 1960s and 1970s used "found footage" as the basis for their formal constructions.[21] This demonstration perhaps points in two directions: first, towards the potential "re-birth" of film material long considered redundant or outmoded, giving it a "second life." And here it is worth noting that Tate & Lyle Sugars were pleased that the films elicited such interest among young filmmakers. But the project also potentially offers material points for analysis and interrogation, which might yield new insights into the actual processes shown, as part of an expanded conception of "visual history."[22]

A Dynamic Archive?

The overall aim of the *World in a Cube* project was to test a "dynamic" approach to film research, which might overcome inertia or resistance to investigating film collections that do not promise conventional aesthetic or historical rewards. We were lucky, in that the small proportion of films sampled and digitised proved rich in stimuli for those to whom they were shown. The potential to insert these, and no doubt others from the T&L archive, into networks of further dissemination and research is clear. In this respect, they could be seen as joining a tradition that stretches back to the 1930s, when a film sponsored in 1935 by the Commercial Gas

Association, with the unprepossessing title *Housing Problems*, became a cornerstone of the tradition of "British documentary" and is still widely shown and quoted today.[23]

But they could also be seen as inaugurating a new era, when such collections are considered not merely within the canon of "film history," but as a resource that can inform future research and creation in other fields, being used in many different ways as a part of the fabric of our industrial heritage. Just as the artist Yinka Shonibare uses "colonial" fabric to create artworks that challenge our sense of linear history, might not *British Refined*, *Attitudes* and *Simunye* once again play a living, provocative part in our audiovisual culture?

Notes

1. At this stage, Frances Bull, an external researcher and volunteer, was looking after the company's collections while undertaking her PhD on Tate & Lyle's relationship to nationalisation.
2. The Mitchell and Kenyon films were first rescued by a local film enthusiast Peter Worden, and transferred to the British Film Institute in 2000, where their restoration and interpretation were overseen by a team led by Vanessa Toulmin of Sheffield University. See https://en.wikipedia.org/wiki/Mitchell_and_Kenyon.
3. See the AHRC project "Colonial Film: Moving Images and the End of Empire," http://www.colonialfilm.org.uk/; Lee Grieveson and Colin MacCabe, eds., *Empire and Film* (London: Palgrave Macmillan on behalf of the British Film Institute, 2011); Lee Grieveson and Colin MacCabe, eds., *Film and the End of Empire* (Basingstoke: Palgrave Macmillan, 2011).
4. The term "industrial," used in the USA for sponsored documentary, is considerably better.
5. See the biographical entry for Stollwerck in "Who's Who of Victorian Cinema," http://www.victorian-cinema.net/stollwerck; also Martin Loiperdinger, *Stollwercks Geschäfte mit lebenden Bildern* (Frankfurt am Main: Stroemfeld/Roter Stern, 1999).
6. An early advertising film for Vinolia soap, made in 1897 by C. Goodwin Norton, and *A Visit to Peek Frean & Co's Biscuit Work*, made by Cricks and Martin in 1906, are two of the earliest promotional films for British companies to survive.

7. Martin Loiperdinger has curated a selection of early German advertising films produced by Julius Pinschewer: "Classics of Advertising Films," https://absolutmedien.de/film/529/Julius+Pinschewer+%E2%80%93+Klassiker+des+Werbefilms.
8. *TurkSib* was singled out for praise by Grierson, and widely shown in the early 1930s in Britain, no doubt influencing many members of the emerging documentary film movement. See notes by Henry K. Miller for *The Soviet Example: from Turksib to Night Mail*, directed by Victor Turin (London: British Film Institute, 2014), DVD.
9. See for instance: Ian Aitken, ed., *The Documentary Film Movement: An Anthology* (Edinburgh: Edinburgh University Press, 1998); also his *Film and Reform: John Grierson and the Documentary Film Movement* (London: Routledge, 1990). Other accounts, among many, are: Elizabeth Sussex, *The Rise and Fall of British Documentary: The Story of the Film Movement Founded by John Grierson* (Berkeley: University of California Press, 1976); and Paul Swann, *The British Documentary Film Movement, 1926-1946* (Cambridge: Cambridge University Press, 2008).
10. Patrick Russell, senior curator of non-fiction at the British Film Institute, was extremely generous with practical help and advice during this project, and his books and DVD sets of British documentary films are an invaluable resource. See, especially, Patrick Russell and James Taylor, eds., *Shadows of Progress: Documentary Film in Post-War Britain* (Basingstoke: Palgrave Macmillan, 2010).
11. The company was created from the merger of Henry Tate & Sons and Abram Lyle & Sons. Its refinery was opened in 1878. See the company website: http://www.tateandlyle.com/aboutus/history/pages/history.aspx.
12. *British Refined*, directed by William J. Bassett (London: Thames Refinery Film Unit, 1960). There are two versions of this film, one English and one West African.
13. *Attitudes*, directed by Michael Radford (London: James Archibald for Tate & Lyle, c. 1972–76).
14. *Simunye—The Third Mill*, directed by Peter Grossett (London: Tate & Lyle in partnership with the Royal Swaziland Sugar Corporation, early 1980s).
15. *A Family Affair*, directed by Michael Johns (London[?]: Robert Angell in partnership with Puritan Films, 1959).

16. For details of the research process and outcomes, see Eleni Liarou, "World in a Cube—Project Report" (2013), http://www.creativeworkslondon.org.uk/wp-content/uploads/2013/11/NMN-Creative-Voucher-Final-Report.pdf.
17. This and all other comments included here are from transcripts of discussions included in the project's final report, ibid.
18. The Community Focus Group was held on 14 June 2013, comprising eleven participants, including one Tate & Lyle ex-employee, and people who live and/or work in East London.
19. For a discussion of Ruiz's film, ostensibly made as election coverage for French television in 1978, see Ian Christie, "Ruiz dossier," *Afterimage* 10 (1981): 112–13; also Adrian Martin's account in *Rouge*, online at http://www.rouge.com.au/2/great.html.
20. Submissions were judged by members of the project's advisory group, and two prizes were offered of £200 and £150, along with accompanying publicity. The winning entries were invited to attend the project's final event in early October where their work was presented to an influential audience, before being published online.
21. "Found footage," removed from its original context, has been the basis of many schools of avant-garde filmmaking since the 1960s, notably in the UK, Italy and the USA.
22. See Elizabeth Edwards, *The Camera as Historian* (Durham: Duke University Press, 2012).
23. *Housing Problems*, directed by Arthur Elton and Edgar Anstey (London[?]: British Commercial Gas Association, 1935), has become one of the foundational film of the British documentary tradition. See, for instance, BFI Screenonline http://www.screenonline.org.uk/film/id/513807/.

Consumer as Producer; Value Mechanics in Digital Transformation Design Process, Practice and Outcomes

Karen Cham

Digital Transformation Design (DTD) is a digital-first, design-led, human-centred industrial method for engineering transformation of complex human-centred systems, such as multi-platform global marketing campaigns; big organizational infrastructures; markets and economies; virtual worlds and simulations. Any online system has the capacity to change what happens "in real life" (IRL) by means of the user experience (UX), that is, a person's total experience using a particular product, system or service and there are many good and bad examples of this.[1] In technology-led "reductive" innovation, where a technological element is used as the basis for a UX, what is commonly known as "disruption" results, that is, the unwanted effects of rapid and ill-, or often un-thought-out change. At worst, value chains are decimated as companies collapse, livelihoods are lost and communities are destroyed and even for the "disruptors," as legislation is ignored, or bizarrely, assumed to be inapplicable, long-term gains in a stable market seem unachievable. Conversely, "transformation" is where the significant sociocultural aspects of technology are accounted for, and DTD requires designing multi-stakeholder engagement mechanics into complex multi-touchpoint ecosystems, on a micro- and macro-level

K. Cham (✉)
University of Brighton, Brighton, UK

simultaneously, ensuring future-proof co-evolution of the tool *and its context*. Not easy, not quick and not cheap, but providing sustainable evolution and at best, engineering desired changes in behaviour.

DTD therefore relies on successful migration of legacy systems of all kinds, personal, social, cultural and technical and it does this by designing, first and foremost, for the "emotional engagement" of end users, without which there is no agency to the system and no change will result. Measuring this type of engagement is long established, beginning with the use of eye tracking in human-computer interaction (HCI) many years ago, and it provides actionable user insights as part of the "agile" user-centred iterative digital development process. These insights are understood as being into "system two" cognition, the cognition of the irrational limbic system, a type of engagement known to be paramount to decision-making processes and only activated by complex semantic, social, aesthetic and cultural affordances, collateral that constitutes the "emotional capital" of any artefact or product; ritual, process or service. This emotional capital provides an indication as to the human "value mechanics" that must be isolated and incorporated into the UX as affordances to accelerate any successful DTD process.

This chapter contextualizes a research and development project, based on DTD and funded by Creativeworks London in 2013 as part of their call, "Co-Creation: Consumer as Producer" that looked at "blurring the boundaries between consumption, customization, production and creative collaboration" by focusing upon the democratization of production afforded by digital media. The call asked specifically for research projects that would expand the role of the end user or consumer in the production process. The advantages to undertaking practice-based academic research with a commercial partner are that the company receives support for Research & Development activities that they may not otherwise be able to undertake and the University can demonstrate the impact of their research expertise. This project aimed to explore the potential for interaction between high-end fashion accessory designers and their customers *in the design process* as part of a prototype product customization platform and the possibilities afforded by integrating "user-generated content" (UGC) into the design process. In file sharing, UGC is often relatively unconstrained, disrupting only the profit chain; in social media, UGC has come to be understood by major commercial players as "earned" media in recognition of the power of public customer feedback; however in product design, UGC was at the time, largely constrained to superficial options such as a palette of colours, customized elements and items for the end user to select pre-order. The design research therefore, aimed to address fundamental issues around the notion of mass customization for creative industries above and beyond this "user completion model" to understand how, where and in what ways users might contribute to the design process in terms of real digital co-design; in complex interactive authoring systems, some sort of architecture or grammar must constrain and enable UGC in such a way as to maintain systemic coherence *in the process and the output*.

Furthermore, as the commercial partner was an online service sourcing high-end luxury branded fashion accessories, it was even more important that any foray into UGC did not *disrupt* the value of the product. The fashion industries' luxury brands have long engineered a delicate and highly lucrative balance between accessibility and exclusivity,[2] providing the core value mechanics of their entire industry, with digital co-design demonstrating the potential to disrupt that delicate balance entirely. It already is evident from services like Spotify and Netflix, that ultimate "horizontal" accessibility decimates the value of the content absolutely, as the concept of "ownership itself relies on the concept of scarcity."[3] Concurrent to this project, eBay appointed guest "curators" with the aim of explicitly creating a sense of meaning, value and ownership in its sea of junk; with Amazon and ASOS not far behind, as mass accessibility has inevitably resulted in a bankruptcy of acquisition mechanics across the board. The design research questions were therefore around maintaining overall value but also specific *brand value* in a UGC context. This is a complex and unresolved area, and the project that was funded promised to explore all potentials for browser-based interaction in the design process between high-end fashion accessory designers and their existing and potential customer bases, within the parameters of each brand. This could lead to a prototype tool that would have the potential to provide valuable market insights for the designers, increase levels of "emotional engagement" with their brand, expanding their reach and incentivizing their customer bases. The research aimed to address fundamental issues in the notion of any type of co-design for high-end fashion, by establishing the "cultural capital" of each brand, for example, establishing where the brand value is in the individual brands, their products, their process and their market. We aimed to investigate how digital co-design methods might maintain, augment and transform that brand value; what lexicons and shape grammars might inform parametrics and generative design principles for specific brands; and how such co-design opportunities could be integrated into digital tools and marketplace. By using emotion recognition technologies to gather quantitative data we hoped to investigate specific branded "user experiences" (UX) of the prototypes, to "differentiate co-design and mass customization from a user completion model within the realm of product design."[4]

This Creative Voucher project aimed to reveal significant issues such as the inherent conflict between mass market commercial demands and high-end design and how to maintain the dynamics of high-end fashion value in a user-generated context; the fundamental and inherent conflicts between accessibility and value. In practice, what actually happened was some sort of Derridean feedback loop, where the project dissolved into competing perspectives on the perceived value of the cultural capital of the process and project itself. The commercial partners were not comfortable giving the researchers contact with the designers; questioned various proposals of what the design process might be and the possibilities the tool might offer their business; considered the Research Assistant to be their digital assistant for any issue on a daily basis; and sought to advise the lead researcher on basic technical issues. To explain what the project might have achieved, this chapter thus sets out the background of Digital Transformation Design, pointing towards a working methodology that can support future commercial/academic collaborations, in the hope that academic expertise can indeed drive the marketplace for commercial partners.

Design Practice

As discussed above, DTD is a digital first, design led, human-centred industrial method for engineering transformation of complex human-centred systems, such as multi-platform global marketing campaigns; big organizational infrastructures; markets and economies; virtual worlds and simulations. In contexts such as these, the design of the UX is engineered explicitly to exploit both neural and social plasticities and affect change. Transformation is the converse of digital disruption, which is a technology-led imposition upon existing ecosystems of value chains, stakeholders and relationships that brings unwanted disruptive changes. Examples of digital disruption include Kodak, where media technology moved so fast as to disrupt the core business model faster than the company could "pivot"; Blockbuster and HMV similarly and

Uber, where the tool has decimated existing livelihoods and then its own business model by not even accounting for legislation in some deployments.

DTD has evolved from "User Experience Design," a complex, new and evolving field, which is currently defined as concerned with "experiences created and shaped through technology...and how to deliberately design those." The International Organization for Standardization defines "user experience" as "a person's perceptions and responses that result from the use *or anticipated use* of a product, system or service."[5] Commercial UXD is often defined as a subset of the broader fields of experiential marketing and customer and/or brand experience design. It was Brenda Laurel, in her 1991 book *Computers as Theatre*, who first used the term "user experience" as a means to expound an embodied experience of interaction with machines.

> Thinking about interfaces is thinking too small. Designing human-computer experience isn't about building a better desktop. It's about creating imaginary worlds that have a special relationship to reality-worlds in which we can extend, amplify, and enrich our own capacities to think, feel, and act.[6]

Two years later Don Norman, who was appointed as one of the first ever User Experience Architects at Apple, is quoted as saying:

> I thought Human Interface and usability were too narrow: I wanted to cover all aspects of the person's experience with a system, including industrial design, graphics, the interface, the physical interaction, and the manual.[7]

There are many ongoing debates as to whether an "experience" can be "designed" at all, whether a UX designer just designs *for* the experience, and how any of it differs from *design* per se. It is fair to say that as a result of the sheer velocity of technological change, in recent years practice has led theory in all fields of digital design, as recent developments include mobile, ubiquitous, social and tangible applications, products, services and spaces that include, but are not limited to, websites, mobile phone apps, digital television, interactive artworks, computer games, software and "smart" products and environments, the "Internet of Things," the "Internet of Place," and virtual and augmented reality. Digital media design is often for interactive products and services, and it is that interactivity that has caused many people some consternation.[8] The term "interactive" is specifically used here to refer to "a machine system which reacts in the moment, by virtue of automated reasoning based on data from its sensory apparatus."[9] For a holistic consideration of the users' experience, good UXD should aim to optimize the integration of functionality and aesthetics in digital interaction to reinforce and promote the communication goals.

"Human-Computer Interaction" (HCI), was the practice that first explicitly addressed designing for the "human factors" in our interaction with machines. The term itself was first used in the mid-1970s and popularized in Thomas Moran and Allen Newell's "The Psychology of Human-Computer Interaction."[10] It is multidisciplinary, drawing upon computer science, cognitive psychology and ergonomics amongst other fields. Significantly, it established itself around 1980, concurrent to the advent of personal computing, when new and diverse non-specialist user groups started using computer systems. Whilst HCI, focusing upon the purely technical function and basic performative "usability," is often misunderstood, badly represented and sometimes poorly applied, it embodies the concept that working with an interactive computer system takes place in "a dialogue between the user and the computer" which is still an irrefutable paradigm in daily practice.[11]

Irrespective of any amount of integration with peripheral devices, digital media is marked out by one key characteristic; that of interactivity; it is therefore still "user interaction design" (UID), that is, at the root of designing any UX. "*User* interaction design" (UID), is a term used in the study, planning, and design of the interaction between people and computers, which grew out of HCI. In what is considered by many to be the definitive textbook on UID, *Interaction Design, Beyond HCI*, Jenny Preece, Yvonne Rogers and Helen Sharp importantly define UID as including many academic disciplines in addition to those associated with HCI, such as design, informatics, engineering and sociology.[12] In parallel, "Interaction Design" refers to the shaping of products and services with a specific focus on the interaction between people and *the designed object*. In *Thoughtful Interaction Design: A Design Perspective on Information Technology*, Jonas Löwgren and Erik Stolterman firstly define the tradition of interaction design as it evolves out of user-centred product design.[13] This perspective is manifest in the approach of the Royal College of Art's seminal Design Interactions MA, Donald Norman's book *The Design of Everyday Things*, and Durrell Bishop's legendary marble telephone answering machine (1992), a tangible interaction application that gamified the message leaving and retrieving process using marbles.[14] It is therefore also User-Centred Design (UCD), developing out of a product, that pioneered "Human-Focused Design."[15] Digital is a convergence of "television, telecommunications and computing,"[16] so UX designers must work with computer science, product design, graphics and media production techniques and methodologies to create engaging products and services.

"Web 2.0," as it came to be known, added hitherto unforeseen levels of complexity to the fundamental HCI two-way dialogue by facilitating the advent of UGC as we know it today. In effect, this allowed various interpretations of a message or artefact to be apprehended, adapted, amended and fed back into the source system, presenting problems on any number of levels. This phenomenon was best described by Bowman and Willis' in 2003 as an "emerging media ecosystem" as part of their "WeMedia" manifesto, a seminal analysis of the news reporting value chain in the age of user-generated content.[17]

Later, the true impact of a global peer-to-peer decentralized news network was manifest when the publication of a cartoon of the Prophet Mohammed in the Danish press became an international communications event, sparking riots after it "went viral," spreading across the globe and reaching audiences it was never intended to reach out of context and in breach of the core taboos of sacred legacy systems. Tools like Trip Advisor meanwhile, have created accountability for the hospitality industry at a level of previously unimagined visibility, impacting quite profoundly on small businesses and global brands alike, and leading to the concept of "bought, owned and earned media"[18] across a constantly evolving ecosystem of touchpoints.

It is only as a result of these "disruptors" that we have recognized that a representational system has the capacity to change what happens "in real life" (IRL). Traditionally, the media effects debate stalled at any true understanding of the symbiotic relationship between content and behaviour, the territory now inhabited by User Experience Design (UXD), that is, designing a person's total experience of a particular product, system or service. As discussed above, transformation is where the significant sociocultural aspects of technology are accounted for, and DTD requires designing multi-stakeholder engagement mechanics into complex multi-touchpoint ecosystems, on a micro- and macro-level simultaneously, ensuring future proof co-evolution of the tool *and its context*.

So if we are to design a transformative, rather than disruptive, co-design dialogue; a nested complex system of interactions in the process, the object and the outcome, what type of meta-design paradigms can we use to enable success? Whilst admittedly handbag design doesn't carry the societal risks of journalism, for product designers, user-generated content poses a huge risk to their value chain. Mass customization, co-design and collaborative innovation platforms all risk "design by spambot" as the "mechanically-reproduced artefact"[19] is dismissed in a discourse where value is still equated with authentic concepts of authenticity and originality, usually anchored in production techniques. UGC potentially negates the exclusivity essential to establishing value; not only is the digital artefact accessible to the masses, it is here shaped by audience input; a product of "the mass" themselves. It doesn't take much to envisage the design equivalent of folksonomies, for example, at worst, a minestrone of conjecture and asides, the very opposite of the aim of any type of design.

Design is an oft-used but ill-defined word. As taught in British art schools, and practised in the UK creative industries, design practice finds its roots in the industrial design methodologies of the Bauhaus, a revolutionary art school founded in Weimar in 1919. The Bauhaus was distinguished by its internationalism, cosmopolitanism and artistic diversity.[20] It operated as an artists' collective, focused upon design practice in an industrial age and espoused the belief that *design could improve society*. All students were trained in a general approach to the basics of design in all contexts, with a concentration on industrial problems in their social context, mechanical tools and mass production. The original Bauhaus manifesto was aimed at building a design curriculum based on a "synthesis of art, science, and technology [and] the fulcrum…was the preliminary course,"[21] a formalist approach to design process encapsulated in the Modernist ethos of "form follows function," "truth to materials" and "economy of design." The "Basics" as it came to be known, favoured an "economics" or "purity" of design that advocated that the designed object should function as well and as simply as possible, setting out the case for a basic usability and putting the user at the centre of the design process.

Additionally, the teaching of basic design was condensed into exercises with a focus on a research-based approach to problem solving, within the framework of specific constraints. MacLean et al. pointed out that the final output of a design also included what they called "design space"; a body of knowledge about the artefact, its environment, its intended use and the decisions that went into creating the design.[22] The "Point, Line & Plane" approach that was published much later[23] added a fundamental lexicon of geometric elements from which all other forms could be generated; a "constructivist" approach to design that clearly underpins parametrics and generative design methods today.

Johannes Itten's "preliminary course" at the Bauhaus aimed to introduce students to the fundamental design problems of form and materials, and the basic laws of design. These fundamentals were also known as "Vorkurs," or "Grundkurs" at the school of Ulm, became the "Basics Course" at the New Bauhaus in Chicago, after Moholy-Nagy accepted an invitation from Chicago's Association of Art and Industry to re-establish his work there in 1937 as the Nazis had closed the Bauhaus. It is Louis Henry Sullivan the "father of skyscrapers," an influential architect and critic of the Chicago School, a mentor to Frank Lloyd Wright, and an inspiration to the Chicago group of architects who is credited with the design mantra "form follows function" and from the late 1930s it was the Harvard Graduate School of Design that played a crucial role in shaping international modernism, alongside Walter Gropius' transformation of Harvard's old Beaux-Arts School. It is this hybrid approach to industrial design in the USA that eventually led to IDEO and the d-school at Stanford and their "Design Thinking" movement that presupposes design problem solving can be applied in any context as a human-centred approach to solutions.

The notion of design as a "way of thinking" can be traced to Herbert A. Simon's 1969 book *The Sciences of the Artificial*, and Robert McKim's 1973 book *Experiences in Visual Thinking*. Rolf Faste expanded on McKim's work at Stanford University in the 1980s and 1990s, teaching "design thinking as a method of creative action." Design thinking was adapted for business purposes by Faste's Stanford colleague David M. Kelley, who founded IDEO in 1991, a firm best known for pioneering an "expanded" view of design. Unfortunately, in the last few years "design thinking" has also been adopted with "missionary zeal" by many who have no idea of its provenance nor its rigour. In fact many believe, it has "little to do with what designers do" or indeed "what is taught in design schools" to the extent that it has become an open-ended signifier, meaning anything in any context for anyone with any purpose. Very much akin to the term "gamification," "design thinking" is now operating as an autonomous ideology. Most recently, this semantic bankruptcy led to the term being registered as trademark with the US Patent and Trademark Office in class 41—meaning that the right to use the phrase in educational settings is owned by Stanford, a small and perhaps necessary step towards standardization and quality control of an important emerging practice.

It is in Ittens Basics course, and its evolution through IDEO, that we find the roots of today's "Design Thinking" movement, with the notion of design basics that are domain agnostic and that provide the roots of *Sprint0*, the preliminary problem definition phase in digital production today. However, it is also in the Bauhaus, in 1919, that we find the foundations of a user-centred, research-informed, usability-orientated, context-specific, analytical problem-solving, industrial design practice that accounts for generative systems and is focused on social transformation. It is here, that the most advanced of Digital Transformation tasks can find its methodological basis.

Process, Meaning and Value

In order for DTD to be a manifestation of design thinking, the problem-definition phase of a project is of paramount importance and it always comes first, or as its name implies, prior to the beginning. It is absolutely imperative that a design process begins by defining the problem, not by assuming any solutions. It is here that "design thinking" is perhaps at its best. It is an analytical and systematic integration of divergent and convergent mental processing that integrates the rational and the intuitive, towards defining the exact nature of the problem at hand. Digital disruption is always technology led—a product or service goes to market on the basis that the technology can do it. Whether or not the technology should do it and whether it solves the problem at hand is not addressed. *Sprint0* is a paid analytical evaluation phase where all variable elements of a problem, such as stakeholders, social and technical legacy systems, budget and time constraints, and all other elements are evaluated in the context of desired outcomes. The idea-generation phase is then a divergent process based on the tangible facts that define the problem and that aims to best solve that problem.

Digital production runs in "sprints," phases that are iterations known as an "agile" development process, one that relies upon research-based decision-making and is entirely user centred. The primary source of research data is demographics on indicative user groups. These are translated into working User Profiles that underpins User Journeys—indicative human-centred narratives that define how your indicative user groups come across your touchpoints—*prior to the design of the system*. These journeys, defined in the light of the problem definition phase, then define the architecture for first iteration, *from the middle out*. Through the agile development cycle, these iterations are tested upon users from the target group and changed to meet the findings. Traditionally, some biometric material has been included in the form of eye tracking. There is a long history of quantitatively evaluating where engagement might lie in the HCI tradition of using eye tracking, that originated from trying to understand how to put an interface together in such a way as to direct the user's attention successfully. Anchored in HCI, eye tracking was traditionally focused on measuring efficiency and task performance of a system, however, digital systems that can rely purely on functional efficiency are now almost entirely history.

Löwgren, Stolterman and Löwgren importantly defined an "affective" UXD as design that aims to elicit positive responses such as "feeling at ease, being comfortable, and enjoying the experience or motivating users to learn, play, be creative, or be social."[24] It was in 2009 that Eric Shaffer, Founder and CEO at "Human Factors International," and one of the first people to recognize that user studies would be a key issue for computing, stated that the interactive online environment offers "far more opportunities to influence customers' decision-making than traditional advertising or marketing channels do" and termed a new level of influential UXD as designing for "persuasion, emotion and trust" or "PET."[25] In terms of CX, designing for PET, using successful incentivization techniques of any kind, leads to an increase in what is termed "conversion rates," that is, quantifiable returns on how many users have undertaken the desired result, for example, subscribed/purchased and so on, and where, when and how that occurred. This data is then used to generate "predictive analytics," or more accurately, algorithmic patterns of user behaviours that provide actionable insights into how future users might behave in order to better inform UX designers how best to design for "conversion" in the future. DTD is a good-quality, design-led UX process that designs for

PET by integrating user insights of all kinds within the iterative development cycle.

However, as digital services operate as complex socio-technical mediated ecosystems, distributed across multiple co-evolving touchpoints, the value of a brand, product or service is easily dissolved through multiple ongoing instances of user generate content (UGC) as computer systems cannot parse *meaning and value*, they can process syntax but not semantics and so the *noise* in the message increases overtime, very much as the meaning of a message is lost during repetition in "Chinese whispers" (exponential increase in Shannon entropy).[26] For this reason some sort of semantic framework, architecture or grammar must constrain and enable UGC in such a way as to maintain systemic coherence *in the process and the output*. In artistic compositions, the design of open structural relations, rather than closed objects, finds its roots in systems art, and the dynamic capacity of digitally interactive systems in use, places digital interactivity well within the realm of complex systems science. This convergence has been established by the author as a "reconstruction" of the post-structuralist "death of the author," providing a theoretical starting point to allow multiple users to participate in a dialogic process that demonstrates self-organization and emergent behaviours.

Visual communications that are digitally interactive in this way are participatory, navigable in a non-linear manner and/or open to user generated content and require different design methodologies. The author has previously proposed that designing for digital media is best approached by an integration of poststructuralism and complex systems theory:

> the designer must successfully integrate visual communication design, information architecture and usability by purposefully designing for semiotic autopoeisis 5; a fundamental dialectic between structure and function must be designed *into the system and its use*. Such a proposal requires good UX designers to design diachronic grammatical structures that can adapt and evolve whilst consistently providing a coherent synchronic experience under multitudinous variables. Good user experience design for digital media visual communication systems requires designers to *paint with language and leave it wet.*[27]

Once users begin to "paint with language," the constructed representation, of a brand, for example, becomes *rhizomatic*; that is, it becomes complex and co-evolving and demonstrating emergent behaviours, in line with Gilles Deleuze and Félix Guattari's (1972–1980) philosophical definition of the rhizome as

> characterized by ceaselessly established connections between semiotic chains, organizations of power and circumstances...a rhizome has no beginning or end; it is always in the middle, between things, inter being, intermezzo...a rhizome is an image of thought that apprehends multiplicities.[28]

This is not least as it is experienced across multiple platforms. In branded multi-platform UX, research undertaken by Raida Shakiry under the supervision of the author, demonstrated that a "dual process" approach was required to evaluate to what extent this representation is present; that is, we must quantitatively measure both cognitive *and emotional* engagement to evaluate engagement in the multi-platform branded user experience. In contemporary UX practice eye tracking is now used in combination with EEG and implicit response testing as part of neuromarketing, as a means of generating actionable insights as part of the agile development cycle. From the technical perspective only, it cannot account for the literacy of complex visual messages and often comes back with junk insights such as filling your content with faces as there is most emotional engagement when people's faces are featured. UX is however currently recognizing, that "storytelling" is important and generating emotional engagement in narrative isn't that simple. In particular, branded storytelling across multiple platforms is particularly difficult to maintain. In DTD, the actualization of emotional value mechanics, as part of the development cycle, is of paramount importance, as without it the system has no agency and no transformation will occur.

"System two" cognition, the irrational limbic system, is paramount to decision-making processes and is only activated by complex semantic, social, aesthetic and cultural affordances that constitute "emotional capital"; these are the human "value mechanics" that must be isolated and incorporated into the User Experience (UX) as affordances in any successful DTD process. There are a number of ways of establishing affordance by actuating value mechanics during the development cycle in digital transformation design. One is through modelling the brands' values explicitly. For example, if a key brand value is accessibility, making sure the whole UX is accessible. Another way is through user testing, using biometric data to isolate branded affordances in combination with a sematic architecture developed as a rhizomatic architecture from a convergence of poststructuralism and complexity. The work for Creativeworks London was then, very much a design and build of the "space of possibility" in "complex media."[29]

Case Study

The first contact between the partners in this Creative Voucher project happened when the entrepreneur approached the author some time prior to the Creativeworks London call, looking for an intern. I explained that any work proposed had to meet significant learning outcomes for the postgraduate students in addition to providing a minimum stipend. The work requested and the rates offered were not, however, in the end commensurate with the Digital Media Kingston programme.[30] As I regularly worked as a design consultant through Kingston University Enterprise Ltd, I thus drafted a response that suggested ways in which the work she wanted doing could meet high-level design research aims and when the Creativeworks London call was released, I contacted the entrepreneur and suggested we apply as the project I had scoped in response to their enquiry met the terms of the call perfectly.

We were of course delighted to win an award. At the outset, however, the project was delayed by six weeks through the commercial partner proposing an IP agreement with the University, to which it was unable to agree and before any IP had been generated. This was the start of a series of miscommunications and misunderstandings that undermined our chances of a successful outcome. The entrepreneur refused me any contact with the designers saying there was nothing they could tell me that she did not also know. The entrepreneur, as partner on a project that was intended to be co-created and collaborative, significantly underestimated the extent of my digital research expertise. This is 30 years into my design career and over 20 into digital; I designed my first website three years after Tim Berners Lee, but using an image as an interface to a narrative; I created a touchscreen non-linear video the same year, won EU recognition for the digital micro-business model two years later and established *Sprint0* on the job, three years before the publication of the Agile Manifesto. A quick Google tells you most of this, and also brings up my publication record, for Intellect, Routledge and IEE.

I had to resolve to investigate the potential for user-generated content in the design process of high-end accessory designers independently of the designers already working with the entrepreneur, through our own staff and alumni at The Design School at Kingston University, which is recognized as a global leader in fashion design education and whose alumni include leading designers such as Sophie Hulme. Sophie was keen to participate, but on the grounds that her work on the project was not known publicly as it could damage her brand. I contacted a number of other designers across the spectrum, including Samantha Ward of Yoma and Jacqui Markham, Global Director of Design at Top Shop, and explored what a tool might look like that allowed designers to set bespoke preferences to gather market information; or allowed crowd sourcing of design direction; voting thorough to manufacture; users-created look books; being invited to co-design and so on. I then drafted a Process Flow Diagram to describe the high-level architecture we would have to use as a starting point for the entrepreneur to discuss with the designers how, where and when users might participate in their individual processes. The principle being that Digital Transformation Design of their products, services and business models must be engineered in such a way as to preserve and accelerate their individual design mechanics in bespoke ways at agreed touchpoints. The Process Flow Diagram (see Fig. 1) suggests ways in which different users might engage in the design process beyond a user completion model. The project aimed to address

- participatory design frameworks for individual designers and their collections;
- how true co-design methods might be integrated into mass customization tools;
- what parametrics and generative design principles for fashion accessories might look like.

Figure 1 was referred to by the technical partner in the business as "spot the difference," as potentially, from a technical point of view, the back end function to enable UGC would be very similar at each stage of the design process. However, from the dual users' point of view, the customer and the designer, the type of convergent collaboration each point of interaction enabled would be entirely different, idiosyncratic,

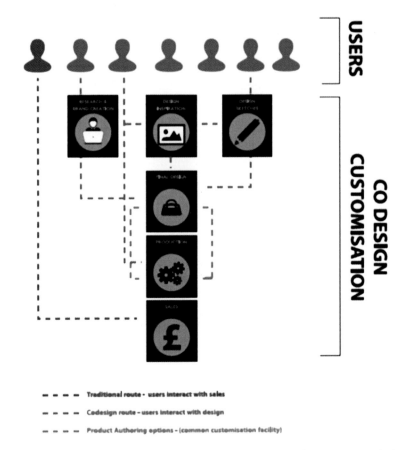

Fig. 1 Process flow diagram that differentiates co-design for a user completion model (2013)

complex and potentially disruptive. For me, it is in moments such as these, where people, media and machines converge, that real design research begins.

Unfortunately, on the grounds that the entrepreneur and her team believed that "designers start with a shape" and that interaction at any stage is *the same thing*, the project effectively stalled at this point and I realized I would have to troubleshoot a way forward. My Research Assistant had been doing another useful job meanwhile undertaking a Competitor Review looking at what tools were on the market, their mechanics, users and outcomes and so I decided he could support the client to develop their own copy of existing products whilst I independently undertook the design research; hoping that I could converge the two later in the development cycle.

It was then shortly after this that the client made a number of urgent calls, texts and emails to me concerning the fact that designers don't want mass customization tools…because it can damage their brand. She decided we should proceed to build a tool that she could sell on in any context and the brief for this repeatedly reacted in line with the market; exactly why the agile development process is as it is. My RA was a young postgraduate who had shown excellent industry-facing research skills in his final MA User Experience Design project developing a full service design for Nike's smart football boot; he was a thorough, patient and diligent student. He began working in the local coffee shop near his home which saved the project time and money. The client bumped into him there one day; took an interest in his progress and offered some direction. She then asked him to undertake other digital jobs that were not related to the Creative Voucher project; expressing the view that because he was being funded by the voucher he worked for her. This was not the relationship between researcher and SME that was anticipated by the Creativeworks London Creative Voucher scheme. The Research Assistant thus felt he had to step down from the project. The client then told me she had one designer who makes bespoke products who would work with us; she put me in direct contact, but then interrupted my preliminary enquiries as I was enquiring about design process, materials, manufacturing model, turnaround time, targets for growth and brand values, saying that she basically wanted market insights, thus arresting my investigations that would underpin the functionality of the tool and its outcomes. I appointed an experienced front-end developer and put him in touch directly with the client; briefing him to build whatever the client wanted on time and on budget, which he did. On handover, she expressed disappointment that the one individual designer she had managed to secure interest from was complaining that the tool would not enable cost-effective manufacturing, which of course we knew, because we had been unable to design those requirements into the outcome after our research was arrested.

Conclusion

Without the preceding 5000 words that summarize 100 years of design history, 30 years of design practice, 22 years in digital, 15 years as a design academic, and 7 years of my own education in design, the partner entrepreneur on this Creative Voucher project had no idea of the processes required to achieve the suggested aims. This significantly hampered the kind of co-creation that had been anticipated and desired. Whilst it could be argued that a quick Google search would have revealed the expertise behind my role, and indeed, what might be gained from it, it is I believe, also paramount in building a successful collaborative project to provide examples of previous *process*, not outcomes, to serve as indicative deliverables above and beyond project milestones.

UXD has evolved as a means of solving the problems that arise if you approach a digital design from a technology-led or business requirements–led perspective; a successful digital build has to be design-led and user-centred. Digital Transformation Design put the disruptive potential of digital centre stage and accounts for it—by design. Some useful research was undertaken in the end on this project, however, as to how to maintain the dynamics of high-end fashion value in a user-generated context, and other fundamental and inherent conflicts between accessibility and value. This work did indeed reveal significant inherent conflicts between mass market commercial demands and high-end design. The entrepreneur in the end had total faith in responding to the market but none in design itself to drive that market; so no shared understanding of the economic value of innovation could be achieved across the project.

Notes

1. Karen Cham, "Virtually An Alternative? The Medium, The Message and The User Experience: Collective Agency in Digital Spaces and Embodied Social Change" (Fifth LAEMOS Colloquium on Organization Studies Constructing Alternatives: How Can We Organize for Alternative Social, Economic, and Ecological Balance?, Havana, Cuba, 2014), http://laemos.com; Karen Cham, "Reality Jamming: Beyond Complex Causality in Mediated Systems" (ISEA 08, Singapore, 2008), http://www.isea2008singapore.org/abstract/i-1/p338.html.

2. See http://www.businessoffashion.com/articles/intelligence/the-luxury-brand-balancing-act.
3. See http://www.theguardian.com/media-network/2015/jul/20/netflix-spotify-streams-diminishing-value-digital-content.
4. R. Bernabei and L. Power, "Differentiating Co-Design and Mass Customization from a User-Completion Model within the Realm of Product Design" (The 2nd International Conference on Design Creativity, 18–20 September 2012, Glasgow, 2012): 227–233, https://www.designsociety.org/publication/32515/differentiating_co-design_and_mass_customisation_from_a_user-completion_within_the_realm_of_product_design.
5. Marc Hassenzahl, Kai Eckoldt, Sarah Diefenbach, Matthias Laschke, Eva Len, and Joonhwan Kim, "Designing Moments of Meaning and Pleasure: Experience Design and Happiness," *International Journal of Design* 7, no. 3 (2013): 21–31.
6. Brenda Laurel, *Computers as Theatre*, 2nd ed. (Boston: Addison-Wesley Educational Publishers, 1991).
7. Donald A. Norman, *The Design of Everyday Things* (New York: Basic Books, 2002).
8. Karen Cham and Jeffrey Johnson, "Complexity Theory: a Science of Cultural Systems?" *M/C Journal*, 10, no. 3 (2007): 21–34.
9. S. Penny, "From A to D and Back Again: The Emerging Aesthetics of Interactive Art," *Leonardo Electronic Almanac* 4, no. 4 (1996), http://www.leoalmanac.org/wp-content/uploads/2012/07/LEA-v4-n4.pdf.
10. Stuart K. Card, Thomas P. Moran, Allen Newell, *The Psychology of Human-Computer Interaction* (Hillsdale: Erlbaum, 1983).
11. Manuel A. Pérez-Quiñones and John L. Sibert, "A Collaborative Model of Feedback in Human-Computer Interaction" (Proceedings of the SIGCHI Conference on Human Factors in Computing Systems. ACM, 1996).
12. Jenny Preece, Yvonne Rogers, and Helen Sharp, *Interaction Design, Beyond HCI* (New York: John Wiley & Sons, 2002).
13. Jonas Löwgren and Erik Stolterman, *Thoughtful Interaction Design: A Design Perspective on Information Technology* (Cambridge: MIT Press, 2004).
14. Norman, *The Design of Everyday Things*.
15. Löwgren and Stolterman, *Thoughtful Interaction Design*.

16. Bernabei and Power, "Differentiating Co-Design and Mass Customization."
17. Shayne Bowman and Chris Willis, "WeMedia: How Audiences are Shaping the Future of News and Information" (The Media Centre at the American Press Institute, 2003), www.hypergene.net/wemedia/download/we_media.pdf.
18. See http://www.digitaslbi.com/global/.
19. See Walter Benjamin, *The Work of Art in The Age of Mechanical Reproduction*, trans. J. A. Underwood (London: Penguin, 2008).
20. Anita Cross, "The Educational Background to the Bauhaus," *Design Studies* 4, no. 1 (1983): 43–52.
21. Stefano Delle Monache, and Davide Rocchesso, "Bauhaus Legacy in Research Through Design: The Case of Basic Sonic Interaction Design," *International Journal of Design* 8, no. 3 (2014): 139–154.
22. Hong Zhu, *Software Design Methodology: From Principles to Architectural Styles* (Oxford: A Butterworth-Heinemann, 2005).
23. Vasilii Kandinsky, *The Life of Vasilii Kandinsky in Russian Art: A Study of "On the Spiritual in Art,"* ed. John E. Bowlt, trans. Rose-Carol Washton Long (Newtonville: Oriental Research Partners 1980).
24. Löwgren and Stolterman, *Thoughtful Interaction Design*.
25. Eric Schaffer, "Beyond Usability: Designing Web Sites for Persuasion, Emotion, and Trust," *UX Matters*, 26 January 2009, http://www.uxmatters.com/mt/archives/2009/01/beyond-usability-designing-web sites-for-persuasion-emotion-and-trust.php.
26. Jianhua Lin, "Divergence Measures Based on the Shannon Entropy," *IEEE Transactions on Information Theory* 37, no. 1 (1991): 145–151.
27. Karen Cham, "Architecture of the Image" (Electronic Visualisation in the Arts, EVA Conferences International, British Computer Society, London, 2011), http://ewic.bcs.org/content/ConWebDoc/40614.
28. Gilles Deleuze and Félix Guattari *Anti-Oedipus: Capitalism and Schizophrenia*, trans. Robert Hurley, Mark Seem, and Helen R. Lane (New York: Penguin 2009).

29. Karen Cham, "Reconstruction Theory, Designing the Space of Possibility in Complex Media," in "Performance Play: Technologies of Presence in Performance, Gaming and Experience Design," eds. Lizbeth Goodman, Deverill, Esther MacCallum-Stewart and Alec Robertson, special issue, *International Journal of Performance Arts and Digital Media*, 2 & 3, no. 3 (2007): 253–267.
30. See https://blogs.kingston.ac.uk/dmk/.

Goldsmiths Digital: Research and Innovation in the Creative Economy

Mick Grierson

Academic research, in its purest form, is about changing how we understand the world. Sometimes this involves an entirely new philosophical, logical, or aesthetic principle. On other occasions, it sheds light on how different types of existing knowledge can combine. Or it may be characterised by new observations emerging entirely by accident, and that we as yet cannot explain.

In general, we understand innovation differently. We might say that innovation is about changing the way things are. The concept of innovation brings with it the notion of a new way to do something—not just a new way to understand it. In this sense, innovation implicitly requires practical outcomes and impact. This impact can be in any area, even the nature of research itself.

It is clear that academic institutions should be active in both research and innovation. The 2015 Dowling Review of Business-University Research Collaborations states that "use-inspired research" drives new insights in fundamental research, and that greater funding of collaborative research and development, supported by "pump-prime" funding, is required in order to deliver improved economic impact and more valuable research in general. It also states that the current strategy is not well coordinated.[1]

M. Grierson (✉)
Goldsmiths, London, UK

However, there have been some attempts to explore how collaborative research and development (R&D) might work better. In the past few years, projects such as Creativeworks London, and other similar, related enterprises including London Creative and Digital Fusion, and the NESTA, AHRC, ACE Digital R&D fund, have provided excellent opportunities to explore and better understand how institutions can more effectively collaborate with non-academic partners.[2]

In 2014, in direct response to these opportunities, I set up Goldsmiths Digital, a research-led practice initiative to provide consultancy and contract research services to the Creative Economy sector, the primary outputs of which would be software and hardware prototypes.

In order to better understand the motivation behind this decision, and what has been learned as a consequence, it is important to have a more complete understanding of what is meant by the "Creative Economy."

WHAT IS THE CREATIVE ECONOMY?

Of the 32 million jobs in the UK, more than 9 per cent of them are classified as existing within what is described as the "Creative Economy," with approximately 28 per cent of these being in London.[3]

More than half these jobs are regarded as existing within the core Creative Industries. They alone contribute an estimated £71 billion per year to the UK economy. In fact, the Creative Industries have been growing approximately three times faster than the entire UK economy in recent years, outperforming almost every other sector.

This is a success story, especially when one considers that the financial services sector, itself in receipt of over £1000 billion in public funding between 2007 and 2010,[4] is shrinking by as much as 10 per cent each year.

The Creative Economy incorporates advertising, marketing, architecture, crafts, design, film/TV, publishing, museums, galleries, libraries, music, performing and visual arts, and information technology. Of all fields that form part of the Creative Economy, the largest in terms of jobs is information technology, software and computer services, otherwise known as the "Creative Technologies Sector."

The Creative Technologies sector represents almost one-third of all Creative Economy jobs. It is also directly responsible for almost half of all economic value in the sector, contributing over £30 billion per year to the UK economy, and almost half of all Creative Economy exports.

Given the high impact of technology across the Creative Industries, it is fair to assume it has a large indirect effect on the Creative Economy overall. For example, music technology is worth the same in economic terms as the entire recording industry it supports. Similarly, TV, film, advertising, marketing, and design, depend on outputs from the Creative Technologies sector, with digital marketing being a core aspect of contemporary business growth.

One might argue that given the positive performance of the Creative Economy, Creative Technologies are a significant, driving force in the UK. What is certainly true, is that the importance of the Creative Technologies sector can be easily underestimated. What is perhaps worse is that, in academia at least, we are not entirely sure what Creative Technology is, or how we should encourage it.

Understanding Creative Technology

It is more or less straightforward that Creative Technology is a core part of our economy. However, it is also clear that Creative Technology is an interdisciplinary practice. This makes it very difficult for academics to understand what it is, because usually, academics explore known areas of research within traditionally accepted disciplines.

What is perhaps more problematic, is that it operates across the boundary of science and art. In the field of Creative Technology, there is perhaps no difference between a professional flautist, and a computer programmer who makes music. In each example, they rely on advanced knowledge of challenging techniques to create art: on the one hand, programming a computer, and on the other, manipulating a complex acoustic device. And sometimes she does both at the same time.

I argue that the separation of art and science in our culture is a core reason for our inability to understand Creative Technology. This divide has both produced, and is also reinforced by, perverse incentives impacting upon academic research. One such incentive is the perceived meaning and value of research in different academic fields—a subject of recent reification across academia, both by the 2014 REF (Research Excellence Framework), and studies such as the AHRC cultural value project. For example, I have said that the Creative Technologies sector is one of singular importance to the UK economy. However, it is not clear that we are able to reward best practice in this field in the same way as in other academic fields. Conversely, it is arguable that we absolutely should. So who do we incentivise to generate academic research and innovation in Creative Technologies?

Incentivising Creative Technologies Research

One might assume that we incentivise and reward computer science via the Research Excellence Framework for its contribution to the field of Creative Technologies. However, an analysis of the 2014 REF results demonstrates that applied, interdisciplinary fields of computer science, including those specifically intersecting Creative Technologies, were generally not considered as being of high quality. Alan Dix, a respected member of the 2014 computer science REF panel, has demonstrated that it is orders of magnitude harder to get an academic output rated as world leading in fields intersecting Creative Technologies than in all other fields of computing.[5]

Therefore the REF does not reward academic innovation in fields of computing that are currently driving Creative Technologies. Instead, such innovation is penalised because it is not seen as core to the discipline, and not sufficiently scientifically motivated. It cannot be assumed that this view is as prevalent at research council level with respect to computer science and engineering (within the EPSRC for example). However, it is more or less clear that the REF represents the views of the academic community, and that the academic community is responsible for evaluating grants. Therefore, it may well be the case that Creative Technologies research and innovation, unless entirely articulated within specific fields of computing or engineering, may struggle to be rewarded.

One might also assume that Creative Technologies are incentivised and supported by the research councils through Innovate UK. There is some truth to this. For example, Innovate UK has specific Creative Industries funding calls that seek to cement alliances between research organisations and creative business, to drive innovation. However, SMEs operating in Creative Technologies sectors, specifically those working on software and services for the Creative Industries, might struggle to find time to apply for funds, and what is more, might be unable to find the required 50 per cent match funding in order to satisfy the eligibility criteria.

In the case of the Goldsmiths Digital Firefly project, where the Creative SME was unable to meet the match funding requirements, they were able to raise the remaining 50 per cent through the organisation of their own crowdfunding campaign. As part of this campaign, it was advertised that they had already raised half a million in funding from Innovate UK. However, strictly speaking this was not in fact true. If they had failed to meet their funding target as part of their campaign, their Innovate UK funding would have been withdrawn.

So it is not clear that Innovate UK incentivises innovation in the Creative Technologies sector very well. In Paul Nurse's review of the research councils, he supports Dame Ann Dowling's view that the process is too complex and difficult for SMEs to engage in.[6] Both Nurse and Dowling state that greater interdisciplinary collaboration, including between the research councils and Innovate UK, is necessary. Further to this, Nurse recommends that the current portfolio of grants be further restricted to a series of loan opportunities. Although this does not disadvantage academics directly, it does not incentivise them, and may make it more difficult for them, and their partner SMEs to benefit from such schemes in the future.

On the other hand, it is possible that there are those in the arts and humanities who fear that creative technologies may represent "science by the back door." Creative Technology requires programming, and programming is traditionally seen as an approach that engineers and scientists take to conducting their research. However, one only needs to briefly browse kickstarter.com to see the indelible impact creative coding and the maker movement are having on culture.

The AHRC's cultural value project report does not represent either of these movements as significant areas of culture in the arts or humanities. Nor are there many practical, innovation-specific outcomes in Creative Technologies specifically funded by the project. It must be understood that the focus of the AHRC cultural value project and its associated report is on cultural value specifically.[7] However, it does not draw significantly from the impact Creative Technology is having in the arts generally, and this might be interpreted as an unwillingness to engage with overtly technical forms of culture, and by extension, innovation in general. However, my own research in creative technology has been well supported by the AHRC in the past, and so I would argue that this is possibly just an oversight caused by the need to represent the vast range of diverse research across the arts and humanities.

It seems that the research community is unclear regarding how it might best support and incentivise interdisciplinary work that sits at the intersection of art and science. Given that this is precisely where research and innovation in Creative Technologies are placed, and the contrast with respect to their importance to the UK economy, it is fair to say that anything we can do to incentivise such work brings great benefits to the academic community, the economy, and society generally. As such, academia can align its research evaluation, innovation, and incentivisation processes with what is happening outside academia.

Goldsmiths Digital

As I have already mentioned, Creativeworks London and associated schemes represent an attempt to do precisely this—align academic research with external partners for the purpose of innovation. The philosophy of awarding small amounts of funding to seed a large number of projects might easily be shown to result in failure, as many projects will undoubtedly come to nothing. However, in the case of Goldsmiths Digital, these opportunities enabled me to embark upon a project to better understand how we might more effectively align our research and innovation processes with what is happening in the marketplace.

In fact, Goldsmiths Digital has been a very successful commercial endeavour, substantially supported by Creativeworks London and related initiatives. It has generated over £210,000 in commercial income, creating over £70,000 in student bursaries, and £44,000 for temporary staff. Much of this funding came from Creativeworks London and London Fusion. Further to this, it directly led to substantial FEC grants: NESTA digital R&D project Soundlab worth £130,000, Innovate UK project firefly worth £500,000, and the European Commission Innovation project RAPID-MIX, worth €2.2 million. It has also resulted in the creation of spin-out companies, successful crowdfunding campaigns, and a US interface design patent. Creativeworks London, and other related AHRC initiatives, have been a very important part of this success.

The Goldsmiths Digital project began with the definition of three specific definitions of purpose: Understanding the Gap, Prototyping as Research, and Generalised Accessible Design.

Understanding the Gap

This area of focus emerged from the understanding that, as has already been mentioned, academic research in both the sciences and humanities can often fail to find impact in the public eye in terms of economics and culture. Goldsmiths Digital seeks to understand and express the nature of the gap between what the academic community considers excellent research, and what is considered useful by industry and the wider public. It is my aim that such an understanding will aid in the development of future research that more successfully meets the needs of public funding initiatives. In addition it is intended that this work will underline the need for greater public funding in pure research, without compromising in quality, whilst also developing a better understanding of the requirements of innovation.

Prototyping as Research

Prototyping is an effective research method that can lead to innovative outputs of high value and high impact. Goldsmiths Digital aims to treat prototyping as a form of research in the wild, articulating notions of research-led and research-informed practice through the paradigm of the prototype. Prototypes are evaluated using a range of appropriate and existing methods. In addition, emerging evaluation methodologies, such as industry-focused, iterative user-centred design, form a core part of our research agenda.

Generalised Accessible Design

We treat research in accessible design as a real-time, in the wild method for the production of better prototypes. Working with disabled and non-disabled communities equally may lead to innovations that are more easily reproducible, more easily deployable, and therefore more effective. This follows on from our existing research exploring how "trickle up" design research, where users with very specific interaction needs help to evaluate the usability of prototypes for non-disabled users, leads to more deployable and usable creative technology.

These three areas of focus continue to act as guiding principles for Goldsmiths Digital. However, they are not intended to be all encompassing or prescriptive. Instead they should be regarded as starting points for articulating an approach to research and innovation in creative technologies.

In some cases, the larger-scale Goldsmiths Digital projects, such as the Digital R&D funded *Soundlab Framework*[8] collaboration with Heart n Soul,[9] eventually came to embody these principles entirely. For example, *Soundlab Framework* has operated a user testing service for mainstream Music Technology companies, providing feedback on their products from musicians with physical and learning disabilities. *Soundlab* also won the 2016 Music Teacher award for best Special Educational Needs Resource. It additionally led to the publication of a conference paper at SIGCHI 2015, representing the first time Interactive Machine Learning had been used to create interfaces for the disabled.[10]

Soundlab grew out of the Creativeworks London project, *Cheeseburger Man*. It is worth exploring this project as a case study, as it effectively demonstrates how partnerships brought about through such funding can lead to larger-scale outcomes. In addition, it is useful for understanding the challenges involved in Creative Technologies development.

Creativeworks Case Study: Heart n Soul

Cheeseburger Man was a Creativeworks London project. The goal was to create a brand awareness remix app to support the release of an album by *The Fish Police*.[11] *The Fish Police* is a band fronted by autistic rock star, Dean Rodney, who works closely with Heart n Soul, the Deptford-based disability arts charity. I continue to enjoy a fruitful association with Heart n Soul due to my collaboration with them on the 2012 Paralympics *Unlimited* exhibition, *The Dean Rodney Singers*.[12]

Cheeseburger Man involved the design and delivery of an iPad app that would allow users to interactively remix a *Fish Police* recording, and upload their remix to a website. The fundamental resource required to complete such a project is a creative programmer. Furthermore, you need a creative programmer who is able to understand the importance of the design process. As a researcher with a focus on exploring prototyping as a method of research, and as course leader for the only Creative Technology degree programme in the UK at the time, this was one resource I was confident I could find.

The total cost of producing this sort of app in the commercial marketplace is approximately £40,000. Therefore, we were committing to create the same identical experience that you might get for that price, but for only 25 per cent of the cost. This is of course a challenge. However, this challenge would allow us to test the robustness of our creative application development framework, which we specifically developed for such a purpose. This effectively aligned our goals with that of the project partner, allowing us to prototype and further refine our development framework.

The most important aspect of the project, as with all technology projects, was establishing an appropriate level of scope with respect to the desired features. The reason such a project would normally cost £40,000 is precisely because that is how much it costs to pay a creative technology developer to design and build an app. Our existing framework would simplify the process of development. *Heart n Soul* would take care of marketing and launching the app.

Feature Creep

What we were desperate to avoid was the inevitable negative impact of "feature creep," which occurs in all projects of this kind. "Feature creep" is the single most destructive element in all technology collaborations. It is often caused by the lack of understanding people can have—scientists, artists, and entrepreneurs alike—with respect to the complexities of software development.

Software requires significant planning, and is a deeply time-consuming process. Once a decision is made regarding the requirements for all specific functions, a time cost can be calculated. This is usually measured in days, and can only be an estimate based on how long each function will probably take to implement. If new functions need to be added part way through implementation, this can sometimes result in an entire rewrite of all the software, potentially from scratch.

It is perhaps easier to understand why this is so if you compare the process to building a house. Once it has been decided where everything will be placed, foundations can be laid, walls constructed, windows, doors, and roof added, plumbing, gas, electricity, flooring, and furniture fitted. If you then decide to move a room, this might mean that the build could take three times as long. It may in fact require a change to the foundations. It is of course unethical to expect this work to be done for free, so it should be assumed it would also cost three times as much.

The Specification

In order to prevent such disasters, it is usual to agree to a specification, at least in principle, before any software is written. This is particularly the case for projects with a limited budget, as it is much more likely that you will run out of money.

It must be stressed, that in my entire career as a creative technologist, agreements over specifications represent a crucial point of failure. That is to say, when relationships break down between partners, it is almost always, without fail (except in circumstances where your staff go missing), due to the client partner either refusing to agree to a specification (for example, attempting to delay decisions about how software should function until after it has been built), or attempting to engineer some means by which they can alter the specification after it has been agreed, or worse, after work has already begun. This is nothing to do with the difference between academia and industry, science and art, or individual disciplines—it is identical across all such boundaries. Clients will always attempt to force developers to build software outside of what was previously agreed. They almost universally feel they should be able to improvise new features during every phase of the development process. Imagine that a client was behaving this way whilst you were building their house, and you get a little closer to seeing the problem.

My hypothesis was that rapid development frameworks, combined with quick prototypes, might offer a suitable starting point for mitigation of this issue. The hope was that our framework would absorb some of the pain by making it possible for us to rapidly prototype the application in between phases of user testing. As a development approach, this worked very well, and we now use this as a core technique in our research. However, it was only the case because we had spent the previous three years working on a framework to support precisely these sorts of creative application development issues.

Evaluation and Reflection

The project was a success in the sense that the final app was loved by the people we made it for. We followed a user-centred design approach, with iterative development and rapid-prototyping based on our framework. The app ended up with some great features, and drove development in our prototyping research. We also used what we learned to successfully apply for further funding.

However, our framework, although successful in delivering the app, did not prevent all the pain. Specifically, there were some features that we could not anticipate, and as a result, these needed to be built from scratch. Also, we found that the amount of time required to build and maintain such a framework was a significant cost. It is likely that, for most developers in Creative Technology fields, where appropriate RAPID frameworks are not available, very tight specifications will remain necessary.

It can also be argued that just because you have tools that speed up your development, this does not mean that clients should feel more relaxed about demanding regular changes to agreed specifications, or refuse to sign off materials that have already been agreed in principle. These are clearly bad business practices that result from inexperience across UK academia and industry with respect to technology development in general.

However, we found that the basic principle did save time and money. Goldsmiths Digital went on to develop a number of core technologies that were then used in the deployment of a range of similar projects across the creative sector. It was not always possible to repurpose everything, and new technology had to be continually developed, but the main result was an ever-growing repository of deployable, reusable software elements.

A great deal of our current work is now in the creation of frameworks that speed up the development process in order to provide more flexibility at the prototype stage. In particular, we have identified a number of desirable software features which are difficult to engineer, and are working to make these more accessible to more people. This is the rationale behind our Horizon 2020 innovation action, RAPID-MIX, for example. As a result, our machine learning systems are now being used as rapid development tools by Google, Microsoft, the BBC, and many others.

I would propose that the needs of a great many SMEs could be met in this way. In particular, where funding policy dictates that public funds support a small number of UK SMEs to develop their products in areas that are largely similar, such as big data for example, it would be wise to support teams of experienced academics to develop core frameworks that provide said functionality and demonstrators to as wide a community as possible.

Such frameworks could then be licensed and promoted to a much larger number of SMEs, accelerating growth and competition in the marketplace around policy-critical innovations, instead of simply supporting one SME with a large grant. This would cost the same, or possibly less in terms of public funds, but could have a much wider benefit across the industry. It would also allow academic institutions with the right experience to diversify their income via licencing.

Conclusion

Funding such as that offered by Creativeworks London has been vital to the success of the Goldsmiths Digital project. The initial project preceded approximately 40 further collaborations, leading to a high number of innovation outcomes, and further funded research with organisations such as Heart n Soul and many others including Google and Microsoft.

Goldsmiths Digital continues to grow. We are about to employ a Project Coordinator to handle communications with clients, and manage staff. Goldsmiths as a whole has been hugely supportive of the initiative, and it is hoped that new staff will grow the business to aid income diversification, a core element of our developing academic future.

However, what is unclear is precisely how the wider academic infrastructure should incentivise and reward such success in the future in terms of quality assessment and funding.

The barriers separating traditional academic disciplines, dividing the arts and the sciences, remain in place. These barriers perversely incentivise narrow fields of research that lead to largely abstract outcomes, widening the gap between research and innovation.

Whereas in engineering, practical outcomes may be celebrated, in the arts they are denigrated, and work in the intersection of arts and computing is rated amongst the least important in the sector.

Yet, this offers a poor parallel to real-world economics. As such, academia cannot account for or understand innovation that depends on creativity and technology in equal measure, yet this is a driving force in our economy.

But there may be light at the end of the tunnel. Academic research, in its purest form, is about changing how we understand the world. Sometimes this involves an entirely new philosophical, logical, or aesthetic principle. On other occasions, it sheds light on how different types of existing knowledge can combine. Or it may be characterised by new observations emerging entirely by accident, and that we as yet cannot explain. You can often find such things right under your nose.

Notes

1. See http://www.raeng.org.uk/publications/reports/the-dowling-review-of-business-university-research.
2. See Tarek Virani, "Mechanisms of Collaboration Between Creative Small, Medium and Micro-Sized Enterprises and Higher Education Institutions: Reflections on the Creativeworks London Creative Voucher Scheme" (Creativeworks London Working Paper No. 4, Creativeworks London/Queen Mary, University of London, 2014), https://qmro.qmul.ac.uk/xmlui/bitstream/

handle/123456789/6542/PWK-Working-Paper-4-SEO. pdf?sequence=2.
3. See https://www.gov.uk/government/statistics/creative-industries-economic-estimates-january-2014.
4. See https://www.nao.org.uk/highlights/taxpayer-support-for-uk-banks-faqs/.
5. See http://alandix.com/ref2014/.
6. See https://www.gov.uk/government/uploads/system/uploads/attachment_data/file/478125/BIS-15-625-ensuring-a-successful-UK-research-endeavour.pdf.
7. See http://www.ahrc.ac.uk/documents/publications/cultural-value-project-final-report/.
8. See http://www.makeyoursoundlab.org.
9. See http://www.heartnsoul.co.uk.
10. Simon Katan, Mick Grierson, and Rebecca Fiebrink, "Using Interactive Machine Learning to Support Interface Development Through Workshops with Disabled People," in *CHI '15: Proceedings of the 33rd Annual ACM Conference on Human Factors in Computing Systems* (New York: ACM, 2015): 251–254.
11. See http://www.thefishpolice.com.
12. See http://www.heartnsoul.co.uk/category/artists/details/dean_rodney.

Getting Inside the Creative Voucher: The Platform-7 Experience

Andy Pratt and John McKiernan

As with the others in this collection, this chapter explores the experience of using a creative voucher. However, here we take a different perspective by reflecting on the process rather than outcomes. In this chapter we view the voucher—and the policy of vouchers—as part of a wider process that may, or may not, engender knowledge exchange; which in turn may, or may not, be incorporated into a final product or process. Connectivity and time are necessary, but not sufficient, to explain knowledge exchange. The argument, as illustrated by the chapter, is that the other processes (intended and unintended) that surround (or constitute) the voucher need to be included in what we might call the "voucher experience." This experience is where and when a relationship, knowledge and understanding are created; the situational dimension may in turn constitute which knowledge is coded as useful by participants. This situated and contextual work is not peripheral or of secondary importance: it is central. Accordingly, we want to stress that people as well as cultural products were involved in this

---

A. Pratt (✉)
City University, London, UK

J. McKiernan
Creative Publics, London, UK

© The Author(s) 2017
M. Shiach, Tarek Virani (eds.), *Cultural Policy, Innovation and the Creative Economy*, DOI 10.1057/978-1-349-95112-3_7

voucher, and it is the human interaction that we stress rather than products, or disembodied and decontextualized knowledge.

The protagonists in this voucher are John and Andy. John acts as a producer and curator for Platform-7 Events, an arts organization that focused on time-limited abstract art interventions and installations in public spaces. Andy is an academic who studies the social and economic processes of the cultural economy; he is particularly interested in how culture in made (what is commonly called "creativity" or "innovation"). The challenge at the outset is to identify what the voucher could "do" for each person and their practice. As we will see, the project produced some reflection for John on his development of practice, as well as the potential of universities to be part of that process. For Andy, it developed an understanding of art practice and the challenges of evaluation, or understanding of knowledge. Andy and John decided that it would be of benefit to communicate some aspects of the experience in written form: John might be able to use it to communicate to others his "process"; Andy would hope to illustrate what "knowledge exchange" looks like in practice. As we will see, this may seem an unremarkable outcome, but when viewed in the context of the way in which we conceive of knowledge, and its "diffusion," let alone how this is instrumentalist in policy and organizational forms, it offers a potentially disruptive moment that we may learn from.

We also suggest that one could read and write the other chapters in this book in many other ways too; not simply through a more formal lens of evaluation and outputs. So what of this disruptive moment thus produced here, and in other chapters? On its own this means nothing, it is not exceptional. However, the insight of other ways of looking, and valuing, is the potential here. Given that the bigger objective of Creativeworks London was to engage the humanities and the cultural economy this gives one insight into ways that both the humanities and art practice, can "speak back" to the normative and objectifying methods of evaluation: illustrate that the methods can obscure more that they reveal. It may also encourage us to examine the (assumed fixed) objects of other types of innovation and knowledge transfer which might turn out not to be as fixed and impermeable as they have been characterized.[1]

The chapter is broken down into three sections. First, we get to know Platform-7 (P7) and what it does. This is Andy describing back to John what he does, and what a single project, the case study of the Silent Cacophony (SC) event, sought to achieve. This task was difficult to write in particular as John's practice has evolved, and continues to evolve, it is difficult to avoid writing a career history as well. However, we resisted this for presentational reasons: it does show that the artificial selection of a time-scale changes our understanding of practice. Second, the main body of the chapter concerns the experience of the SC event of the artist participants. We took a conscious decision not to look at the "audience impact" as the focus for John was to reflect upon his own practice and how and why artists were keen to participate. This does not mean that the affective experience of the audience was irrelevant, simply that it was bracketed out so that we could view the practice of knowledge and understanding generated in the event. Finally, we pull together the threads and insights in a conclusion. The methods that we used were interviews and participant observation, Andy was helped by Aysegul Kesimoglu and Kate Mattocks in this exercise. The approach more generally was in the spirit of Participatory Action Research (PAR).[2] Andy was keen that the methods should match the processes and the ethical and moral positions that were being studied, and challenge the privileging of knowledge and research. PAR approaches seek to transcend the boundary of researcher and researched, creating a partnership and a flow and process. Knowledge and "findings" are shared and reinterpreted as a continuous process. Hence, this chapter, in its linear and "objective" form, is a misrepresentation of the process; however, the reader is forewarned.

WHAT IS PLATFORM-7?

Platform-7 activity is driven by a core concept and set of ideas, then artists are encouraged to "run with" the ideas, to test their imaginations and those of the audiences. As we'll see, one of the challenges is to capture the learning and reflection of those in and working on the project itself, and to select and unpack particular aspects of it. In part this is because they are emergent, and in part because their impact or insight is not always immediately apparent. P7 often presents itself as something that hopes not to exist; not in a sense of willed redundancy, but in the sense that it privileges the performance and audience experience and removes the barriers to interaction and questioning. It seeks transparency, and aspires not "get in the way of" the art.

One of the challenging things about P7 practice is that it is (analytically) a mingling of performance art practices and advertising practices. Which is another way of saying it is about communication. This is not an art that seeks to ironize advertising, or reproduce advertising as art; rather it can be seen as "reverse advertising." Advertising usually works through the development of a mono-dimensional and idealized image of the product, which the consumer is led/sold to desire and buy. The tactic is to close down, focus and to segment. The emotional engagement is shallow and passing, but generated to produce desire for the purchase.

Platform-7's practice is the opposite; it is not reductive, but instead exploratory and expansive, one that is resistant to the stamp of a single meaning. It is rooted in an emotional engagement that is brought to the project by the audience; and thus rather than being divided and segmented as audiences they are united by the diversity of their own responses to the practice.

One very strong element of P7's practice is the triggering of memories and emotions, and community, and thus the production of ready empathy for others that have not been previously met, but have a shared experience. It is this production of connection that is critical, and very powerful. Another dimension of P7's practice is material culture, or things; memories and experiences are associated with objects and places, often banal, that we can all recognize in our lives and hence they are powerful conductors of memory and emotion.[3]

What emerged from our discussion and interrogation of John and P7 is that the challenge faced is to consider how these insights and practices, and the information produced, can be used (beyond the event): put simply is there a market/demand for it, if so where? The strongest element is the approach/methodology; and the articulation of emotions and experiences through an experience "unlocking" them. This produces a far more "authentic" range of perspectives and insights about things and places. The exploratory art practice is critical in opening up these different perspectives (although not limiting of them: an invitation to think and feel). This is after all what advertising seeks to do, but arguably, has pursued it in a "lazy" way by telling consumers what to think.

It is for this reason that one area in which Platform-7's work might be seen as useful is in the generation of alternative visions, for planning, redevelopment, for new uses; for political or ethical campaigning (again, which often uses the old advertising model, rather than the "reverse" model implied here). We reflect upon these challenges later in this report after the SC study and see how John is now applying this learning to assist corporations and small businesses in finding innovation and creative recombination opportunities.

The Event: Silent Cacophony

Silent Cacophony (SC) offers an opportunity to reflect upon the two-minute silence practised in the UK as a mark of remembrance of the end of the First World War, and latterly the dead of all armed conflict. The normative commemoration is linked to the symbolic red poppy, and formal state events of memorial at 11 A.M. on 11 November. The two-minute silence is a pause for reflection. This moment has become institutionalized over time, and also with distance from the events and death of protagonists it has become less universally practiced. There is much debate about the symbols, the red poppy and its adoption by the state and linking with national triumphalism, and the formal, state-dominated nature of the event. Such is the nature of invented traditions and culture: they are mutable and change. These issues will become increasingly salient over the coming years (2016–18) with the UK's publicly funded reflection on the centenary of the outbreak of the First World War.

SC represents a novel intervention onto sensitive political and cultural territory. On the one hand, it offers an informal, civil society–based response to the two minutes of silence. On the other, it offers a reflection on the process of reflecting, a particular theme of P7's work. The videos of P7's previous event in 2012 (No Man's Land) offered stark contraposition of the (apparent) public non-observance of the silence, and the (contradictory) silent vigil observed by the artists on the normally vibrant busker spots on the London Underground system. Another layer of meaning was that these stations are proximate to locations bombed during the Second World War. It was the contradiction observed following 2012 that brought together the word play on silent and cacophony, which resonates with inner turmoil and terror of war. Silent Cacophony attempted to capture how, following a sudden traumatic experience, people will often reimagine the moments immediately before the trauma using romantic expressions like "before the explosion it was so calm you could not hear a bird singing."

P7's 2013 event SC took this theme further and explored a variety of other sites in London, again subject to bombing, for a reflection. Artists were given a free rein as to how they structured their intervention: but a critical element of it was that it was time- and space-specific. Artistically, this chimes with the trend to temporary site-specific work and its essential impermanence and reconfiguration of audience as participant. So, SC has high art concepts; as well as engagement with political and social practices; as well as not just being site- specific but engaging in those specificities.

As Platform-7 reported at the end of the event, "Silent Cacophony was a hugely successful project and everyone was really pleased with the outcome. We ended up with 31 London events, 4 around England and 4 internationally, and approximately 135 actively participated in making the event on the day." The gallery of the event is on the P7 website with a number of blog posts and reflections.

As suggested above, part of the temporary site-specific movement in art has been to seek to transcend the audience-artist dialectic, to question the mono-directional and unitary-meaning in art. Some artists see their role as provocateurs, in the sense that they seek to generate a "different way of seeing" or understanding. Others simply want to have a more engaged or democratic dialogue.

As noted above, to an extent the audience was in part fortuitous and part planned (social media had communicated locations, events took place in the public realm and thus were open to chance encounter). From the perspective of our study we were interested in what sort of challenge this presented to artists, as well as P7, and how it was resolved.

Moreover, as noted below, doing something in the public realm requires engagement with public and private agencies that govern such spaces: this was a logistical barrier. In this case, the viability was not dependent on a "paying" audience; funding was derived from grants, or donations (monetary of time). This included some finance for artistic participation, for organizational time and publicity. Of course, one might wish to reflect further on grant application and the raising of finance, without which the event would not happen. And finally, there needed to be a vision, an initiator and management of the whole process.

Overall, what we highlight, and what we explored, was the "hidden iceberg" of activity that sustains any cultural performance. In this sense we take our lead from academic work on cultural production systems that have sought to examine and understand the process of cultural production above and beyond either the artefact or performance, and in so doing explore the range of value and values produced.

LISTENING TO THE PARTICIPANTS

Although the descriptions of P7 and the SC event were generated through extended discussions and reading material, and witnessing events, they inevitably take on an objectifying and distancing element. In this section we hear the voices of those that took part in the production of the SC event. Our interviews with artists generated a wide range of responses; we found that the majority of comments could be grouped around three main themes: place- and time-based activities, curation, and artistic practice.

Artistic Practices

In a simple sense participation in SC is like a small commission for an artist. Of course, employing an artist is generally different to employing a plumber; for the most part the artist is expected to produce the unexpected, to be creative. What is different about commissioned work, from "freely occurring" work is that some form of direction or limitation is imposed externally. The task of the artist is to interpret, and rearticulate, his or her own ideas and experience to "speak to" a new context. Artists told us of their appreciation of P7's curatorial role and methods.

The comments of some of the artists interviewed captured this: "the projects tend to be very thought-provoking and open-ended, and this allows considerable freedom to develop in alignment with my own experience and practice"; "the difference between P7s project and others is the excitement of being challenged, and being able to sink my teeth into something"; "it had the effect of drawing things out of people that they wouldn't necessarily talk about."

This explains why SC presents challenges and opportunities beyond simply being hired (however, for some artists, especially in early career, this was the most important aspect). Artists actively sought out and relished the opportunity to engage with the SC project for a number of reasons associated with boundaries. Primarily they were given a concept and asked to consider how it might be applied in a fixed time, and at an appropriate place. The creative challenge was to interpret the brief, so that it worked in the time and place. In this sense artists were given a lot of choice, which was unusual, and a welcome challenge: in short it was a spur to creativity, they were being "pushed" outside of a comfort zone. Experienced artists liked this in particular. One artist commented, "this project has the potential to take you to new grounds (a different new level) with my [practice] as well. Therefore, there is a strong personal motivation for development." The particular challenge and risk that SC presented was the public and "boundless" nature of the intervention: anything could happen, and anybody could react; this is a unique challenge of performance art. For some artists this was really challenging, or indeed frightening.

However, it was clear from the majority of responses that SC added a new layer of import for participants, namely the fact that others were engaged in related activities at the same time, and the same purpose. Other performances were not seen by most, but the idea of a collective action, and the notion of a "community" doing this was powerful for artists. It is something that many said they seldom gained from their practice, which generally was a lonely and isolated activity (see below).

Place-/Time-Based

As noted above, there is an artistic tradition of time-based arts, time-space and temporary site-specific work. This project, in one sense was a perfect set-up. The timing of Remembrance Day is quite particular, and well known by public and performers. The context was known but open to reinterpretation; and the "stage," the place, was the source of narrative and intervention. But, moreover, as it was taking place in a specific space there was further resonance, revealing the often forgotten palimpsest of pasts in place. This concentration generated for some a very intense reaction or resonance. Such interventions, for some, were powerfully affecting and affective. Both members of audience and performers reported being more deeply touched than they expected; for those with a family connection, or direct of experience of war this was doubly so.

It is perhaps a surprise that such a qualitatively different affect is produced. In part, this can be because it is unexpected; in a formal theatre setting, one is prepared and insulated from the spillover into "reality" by the fourth wall. In situated performances, people may be taken unawares; and performers surprised by the resonance of their actions in a particular context at a special time. The opportunity for new and very affective communication rooted in time- and site-specific practices is clearly an interesting one for all forms of communication and public discourse.

Many of the artists who participated were "impressed by the scale of the event"; this was expressed in part as "being part of something bigger...that they are all becoming a part of one thing". Others mentioned that "you often deal one to one with one institution or theatre. So it's quite intriguing that there is a whole network." For some, this impacted directly on their own practice: "[K]nowing that you are part of a bigger intervention/a collection makes it feel different...as an artist on the day you draw a lot of courage from that...the collectivistic process makes you feel that you can be (if you want to be) more adventurous or more ambitious on the day of the event...I take courage from others who are involved in this with me."

Artists were interested in how so many artists had the same "prompt" from P7, but reacted to it in so many diverse ways, "they had the same words, but they will make something individual out of it." Moreover, the actual practice of community was important in challenging the isolation often felt by artists: it is important to have "a 'wash-up' event and via these events or other collective processes artists from different disciplines find new collaborative projects to work on together," and "they will not be able to assess their collective impact until they all meet each other."

Finally, artists appreciated the logistical preparation and permissions that P7 had established; many not really appreciating, until that time, what was involved. As one artist noted, "[M]y eyes have been opened with respect to the amount of bureaucracy and coordination involved." Another said: "[Y]ou don't usually get an opportunity to perform in a public space."

Curatorial

What was striking from observing the event, and speaking to participants, is the role of curating: functionally speaking, this is what P7 does. Clearly, the immediate engagement and interaction is with the performers. However, the set-up, the brief, and the social coordination, as well as the logistical and communications support, lie with P7, and on the shoulders of John, its principal. There is a challenging issue, one common to many micro-creative enterprises: can the founder be "separated" from the company? In other words, is the principal the greatest asset, or can the organization/company be "spun off"?

John, or any person, taking on a producer/direct role is critical. This is a common role found in the creative industries, the person who must create the brief, convince others of its value, select and encourage participation from the right persons, manage them, as well as make sure that it happens within a logistical and legal framework: moreover, to then become more or less become invisible for the performance itself.

P7 is an efficient and effective machine to produce such events, and John is clearly adept at managing it. Like every successful person in such a role it requires a unique quality with personal relationship management, and some charisma and reputation. John's style is very much towards an open agenda to stretch artists by giving them autonomy. He works on setting the parameters. Participants, from their point of view, sometimes saw this as chaotic and unfocused; but most appreciated the freedom and rose to the challenge, realizing that John was creating an opportunity. This in itself is a much-discussed topic in the literature, and in practice, of how to "manage creativity": it's a delicate balance and it's interactive (not all artists are the same), between too much, and too little, control.

One artist commented, "[S]ometimes it's about one ego, which can be very controlling. In comparison, P7 is not like that. It's not run by one ego. It's very different." The way in which John used his skills as an enabler was particularly valued: "[H]e gives you some stimulus to go away and use. It's a creative producer type of role." For others, it was: "[T]he way John works, in that as an artist I feel very supported, yet free to carry out your own artistic practice in the way I want." His practice works, "in terms of giving courage and making me believe in the process."

The whole set of events was held together by the powerful central concept, and webpage, and its success in articulating a variety of artistic responses. As noted above, the collective power of the network of artists was felt to be important. The webpages were critical in this respect "representing" the network to its participants; something they only saw these in material form at the final post-event party. Nevertheless there appeared to develop a sort of viral element to knowledge about SC and word of mouth was very important in recruiting artists initially.

The fact that John made the network transparent, that people know what others were doing, and he created a social event was registered as significant by most participants, and a spur to wanting to work with P7 again, and/or with others engaged in SC.

In this sense P7, through SC and in common with other P7 projects, created a temporary hub that enabled a significant amount of knowledge exchange of practice and experience; networks that are commonly weak amongst artists working alone, or even competing for funds. This raises an interesting question, again common to all such organizations, that of sustainability. Put simply how to carry the knowledge over from one temporary project to another, and to avoid starting from point zero every time. Arguably, P7 has resolved this problem in its practice through a number of strategies: first, P7 has an extensive online archive of all of its previous activities; this is an unusual and valuable resource; second, the use of web presence and social media, and conventional media in John's practice; third, John's personality and personal networks. These three packages of resources are as important to P7's success as the activities that they promote and curate; again, often this work is more or less invisible when set against the "performance" and "affect" that characterizes P7's work. It is an asset that would be easy to undervalue.

Reflections and Conclusions

This creative voucher, and the reflections on it are complex and multilayered. We indicated at the beginning that the imposition of a linear narrative would do some violence to the narrative. Accordingly, in this concluding section we offer two conclusions: one reflects on the SC experience and P7; the second reflects on the process of interaction and knowledge exchange that the creative voucher represents.

Conclusion 1

SC was a very ambitious project, large-scale, and it needed complex logistical support and planning, and had little room for error in delivery. In this sense, it was a typical project-based event. P7 clearly has the capacity to deliver such activities, whilst at the same time enabling artists to produce challenging work, and focusing a project on a very sensitive and important subject. The study that we have done, that focused not on the audience, but on the producers, offered a variety of insights. An obvious one concerns the work, and the challenges, that underpin such an enterprise and the particular skills needed to manage them.

The unorthodox perspective, to look at process, was in part dictated by P7's practice, namely that SC explored the boundaries of production and consumption, or audience and performer. The objective seemed to be one of producing affective reactions and a stimulus to reflection and insight. This action was amplified by the unexpected nature of performance for the public, by the site- and time-specific resonances of the work. This allowed us to consider "impact" in a wider sense. Interestingly for the performers/ artists there was much evidence of their practice being challenged, which might be expected as normal in artistic management; however, a further element was the collective nature of the action, which was a "virtual" connectivity (a choreography), which impacted on, and stimulated the artists greatly.

Finally, this project explored examples of the boundaries of art and politics, the formal and informal, the state and civil society. It offered challenges to normative interaction; also, it offered some potential lessons to the economic sphere where such relationships—producer/consumer—are in flux.

Clearly, this process is important, if looked at more widely and also across projects, if P7 is to maintain its dynamic. It also has to address the challenge of over-reliance on short-term and risky resource to fund projects (publicly funded commissions). P7 has developed considerable expertise in managing this, and one might want to examine the trade-off of time and effort for this sort of funding as well as the ways in which such sequential and short projects require investment in overarching organizational resources. Aside from the problem of scaling up activities, the balance of short projects and long-term organization is the most common problem that micro-enterprises face. Many do not even achieve it, but others such as P7 find it increasingly hard to resource. The challenges described here are common, and especially acute in creative businesses organized on a project format. Clearly at present, the reliance on short-term funding offers few alternative options. At the margins a proportion of the longer-term costs will need to be "folded back" into each project.

P7 offers innovative artistic practice that is escaping from institutional norms, commodification and pre-interpretation. It offers in civil society realms new modalities of interaction that challenge normative politics, or individualized responses: a more collective response. It offers something very close to the cutting edge of business practice as well: the nexus of pro-sumption. So, we can track this modality of practice across the social, cultural and economic realms. Hence, we can gain insight into practices and processes that extend beyond the scope of this event.

The P7 idea then is not to be didactic, but to generate reflection, and learning. For example, can SC change the way we think about remembrance? Can it offer insights into communication between "producers and consumers"? In what ways do "art" and "artists" have a role? These are bigger questions but they are suggested by this work.

In the broader sense it is clear that SC/P7 are pioneering a model of a more interpretative and open discussion of topics; this is a means of carrying out a public debate, it is also a means for artists to reflect on practice. For artists, SC offered an unlooked for, but clearly needed, sense of community and common purpose. The role of such "hubs" be they temporary or fixed, real or virtual seems to serve an important function in an otherwise fragmented art practice world.

This chapter has stressed that there is much more to look at in "impact" terms that "bums on seats." As has been indicated much of what manifests itself as cultural performance is hidden and unnoticed; but it is a vital resource. We highlighted the logistical and social-media knowledge that is necessary to sustain such activities. We have seen that in the case of P7 it is not just supporting, but can be the animating source of artistic activity. Moreover, we have pointed to the fact that impacts can be interactive and across networks of producers and consumers. In a sense activities such as P7 are testing new territories here.

There are a number of issues that arise as a consequence of the affective impact of P7 and similar organizations' work; that is, to create a resource and support facility for people who are distressed by what the reflection on difficult topics can raise. This is a social problem, but its point of event is at a performance, or following it. Artists and funders might wish for profound impact, but sometimes it can be painful; this has to be recognized. Generally, as noted above, impact and outcomes are conceived of in instrumental ways in terms of attendance, or receipts. P7 achieves this type of result, but far more important is the depth of "affect." The question is how to assess or value such an "impact": in a technical or symbolic sense to get this issue on the "balance sheet." In one sense what this Creative Voucher report has sought to do is to highlight this particular "added value" that P7 activities deliver for artists, their practice and their careers, as well as for the public. In short, we have tried to make visible what might otherwise be peripheral or invisible.

This then leads us to a bigger question of funding regimes (for the arts). As we have noted not only are these short-term, complex and time-consuming to win, but because they are competitive they are also risky in terms of long-term prospects, as well as requiring an increasing diversion of resources into obtaining commissions and grants. As pressures have been put on arts funders they have increasingly required a narrow impact result, one that mimics a variant of the business world.

Ironically, the private sector is increasingly coming to value the sorts of non-quantifiable impacts that arts practitioners are so good at delivering, moreover, many private practitioners across the economy look to the creative sector to provide the vital affective connection that will attract and retain their customers. Thus, it would seem that having identified the contribution of P7, one might conceive of it being successful in engaging private sector clients where funding could be greater.

This brings us to the remaining question: are organizations like P7 sustainable as a business model that is economically viable? On one hand, we can see that money is raised, and events happen. This happens in a sequential manner. It has some sustainability yet does this translate into having a long life? This question is in part related to the boarder funding environment and structure of "art donor agencies." Accordingly, there are clearly potential challenges due to the risks of funding availability, and the reliance on one individual. This is not an uncommon problem to face many small enterprises, not only in the arts; it marks a potential threshold of graduation to a different scale and/or scope of operation: this is a scenario that might be reviewed at this point. On funding the picture is two-sided. On the one hand, P7 has experienced grant writers and has success on the whole. However, on the other hand, the constraints of getting funding undermine and constrain the artistic vision; plus the overheads of grant writing are getting larger. The challenge, that P7 is clearly up to is to continue to keep ahead of the funding environment. A potential difficulty is that the energy that has to be expended in getting funding might erode that of practice.

On the other hand, there is an option to not apply for public/quasi-public funding and self-fund activities. One way to explore this option would be to find part of P7 that can be sold as a service. One extreme was considered of becoming a logistics/event organizer for hire. A more interesting direction was to consider selling the "P7 method" if the method could be codified and explored as applicable to revenue-generating areas. An ideal case scenario might be that P7 could sell some of its knowledge that would create a bulwark against the short-term funding environment. However, as noted above, it was unclear in 2014 precisely which knowledge, and in what form, would be tradable in the case of P7 to achieve this.

What Platform-7 offers are new dimensions of experiences and stories, a way to communicate things that may have been lost, or never before experienced. The power is usually through the articulation of an affective linkage with things and/or places. This is—crucially—not an imposed story, the sort of common practice of advertising or branding. On the contrary, this is a connection that hails from the object/place/people. The result is not a unitary "brand consciousness" but an emotional attachment that works for people in different ways. It is powerful because it draws on a personal memory or feeling and articulates that to the event. We might contrast this with "expressed demand" of economics and product supply. Significantly, the emotional connection that P7 specializes in is precisely what might be regarded as the "holy grail" of current marketing and advertising. Accordingly, it is important to note that evaluation that might be appropriate to product sales may not be appropriate to the depth of engagement; they may be measured or understood as two separate discourses. This challenge lies at the heart of evaluating the "impact" or character of transactions between human beings.

The voucher provided John with a rare opportunity for enhanced reflection and his first real experience of "being the subject" of an in-depth study. Andy's first report for Creativeworks London allowed John to read exactly how others were viewing what he was doing and how it impacted upon artists as well as on a broader constituency. It instilled the confidence that the main research focus of Platform-7 was coming to an end. One further four-month intervention in the City of London in 2014–15 exploring an economy based on consumption and wastefulness completed the Platform-7 journey.

John took the Platform-7 research and partnered with Professor John Wood (Goldsmiths) and Professor Maurice Biriotti (UCL/Yale/Copenhagen) to form Creative Publics. Professor Wood developed the Metadesigners research lab over a twenty-year period and Professor Maurice Biriotti, through his company SHM-Group, uses deep insights into human motivation to help organizations solve complex human-centred problems. Creative Publics has developed a systematic way of identifying innovation and creativity clustering and/or vacancy within organizational structures.

Organizations of all sizes, from corporations to small business are wrestling with understanding how to operate in the new economy that is rapidly unfolding. The idea of one lineal production line, "we make cars" or "we sell insurance" has been or is being replaced by more project-based methods and instrumentalization. Consumers and business customers can no longer be fitted into a one-size-fits-all category; more often each expects adaptation to their personal needs. This requires a creative challenge to interpret the brief, so that it works in a specific time and place, often pushing workers and, moreover, management outside their comfort zone.

By using the learning from Platform-7, Creative Publics provides a pre-defined framework that sets parameters for organizations to recombine existing assets (by assets we mainly refer to people) that identifies innovation and new creative potential. The hidden connectivity that sits dormant between people inside organizations, if harnessed, can provide a rich source of knowledge and exchange. The rise in a relational view of knowledge, one that is made in negotiation and translation, can provide an important source of added value as margins become increasingly squeezed for many businesses. Another key factor that businesses can utilize from the SC interviews is the importance placed on being "engaged in related activities at the same time, and the same purpose" and how the idea of working on a "collective action" acts as a motivator. Keeping participants informed, detailing progress and providing archive materials all act as further bonding tools, delivering common purpose and shared vision.

Conclusion 2

This chapter has focused on the intersubjective production of meaning, one that is situated and embedded in practice. It highlights how the processes are subtle and complex, and are inadequately reduced to a market or quasi-market exchange relation (that is implied in both the voucher notion, and the use of the exchange model of [atomistic] knowledge). This chapter illustrates a different conception, a relational view of knowledge, one that is made in negotiation and translation, in situ. We took this debate a logical step further as we sought to explore our "meta" understanding of this process, that which is the stuff of academic reflection. As the Research Lead of the Place Work Knowledge strand of Creativeworks London that awarded the voucher that John participated in, and used the findings as part of the evolution, Andy wanted both an inside and an outside perspective as a participant as well as a practitioner, subject and object of the research. This involved, putting himself as well as John into the research. As noted above, it was not immediately apparent what knowledge was relevant, or important in their interactions: they developed in an iterative and heuristic manner. This evolutionary approach was facilitated by using the PAR methodology which is focused on collaborative learning.

The project that the voucher was supported by, as well as this chapter which reflects on it, seek to probe the "voucher experience" and to question the normative expectations of the creative voucher: as the "magic key" that will unlock the flow of knowledge between a university academic and a creative practitioner and thereby, it is hypothesized, generate an improved cultural product. We sought to engage with the nature of artistic practice, participatory public art, which challenges many of our received assumptions about objectification and interaction, let alone measurement and evaluation, knowledge and understanding of various individuals and communities. We can point to a mutual learning from a confrontation and renegotiation of what is meant by "evaluation" and "impact." This is where John is situated as a producer, exploring how his methods can change views and perspectives.[4] For Andy, and what this chapter raises in particular, it is the apprehension and method of participatory public art, and what knowledge and affects it generates.[5] Very clearly, this sort of practice breaks all of the conventional boundaries of scientific study: objectivity, separation from society, reproducibility, and this stresses the importance of adopting a sympathetic methodology.

Quite appropriately, we wanted to engage with the various ways in which meaning and knowledge were being produced. We sought to resist the linear, atomistic output-focused "evaluation" straightjacket. This strategy is an integral characteristic of the humanities method: the mutual understanding and reflection on meanings and values. Thus, the objectivity of science that is often applied to the policy experiment of vouchers (of which creative vouchers are a part), can be helpfully and usefully questioned here. This does not mean that outputs and evaluation are not relevant or that one sort of knowledge is a priori better than another. It simply acknowledges that meaning is not fixed and constantly renegotiated. This essay highlights that learning and knowledge generation is an internal and ongoing process of creativity. Art is a practice of continual questioning and experimentation and juxtapositioning, and an exploration of meanings.

One message from the project is that we need to design processes and evaluation in an appropriate manner; one that is consistent with the nature of "the object" and knowledge produced around it: both affects and effects. Normative "evaluations" in effect create a truncated and superficial appreciation of the process. In the example of P7, the process is integral to the outcome. This is what we mean by the title of "getting inside" the voucher (not just inside the process, but inside the meaning making). Inside, first, the voucher experience, whose "wrapper" looked superficially the same, but—as we see in the book, all different; second, a sense of reflecting upon the very nature of knowledge exchange, and what it means in this particular case. A point which, we want to stress, cannot be simply assumed a priori, and has to be engaged with through practice, dialogue and reflection.

Notes

1. Andy C. Pratt, "Do Economists Make Innovation; Do Artists Make Creativity? The Case for an Alternative Perspective on Innovation and Creativity," *Journal of Business Anthropology* 4, no. 2 (2015):

235–244; Tarek Virani and Andy C. Pratt, "Intermediaries and the Knowledge Exchange Process," in *Higher Education and the Creative Economy: Beyond the Campus*, ed. Roberta Comunian and Abigail Gilmore (Abingdon: Routledge, 2016), 41–58; Andy C. Pratt, "Innovation: From Transfer to Translation. Illuminating the Cultural Economy," in *The Elgar Companion to Innovation and Knowledge Creation: A Multi-Disciplinary Approach*, ed. H. Bathelt, P. Cohendet, S. Henn, and L. Simon (Cheltenham: Edward Elgar, in press).
2. Alice McIntyre, *Participatory Action research* (London: SAGE Publications, 2008).
3. Example of another Platform-7 project, The Tights Ball: in the tights project, the tights as an intimate owned/donated object served as hooks for stories. Later the artwork of the "tights ball" (constructed out of the donated tights) became a powerful symbol of waste, and our connection with that; but it is also a striking art object solid and large compared to the light and ephemeral tights: one that can be placed in, and moved around, public spaces and used to provoke yet more debate. Likewise, the making of clothes out of (donated) tights is a potent reuse/reimagination demonstration.
4. A characteristic of John's practice has been to curate events that explore and trouble such easy categories.
5. Claire Bishop, *Artificial Hells: Participatory Art and the Politics of Spectatorship* (London, Verso, 2012).

Devising Bespoke Art and Design Interventions for a Dialysis Community

Rachel Louis and Luise Vormittag

This project was developed through collaboration between Rachel Louis of Vital Arts and Luise Vormittag, Patricia Austin and Sonia Kneepkens of University of the Arts London, Central Saint Martins' MA Narrative Environments Department. Vital Arts is the arts organisation for Barts Health NHS Trust, charitably funded to deliver arts projects for the wellbeing of patients, staff and the wider hospital community. Central Saint Martins is a world-leading centre for art and design education located in the Kings Cross area of London.

The Renal Dialysis Unit at the Royal London Hospital (RLH) is one of the largest in Europe, with over 1200 patients. Patients visit RLH for dialysis three times per week, and each visit lasts five hours. Approximately 80 per cent of patients will not receive a kidney transplant and will be on dialysis for the rest of their lives. The Dialysis Unit at RLH is cramped and crowded. The demographic is culturally diverse. This is partly a reflection of the area but also because some ethnic groups are at higher risk of kidney failure than whites. Through the use of Creativeworks London's

R. Louis
Vital Arts, London, UK

L. Vormittag (✉)
University of the Arts London, London, UK

creative voucher we wanted to explore ways of improving this microlocality through activities and design interventions that engage and enrich patients' experience of being in hospital, creating a positive environment and a sense of place and community. The voucher enabled us to embark on this collaborative journey. It allowed our two organisations to come together in a research capacity to work towards a common goal.[1] Through consultation with people who use the space—patients and staff—we investigated the circumstances and dynamics that shape the experience of being on the unit. We examined participants' wants and needs, and how these might be met by art or design interventions. We looked at which creative activities foster a sense of community and how they do so. We sought processes and outcomes that impact positively on the space; those which engage, stimulate and uplift and continue to inspire patients over multiple visits.

This chapter outlines the collaborative journey that we went through. It is structured in a way that highlights the steps and unforeseen stages of the journey; from project preparation to our conclusions and arrives at the point where we now find ourselves.

Project Preparation

On 10 June 2013 we met with Deanna Gibbs, research consultant for Barts Health NHS Trust, who advised us on how to manage the consultation process within an NHS approved framework. She recommended NHS approved research methods that would work well within our project scope and aims. She brought the "Experience-Based Design" approach to our attention.[2] In particular she recommended using the "Experience Questionnaire" tool, also known as the "Emotional Touchpoints" technique.[3]

We discussed the need to be careful with the language and research processes used within an NHS framework. If we use the word "research" we would need to fulfil guidelines that have primarily been drawn up for medical research. This would involve a lengthy ethics approval process which was neither necessary nor appropriate for our project. We were advised to use "service development" and similar consultancy-type expressions. We also needed to have our project authorised by the NHS Trust's research and development (R&D) department; Deanne gave us guidelines for this. We approached the R&D department with our proposal and consulted the NRES (National Research Ethics Service) guidelines for "defining research." We then registered our project as a "service evaluation" with the Clinical Effectiveness Unit.

We initially set up a project advisory board of senior nurses and the matron. Unfortunately, as part of NHS staff redeployment our main contacts were moved out of the Renal Department in January 2014. We tried, but failed to set up another project board. There was too much flux amongst members of staff. This meant that people were not stable and settled in their roles, and it was difficult to get them engaged in our work. We also set up a private blog to share our notes on the project.

Learning About Kidney Disease, Dialysis and the Ward

Background research on kidney disease and dialysis was conducted by reading patient information leaflets and information gathered online. We then interviewed the Matron of the Renal Department, Ann Granger, on 20 August 2013. Ann had worked with the patients for 17 years and outlined the main facts on kidney disease and dialysis treatment. She also explained key operational facts of the ward at the RLH, gave us a tour, and introduced us to her staff. We explained to Ann that we wanted to gain an understanding of the patients' experience of being in hospital and to explore whether we could creatively support or solve common complaints of the unit. We gained a number of important insights from the interview, listed in Table 1. Table 2 lists common complaints by patients.

Learning About "Narrative Medicine"

We attended the "Narrative Medicine" conference at Kings College London on 20–21 June 2013. "Narrative Medicine" can be understood as a medical approach that recognises the value of people's narratives in clinical practice, research, and education.[4] It is a field that came out of an intersection of literary studies and creative writing on the one hand and the health-care disciplines of nursing, social work, and medicine on the other. This field has been gaining in prominence.[5] According to Charon "[n]ot only medicine but also nursing, law, history, philosophy, anthropology, sociology, religious studies, and government have recently realized the importance of narrative knowledge."[6] Narrative knowledge is understood as the "the stories and plights of others," and is viewed as a way to not only build empathy between practitioner and patient/client

Table 1 Insights from interview with Ann Granger

1. Kidney disease is caused by a large variety of things.
2. Dialysis takes approximately 4.5 hours.
3. After dialysis patients need to stay on the ward to log their weight, temperature, and blood pressure.
4. Some patients feel nausea or dizziness after treatment and need to rest before going home.
5. There are different types of dialysis machines and patients either get a needle in their arm or they have a "line"; a type of plug (usually in chest area) that connects to the machine.
6. Patients tend to know each other well—often they choose the same station every time, preferring to be in a bay with people whom they know.
7. There is the option of single-sex bays, but the majority of patients opt out.
8. Different patients have varying levels of independence.
9. There is a kidney transplant waiting list, but not everybody is suitable for a transplant—and not everybody wants a transplant, as it comes with its own list of medical complications.
10. Patients must keep to a restrictive diet with a very limited amount of fluid intake.
11. Number of stations (70)/patients (350)/shifts (3) on the ward.
12. There is approximately one member of staff to four patients.
13. Frequency of treatment for patients is three sessions per week. Duration of treatment is—five to six hours.
14. Patient transport system is used by approximately 50 per cent of patients.

Table 2 Common complaints by patients

1. The ward is too cold.
2. Patients do not get sandwiches anymore.
3. Televisions do not work.
4. The ward feels cramped.
5. Wait for transport is too long.

but a way to build more "humane and effective" practice.[7] It is increasingly being viewed as an important component of treatment within the medical sciences. Charon states that:

> With narrative competence, physicians can reach and join their patients in illness, recognize their own personal journeys through medicine, acknowledge kinship with and duties toward other health care professionals, and inaugurate consequential discourse with the public about health care.[8]

Even though it stems from word-based creative disciplines it encompasses a broad range of approaches. The mere fact that it has gained such prominence of late lends weight to the growing field of arts and health and the vision and programmes of Vital Arts. It demonstrates that this intersection of the fields of medical care and the arts is an area of increasing research activity as well as practice.

Observing the Ward

Initially, to raise awareness of the project and introduce ourselves, we made posters and leaflets for the ward outlining the project. We also included photos of the team.

We allocated five days to quietly observe the ward and shadow the staff in order to get a sense of the place. Rachel had observed that ward environments differed wildly outside of planned activities and arts interventions. It was important to observe the ward on a normal day, before we introduced ourselves.

The ward is made up of a series of bays with clusters of four or six treatment chairs or beds in a bay. There are ten bays of four, and two bays of six treatment chairs. During dialysis patient activities included: napping, reading the paper, chatting, eating, listening to the radio, and watching films on laptops. There was some chatter between patients but mostly at the beginning and the end, and not during dialysis. During dialysis, patients were sleepy and kept to themselves. While patients are dialysing, staff complete data entry, attend to patients who are having difficulties, restack supplies on trolleys, take phone calls, and help to arrange patient transport.

We found that all the bedside curtains were drawn open, except occasionally when a patient required extra care. Each bed was positioned to face away from the windows (to face the corridor) and had a small table which went over the bed. There was great anticipation surrounding the arrival of the tea lady with her trolley. The atmosphere could be compared to a long haul flight: The humming sounds; it felt cold and overly air-conditioned; there was a sense of boredom before the excitement of the trolley arriving; there was no mobile phone connection except for the occasional very low signal, and no internet connection.

During a patient shift changeover the atmosphere was different. There was activity, chatting, and movement. There was joking and banter between patients and staff. Nurses were being called over just for the patient to say hello. When the patients left, they said individual goodbyes to staff and other patients; hardly anyone just left. They took their time saying good bye to each other. We observed a level of joking and interplay between the staff as well as between the staff and patients. There was a sense of warmth, gentle teasing, and laughter. Overall we had the impression of a community.

Patient and Staff Interviews

During September and October 2013, we spent several days formally interviewing 16 patients and 4 members of staff using the Emotional Touchpoints technique as recommended by the NHS Trust's research consultant. We drew up a timeline and designed some emotional flash cards in order to map both the patients' and the staff's day.

We asked patients how they spent different times of their treatment (for instance chatting, reading, napping) and charted which emotions emerged at different stages. We also asked a few open-ended questions about what they liked to do in their spare time and their "dream place" to undergo dialysis.

We gained a number of interesting insights through the interviews. We found that generally, as kidney disease is a long-term condition, many respondents understood their prognosis. Patients felt grateful towards the hospital and the staff who look after them. With many patients we had the sense that they were putting on a brave face, masking the more troublesome feelings that probably sit behind their jovial exterior. As this is a lifetime condition for many patients, finding a way to cope becomes essential. Many patients felt tired and exhausted during and after dialysis treatment. They described their journey home as troublesome. Many respondents felt cold during treatment.

During dialysis patients would rather not be surrounded by people, especially people from outside of the renal community. Interestingly, there is a strong sense of community in some bays. Many patients try and lie in the same bay when they come for treatment. But along with this sense of community came the understanding that a measure of privacy was important. Most patients were quite oblivious to the ward surroundings. The sky tiles (lightboxes in the ceiling showing photographic representation of the sky and clouds) had hardly been noticed. One patient wished it moved like the sky, because it had become boring and unnoticeable. The Dialysis Unit had only recently opened in 2012, following the closure of the old Royal London Hospital. Most patients preferred the new building/ward, because it is clean and new. Patients confirmed the arrival of the tea trolley as a highlight during treatment. It breaks up the boredom and offers something to look forward to.

The conversations we had were very diverse; some were intense and other times it was difficult to connect. Overall we developed a better understanding of the effects of kidney disease on one's life. Most patients we met were not able to work and it was clear they found it increasingly difficult to have an active life. They felt bound to the hospital and found it difficult to maintain a sense of independence, such as going on holiday.

We interviewed staff at different stages of their profession (one junior sister, one health-care assistant, and two staff nurses). We asked about how their shifts are structured. We mapped this across a timeline—similar to the ones we used for patients. Despite the different levels in seniority, they all had the same flow, according to the three daily patient shifts, morning, afternoon, and evening.

All of the conversations helped us understand that the personal connections on the ward between staff and patients are very important. They help each other, give advice, and keep each other company. There was a real sense of solidarity and empathy.

Taking Stock

During November 2013 we got together as a team to take stock of what we had learned thus far. We began going over all of our collected insights and impressions. We discussed what we thought had and had not worked in terms of the interview process. We then honed in on a number of observations.

As anticipated, a static traditional commission of artwork on the wall would have limited effectiveness, as patients would get used to it very quickly. When discussing the sky tiles, one patient commented: "I've finished looking at this." We thought the same would become true of any permanently installed artwork. Additionally, there were not many surfaces available conducive to art work. We considered surface design, for example, blankets on the beds.

Having noted the strong sense of community on the ward, that patients supported one another psychologically and physiologically, we questioned how we might use the patients' own existing knowledge, skills, and expertise, either to incorporate these into projects or to get them involved in the design and production of an art and design intervention.

In acknowledging the immobile nature of treatment, we kept coming back to the tea trolley. We brainstormed ideas on how we could build on this.

Finally, we considered the change in environment of recent years. This Dialysis Unit opened in 2012 and was situated on the ninth floor of the Royal London Hospital. Prior to that patients had attended two other hospitals, both units were largely situated on the ground floor. Patients commented they used to enjoy people watching and now felt cut off, so high up on the ninth floor. Could we help this feeling of disconnection from the outside world?

Developing Project Ideas

During November 2013 we generated a number of different project ideas. Approximately half of the ideas had to be discarded due to practical difficulties. Table 3 shows the ideas that we discarded and those we decided to develop.

Table 3 Project ideas

Idea	Description	Decision
Mobile art trolley as an ongoing artist in residence programme	Idea: Residency programme with a variety of different artists who engage patients in participatory activities such as knitting, poetry, music. Rationale: Based upon the enthusiasm towards the tea trolley we wanted to enliven and extend this idea through introducing participative, community arts activities as an ongoing activity. Problem: Too resource heavy. It would need constant facilitation by Vital Arts and a constant flow of money.	Discarded

(*continued*)

Table 3 (continued)

Idea	Description	Decision
Blankets	Idea: A selection of warm, colourful blankets to keep patients warm and bring colour into the ward. Designed by an artist in close consultation with patients. Rationale: Many patients complain about being cold. The blanket surface is one of the few "clear" surfaces on the ward—and would lend itself well for a design intervention. The design process could be participatory and allow for patient input. Patchwork? Problem: This idea was investigated in some depth by Rachel Louis. Rachel made inquiries into the logistics of the laundry service and blanket circulation as well as material requirements necessary for NHS infection control. Unfortunately it emerged that separating the blankets for the Renal Ward by the laundry service contractor would not be possible. Additionally large numbers of blankets go missing all the time. The idea of patients "looking after" their own blankets also had to be discarded, as patients do often not have the strength to be carrying an extra blanket with them when travelling in for treatment. (Otherwise they would be doing this already.)	Discarded
Dialysis cookbook	Idea: Create a communal recipe book of patients' recipes and related stories to share with one another. Recipes and stories will be collected by a chef. Rationale: Patients care about their community and like to exchange advice. A number of patients talked about food. Patients receiving dialysis have a restricted diet. There are not any renal cookery books for ethnic minorities (there is only one for very bland traditional British food). This idea utilises the ward's community spirit. It would act as a framework to exchange knowledge and ideas. It would showcase the rich cultural backgrounds and knowledge amongst the patients. This idea could be expanded upon, for example, by introducing banquets via a food trolley with a well-known chef, or by distributing the book to other treatment centres.	Taken to next phase

(*continued*)

Table 3 (continued)

Idea	Description	Decision
Window to the outside world	Idea: Views of local parks, the Thames/the canals/ trees to be live streamed into the ward via plasma screens mounted into the ceiling or onto walls for patients to view as a window to the outside world. Details of streams will be fleshed out with selected artist/advisor. Rationale: Patients are bored and would like to watch something (e.g. TV or people watching). Some commented that they wished the sky panels moved. Most patients' treatment chairs face inwards. Video would not work because patients attend hospital so regularly the loop would become predictable. Research suggests access to and views of nature ("green spaces" and "blue spaces") increases positive effects on well-being.	Taken to next phase

PILOTING PROJECT IDEAS

Dialysis Cookbook

December 2013
Luise Vormittag invited the chef, food blogger, and food photographer Kerstin Rodgers to work with on this project. Kerstin blogs under the name Ms Marmite Lover. We chose to work with Kerstin because Luise had seen her speak at an event and thought her energy and charismatic personality would be welcome on the ward. Kerstin expressed immediate enthusiasm for the project. We consulted with Ann Granger, the Matron, who put us in touch with the renal dieticians at the hospital.

January 2014
We invited Kerstin into the hospital to see the ward and talk through the project. Rachel Louis met with the team of five renal dieticians to introduce the project concept and discuss possible collaboration. The team were delighted, stating it was an ideal project for them to be involved in but they had never had sufficient time to devote to it. They agreed that current cookbooks and recipes for dialysis patients were not reflective of the multicultural demographic.

The dieticians shared information on dialysis patients' dietary restrictions with us. Put simply, patients must dramatically reduce their consumption of liquids, sodium, phosphorus, potassium, and protein. The reality of this is incredibly limiting and complex. Counter-intuitively, this means to avoid "healthy" food:

- Most fruit and vegetables should be avoided (too much potassium and phosphorus).
- Sauces—curry sauce, pasta sauce, salad dressing, gravy and so on—contain too much liquid.
- Some cereals contain too much phosphorus and should be limited to one serving a week, in fact, white bread is better than whole meal breads or crackers.
- Dairy should be dramatically reduced as this is a major source of phosphorus.

This list is by no means exhaustive. In addition, a large number of patients are diabetic, so sugar is off limits: "All the fun stuff" as one patient put it.

In envisaging the project delivery and potential outputs the dieticians requested that they check and analyse each recipe, to ensure we were promoting a renal-appropriate diet. They suggested we look for recipes of Asian curries and African stews, as these were the two most commonly sought after recipes from the ward.

February 2014
Luise and Kerstin spent a day piloting the *Dialysis Cookbook* idea. They spoke with five patients from a variety of different backgrounds. They asked them about their favourite dishes, where they learned to cook them, what their associations are with them, and how they adapt them to suit their dietary requirements.

Some patients assumed that we were dieticians and were reluctant to tell their stories around their food and recipes because they thought they would be told off! We discovered most patients were too exhausted to cook following dialysis. Some patients offered tips to their peers such as batch cooking and freezing portions. On the whole, patients were enthusiastic to share and try new recipes. They were bored with their limited food choices and wanted to try something new. Putting a multicultural dialysis cookbook together became a welcome challenge.

March 2014
Kerstin Rodgers typed up the patients' conversations into recipes. We consulted with the dieticians. Unfortunately not all of the recipes were suitable, even though patients had insisted they were okay for their diet. In discussion with the dieticians we found substitutes for some ingredients. Of the five recipes that we collected, three were suitable, following some tweaking from the dieticians. We were asked to photograph the dishes in portion sizes.

April 2014
Rachel and Luise tested and tweaked the recipes. Kerstin photographed each dish. The dieticians analysed the final recipes and gave us the nutritional content of each portion.

June 2014
Luise designed three recipe cards for print. The team prepared a questionnaire that would be given out with the cards to gather patient feedback.

July–August 2014
The recipe cards and questionnaires were printed and collated into packs of three together with the questionnaire. We spent one full day distributing the packs to patients. Where appropriate we engaged with patients, telling them about the project and collating initial reactions and feedback. We placed packs in the patient's folders for the four treatment shifts that we were unable to distribute to personally. We left collection boxes to collect questionnaires on all four staff stations.

Dialysis Cook Book was presented at the Patient Forum Meeting in May 2014 (Fig. 1).

WINDOW TO THE OUTSIDE WORLD

December 2013

We thought about what kind of views would be appropriate for live streaming into the ward. Although patients had talked about people watching at the local markets, we discarded initial ideas of streaming local views of Whitechapel, as we decided this would be too hectic. We also needed views that would provide some interest during day and evening (for the late shift). Eventually we settled on the idea of wildlife and nature. According

Fig. 1   Selina's Bangladeshi fish curry recipe card

to Ulrich "stressed individuals feel significantly better after exposure to nature scenes rather than to urban scenes lacking nature elements. At the most general level, the results suggest that outdoor visual environments can influence individuals' psychological well-being."[9]

We tried a few different routes (London Zoo, London Aquarium, different local wildlife and nature parks). Finally we found "Wildlife Kate" an environmental educator based in Staffordshire who has a keen interest in Natural History.[10] Kate has over 20 cameras positioned around her garden on different feeding stations and in various nest boxes. Different cameras feature different views, depending on where the activity is. Crucially, there are both night cameras and day cameras. Kate was very keen to work with us on this idea. Over the next few months we developed a few key strategies for how to take this forward and involve Kate with the renal community.

January 2014

We met with Dr Rebecca Ross from Central Saint Martins. Rebecca specialises in digital media and interaction. She gave us advice on how to implement this idea with regards to technical possibilities and requirements. She also advised on potential collaborators, coders, and technicians who would be able to assist us.

February–October 2014

Vital Arts investigated NHS rules and policies for installing monitors into the ceiling of the Renal Unit. This included health and safety, infection control, fire safety department, the IT infrastructure, building installation, building maintenance, and cleaning contracts. As the Royal London Hospital is a PFI (Private Finance Initiative) and not owned by the NHS there is also the additional element of cost and maintenance involved from the landlord, which was also investigated.

Progress was slow. Many departments were reticent to be involved, confused by such an unusual request and things stagnated when we tried to incorporate such a project within the complex IT infrastructure. Seemingly impossible complications arose with more and more frequency. Despite perseverance over many months, securing consent and reaching positive compromises in many instances, we were finally defeated by higher than anticipated set-up and running costs of the project.

Window to the Outside World was presented at the Patient Forum Meeting in May 2014.

THE PATIENT FORUM

While the two ideas were being investigated, Rachel Louis attended the Dialysis Patient Forum meeting to introduce the projects and listen to patient feedback. There were nine patients and two members of staff present. Patients were from across Barts Health NHS Trust—not just the Royal London.

When presented with a mock-up of the *Dialysis Cookbook* cards the response was extremely positive. Patients and staff from other renal wards within Barts Health expressed the desire to be involved in this project too. They were impressed by the professional appearance of the cards and the concept. The chair of The Royal London Hospital Kidney Patients Association (RLH KPA) pledged support and enthusiastically said they would like to help fund the development of this project.

When Rachel presented the idea for *Window to the Outside World*, she was met with a mixed reception. It was opposed by two very vociferous patients. Their main reservations were: it would be boring, nobody would watch it because "everybody is asleep," it would be too expensive.

There were positive reactions from other patients too, but it was difficult for them to be heard. Rachel got the impression there was a feeling people were half excited and half bemused by the "ridiculous" nature of the idea.

FEEDBACK AND INSIGHTS TO PILOT IDEAS

Of the three main ideas, *Dialysis Cookbook* was the only pilot project to be fully executed. *Window to the Outside World* was not feasible within the timeframes and budgets of this project. *Blankets* threw up logistical problems which we were unable to solve. Nevertheless, we gained some valuable general insights in developing this proposal; that the patient forum is a good place to make connections with active members of the patient community. When seeking patient engagement it is a good strategy to engage the most active members of this community, thereby creating a certain amount of momentum. We found that the most active patients were those who attended the patient forum, those who were in self-care (had more responsibility for managing their treatment) and those who were on the evening shift (because they tend to have daytime work or other "active" commitments).

Dialysis Cookbook

We collected 52 completed questionnaires, which constitutes about 15 per cent of the patient population. Staff commented that they considered this to be a high return rate, as there is a general consultation-fatigue amongst the patient group, coupled with a high percentage of patients who report difficulties communicating in written English.

The most optimistic and enthusiastic responses came from patients who were more active.

The feedback on the questionnaires was very helpful. We were asked to include vegetarian recipes, recipes suitable for diabetics, and to include nutritional information on potassium and phosphate. A significant number of recipe cards (approximately 40 sets) were returned to us via the feedback boxes. We believe this to be from patients who were not able to read or understand the cards which were written exclusively in English.

To engage a greater number of patients we would need to pursue this as a bilingual project in Bengali as well as English.

Window to the Outside World

Even without the problems encountered within the Trust, this project seems to constitute an unknown concept for some members of the patient community and there is some scepticism about the value of this project. However, we believe there is still great potential in this idea.

REFLECTIONS AND CONCLUSION

On the whole we consider this a successful project. Before this project Vital Arts had not had the resources or tools to engage in such an in-depth collaborative consultation process.

We approached this project with an open mind, expecting to end up with some ideas for a visual arts/participation arts brief. By engaging with the ward over an extended period of time and by reflecting on our findings with an engaged project team, the nature of the project delivered us to an unexpected point. This strengthens the case for budgeting for similar future consultation processes in future.

Even though we were only able to complete one pilot project, *Dialysis Cookbook*, we feel this project has a lot of potential. The failure to complete *Window to the World* has not been an overall failure. Vital Arts has now got relationships in place that will facilitate future projects of a similar nature, while also having become more aware of the difficulties associated with screen-based/Internet-based creative interventions in the hospital environment.

The relationship between Vital Arts and CSM has been strengthened and we are in conversation with publishers to develop a multicultural dialysis cookbook.

NOTES

1. Tarek Virani, "Mechanisms of Collaboration Between Creative Small, Medium and Micro-Sized Enterprises and Higher Education Institutions: Reflections on the Creativeworks London Creative Voucher Scheme" (Creativeworks London Working Paper No. 4, Creativeworks London/Queen Mary, University of London,

2014), https://qmro.qmul.ac.uk/xmlui/bitstream/handle/123456789/6542/PWK-Working-Paper-4-SEO.pdf?sequence=2.
2. According to the NHS Institute for Innovation and Improvement, the "ebd" approach (experience-based design) is a way of bringing patients and staff together to share the role of improving care and redesigning services. It is being developed by the NHS Institute for Innovation and Improvement as a way of helping frontline NHS teams make the improvements their patients really want. For more information see: http://www.institute.nhs.uk/quality_and_value/experienced_based_design/the_ebd_approach_%28experience_based_design%29.html.
3. According to the Scottish Health Council, a number of story elicitation techniques exist, but "Emotional Touchpoints" has emerged as a rich and useful tool, particularly in older people's care settings. For more information on this see: http://www.scottishhealthcouncil.org/patient__public_participation/participation_toolkit/emotional_touchpoints.aspx.
4. Rita Charon, *Narrative Medicine: Honouring the Stories of Illness* (Oxford: Oxford University Press, 2006).
5. See for instance Columbia University's Master of Science in Narrative Medicine, http://sps.columbia.edu/narrative-medicine.
6. Rita Charon, "Narrative Medicine: a Model for Empathy, Reflection, Profession, and Trust," *Jama* 286, no. 15 (2001): 1897.
7. Ibid.
8. Ibid.
9. Roger S. Ulrich, *Landscape Research: Visual Landscapes and Psychological Well-Being* (London: Taylor & Francis, 1979).
10. See www.wildlifekate.co.uk.

The BeatWoven Project

Noam Shemtov

TRANSFORMATIVE USE AS A FORM OF CREATIVE EXPRESSIONS

Using music in the process of creating textile patterns is a practice that is enabled by recent technological advances. As music is protected under copyright law, such a process of creation might prove contestable where no authorisation from the right holder in the musical piece at issue has been obtained. As discussed below in further detail, the process at issue concerns a textile designer who is utilising another person's work in his transformative creation process, while generating his own original creative expression. The extent to which such practice is permissible might have repercussions that go beyond the interests of the textile designer. More and more transformative uses of existing works are becoming possible due to technological advances,[1] although various forms of transformation uses have been with us for a long time.[2] The ease of access and dissemination that is enabled by the Internet holds a great potential for transformative uses to be practised by hobbyists as well as by professional artists. To the extent that such transformative uses are allowed, they may open new creative avenues, increase the number of creative expressions circulating in

N. Shemtov (✉)
Queen Mary University of London, London, UK

© The Author(s) 2017
M. Shiach, Tarek Virani (eds.), *Cultural Policy, Innovation and the Creative Economy*, DOI 10.1057/978-1-349-95112-3_9

the marketplace and enrich the public space. For such transformative uses to be permissible, the delicate balance between competing interests that our copyright law regime seeks to maintain must not become unravelled. Whether our courts are furnished with adequate analytical mechanisms to engage in such assessment is far from certain.

Appropriation art is a sub-category of transformative use. Appropriation art is a postmodern form of art that raises interesting legal questions. The term is often used in relation to an artistic work where one "borrows images from popular culture, advertising, the mass media, other artists and elsewhere, and incorporates them into new works of art. Often, the artist's technical skills are less important than his conceptual ability to place images in different settings and, thereby, change their meaning."[3] Often, the borrowed images are not a subject matter of intellectual property laws and therefore present no legal difficulties. It is where intellectual property rights are engaged, and in particular copyright law, that a delicate balancing exercise should be conducted. The stakeholders whose interests are to be assessed in such a balancing exercise are the artists of the original early work, the latter artist who makes use of the early artist's work and society as a whole. The artist of the original work has a bundle of exclusive rights in relation to his or her work. The grant of such exclusive rights may be explained by reference to utilitarian doctrines or natural rights-based ones. Under the utilitarian school of thought, copyright is granted over intangible property in order to promote economic efficiency.[4] In a nutshell, copyright law provides a reward system that is intended to generate incentives to create and disseminate the works to the public. Granting an artist exclusive rights in relation to his or her work is intended to enable such rewards by proportioning the creator's return on investment to the commercial success of their work. Against the interest of the artist of the earlier work in having exclusive rights over various forms of exploitation of such work, one may weigh the interest of the appropriating artist. This may be described as utilising an existing resource, namely the earlier work, while engaging in creative expression. To the extent that such an activity is permissible, the creator of such work will be eligible to copyright protection in his or her own right in relation to their work. It is under the prism of public welfare as a whole that the assessment of both sets of interest should be conducted. As the economic objectives of copyright law are intended to further societal welfare, the answer to the question of where does one draw the line between permissible and impermissible uses of exiting works should ideally be informed by public interest. Regrettably, rather than having a flexible judicial tool to enable such assessment, the judicial toolkit, in particular in the EU, is ill-equipped to address such issues. As mentioned above, the utilitarian approach is only one of the two sets of justifications used to explain copyright law. The other justification doctrine is based on natural rights theories.[5] Under the utilitarian theory copyright law is mainly about incentives designed to encourage creativity and dissemination of expressive works. The author's exclusive right and legal entitlement is therefore a means to an end rather than the end itself. Natural law–based theories put at their centre the author's natural right to the fruits of their labour and their inherent dignity as an author. Thus, rather than being a means to an end the authorial right is often considered as an end in itself. But even under natural right theories the interest of the author of the earlier work is assessed against competing interests, whether it is the interest of the public in having sufficient intellectual spaces open to authors who come later,[6] or the interest of the later author as under a natural right theory a claimant's assertion of his or her dignity as an author is perceivable only as long as such assertion may be consistent with the defendant's dignity as an author of an original expression.[7]

Although the creative practice that stands at the centre of this current discussion cannot be described as appropriation art *sensu stricto*, it nevertheless faces similar conceptual considerations as appropriation art does. Fortunately, although the general EU legal position on appropriation may not be favourable, the technical environment that surrounds the creation process that was at issue in the BeatWoven project may provide a more helpful context.

When Music Meets Fabric

Technological developments often have a tendency to test the adequacy of our legal framework. Copyright law is no exception, where on occasions it has been playing catch-up with technology, often with little success.[8]

The creative process at issue in this chapter concerns such an instance, where copyright's legal framework is applied to a scenario that, undoubtedly, was not in contemplation when the relevant legal rules of which our copyright system consists were formulated. From a copyright law perspective, one main question arises: do the rules that make up our copyright regime provide an adequate redress to a copyright owner in a musical work where that work is being converted or transformed into textile patterns? As mentioned, although this question addresses a specific scenario, it is suggested that the answer may be relevant to a wider array of situations, as similar public policy considerations may be applicable where technology enables us to transform a copyright work from one form or medium into another.

The creative process used by BeatWoven transforms music into textile patterns with the help of technology, and a healthy dollop of creative input from a textile designer. The actual production process of the textile pattern derived from the musical work may be described as follows.[9] The designer selects a musical composition represented on an audio file in MP3 format. The MP3 file is then loaded onto a software application, which reads out a live audio spectrum every seventeenth of a second. The output of this process is an array of amplitudes/frequencies, which is received by another software application that processes the samples into shapes based on groups of frequencies, which are predefined but could be tweaked by the designer. Each of the shapes is a representation of the amplitudes and frequencies over time. The colour and the size of a shape are defined by amplitude for a given frequency range. On each iteration, the shapes are rendered into a HTML canvas element and at the end of the track the designer downloads the generated PNG file and saves it. Once the app is closed all data from the track is lost and the only thing remaining is the PNG file containing an array of shapes as described above. At this point the designer starts to add her own creative input. Taking into account factors such as genre, culture, era, sounds and tempo, the designer develops textile design ideas, considering aspects such as yarn choices, colour palette, weave structures, weight of the fabric and the final application of the fabric (for example, wall-hung, upholstery, etc.). The designer will then create mood boards[10] and sketchbooks[11] with reference to those choices. Thereafter the designer will open the PNG file in Photoshop, changing the colour scheme and, sometimes, creating abstract patterning. Once the design process is completed, the file is saved in Tiff (tagged image file format) or Jpeg (an alternative format for compressing image files). Such files are sent to a mill, where they are opened on "weaving software," for the fabric to be made (Fig. 1).

The process above might be described as a translation of musical composition into a textile pattern. However, for reasons that would become apparent as our discussion ensued, such description is better avoided. This is so since our copyright regime proves fairly rigid when it comes to the scope of protection granted therein. Ever since the late nineteenth/early twentieth century, translations are considered to fall within the ambit of a copyright holder's monopoly. It was thought that although translations are not purely literally mechanical and often involve a high level of creative input by the translator,[12] they are nevertheless true representations of

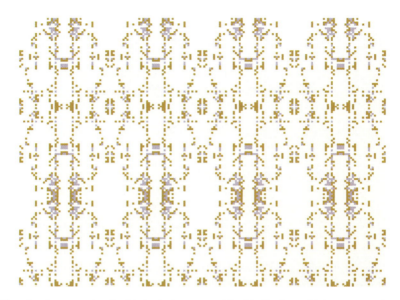

Fig. 1 An example of a fabric design created by Nadia-Anne Ricketts, proprietor and designer of BeatWoven, based on Tchaikovsky's Nutcracker (Tchaikovsky's work is no longer protected by copyright, whose term of protection is 70 years after the author of the work died, and therefore does not pose a problem.)

the original work and enable an interested party to work the translation "backwards" and recover the original work. Be that as it may, the preference to avoid the term "translation" does not stem from a mere attempt to escape the reach of copyright law. The creative process described above is clearly more than a translation in the conventional sense of the word. The *Oxford English Dictionary* defines "translation" in two ways that are of relevance to the current discussion. The first definition is the one that usually springs to mind: "the process of translating words or text from one language into another." The other definition refers to "the conversion of something from one form or medium into another" such as "the translation of research findings into clinical practice." The former definition is a practice that is covered by copyright law, while the latter one is not necessarily so. It is suggested that the creative process at issue is closer to the second definition than to the first one. Moreover, this creative process is far from being a mere conversion. As mentioned, it involves creative inputs by the designer at various stages of the process. Not only does the designer tweak certain variables in the software application, which will affect the resulting shapes, but she also determines the final design by virtue of the creative choices made on the basis of the mood board and sketchbook she has prepared. Hence, the designer ultimately controls aspects such as colour schemes and patterning. Consequently, it is advisable to refer to such a creative process as "inspired by" or "based on" rather than "translation of" musical composition into textile patterns.

Turning Music into Textile Patterns: Legal Viability

The key question in this context was whether the generation of the PNG file by relevant software as part of the creation process constitutes an infringement of the copyright embodied in the musical work. The later created Tiff or Jpeg files or the actual fabric itself, which result from the designer's creative input in terms of modifications made to the PNG file, are of less interest in the present context. This is so since if the answer to the above question is negative, then the work recorded on the latter file formats as well as on the fabric itself are not likely to be infringing since they are even more distant and detached from the music recorded on the MP3 file. If, however, the answer to the above question is yes, then the creative process in question is problematic irrespective of whether the Tiff and Jpeg files and the fabric itself are also infringing. This is so since the creation of the PNG file is essential for the whole process and the presence of an infringing article in the said process would entitle the right holder in the music recorded on the MP3 file to obtain an injunction. Such an injunction will have the effect of bringing the creation and production process of the fabric to a halt.

In the context of UK copyright law, in order to answer the above-mentioned question it was necessary to consider two related questions:

1. Does the work embodied in the PNG file constitute an infringing *reproduction* of the work embodied in the MP3 file within the meaning of S.16(1)(a) of the Copyright, Designs and Patent Act 1988 (UK Copyright Act)?
2. Does the work embodied in the PNG file constitute an infringing *adaptation* of the work embodied in the MP3 file within the meaning of S.21 of the UK Copyright Act?

In my view the answer to both questions is no.

Reproduction

In a nutshell, the software application generates the PNG file by reading the live audio from the MP3 file and then processes it into shapes based on certain groups of frequencies. The resulting PNG file comprises a sequence of shapes arranged on a graph. The question in this context is therefore: whether the visual representation recorded on the PNG file constitutes a reproduction of the music recoded on the MP3 file?

A good starting point would be that "it should be borne in mind that it is not enough to say that the defendant has 'used' the claimant's work. He must have *reproduced* it."[13]

S.17(2) of UK Copyright Act provides: "Copying in relation to… musical work…means reproducing the work in any material form. This includes storing the work in any medium by electronic means." Could it then be argued that the music embodied in the MP3 file is reproduced by the PNG file, albeit in a visual rather than aural manner?

The initial difficulty for anyone arguing that the latter is an infringing reproduction of the former is that under UK copyright law protectable works must fall within the scope of one of the predefined categories. Thus, the form or medium might be of little consequence but the actual essence of the two works is not. In our case the music recorded on the MP3 file would constitute musical work within the meaning of S.3(1) of the UK copyright Act, while the visual representation recorded on the PNG file would be an artistic work under S.4 of the UK Copyright Act and, more specifically, a graphic work under S.4(1)(a). In order to "reproduce" the work recorded on the MP3 file, a court will first need to consider whether the visual representation at issue amounts to a "copy" or a "reproduction" of the piece of music recorded on the MP3.

The general position under English law appears to be that an artistic work cannot infringe the musical copyright in a musical work. For example, in a recent UK case[14] the claimant argued that due to more recent developments in European copyright law, the old UK distinction between literary and artistic works was no longer justified and therefore "reproduction" was "reproduction" irrespective of the various categories involved. Rejecting this argument, the court refused to find that the artistic work in question (that is, a tartan fabric pattern) infringed the copyright in the literary work (the loom ticket, which comprised various instructions and measurements).

Applying this rationale to our scenario, the court is not likely to hold that the artistic work embodied in the PNG file infringes the musical copyright embodied in the MP3 file. Hence, in order to find that the work recorded on the PNG file infringed the work recorded on the MP3 file, a court might first need to consider whether the PNG file contains music.[15] UK copyright law defines the term "musical work" under S.3(1) CDPA as follows: "'musical work' means a work consisting of music, exclusive of any words or action intended to be sung, spoken or performed with the music." In short, a musical work consists of music. This, in turn, requires a definition to the term "music," which UK Copyright Act does not provide. Music, however, was defined in the Court of Appeal decision of Sawkins as "combining sounds for listening to," which "is intended to produce effects of some kind on the listener's emotions and intellect."[16] Since the visual representation recorded on the PNG file does not combine sounds nor is it intended to produce any effect whatsoever on a listener (it is not intended to be perceived aurally), the PNG file does not embody music in the legal sense of the term. Therefore, it followed that the PNG file in not likely to infringe the copyright in the musical work embodied in the MP3 file.

If the PNG file did not constitute a "musical work" within the meaning of UK copyright law, could it be argued that the MP3 file embodied an artistic work (over and above the musical work that is undoubtedly embodied therein)? If the answer to this question was in the affirmative, the assessment of infringement would have been more straightforward as it would then boil down to whether the visual representation on the PNG file infringes the artistic copyright in the MP3 file. In other words, since both works would fit into the same category of protectable works, namely "artistic work," an assessment of infringement will not face the above-mentioned obstacle of the works belonging to different categories of protectable works.

At first glance the proposition that a musical MP3 file might be considered as an artistic work under UK Copyright Act appeared odd as it did not seem to fit into any of the sub-categories of artistic works as defined under S.4 of the Act. However, in the case referred to above,[17] which concerned an infringement of a tartan fabric pattern, the court found that a "ticket stamp," which consisted of instructions as to how to set up a loom in order to weave a particular fabric pattern, was not only a literary work but also an artistic work. This was mainly due to the fact that an experienced fabric designer could visualise the appearance of the fabric in question when examining the said "ticket stamp." Could it therefore be said that the music embodied in the MP3 file was also an artistic work if an expert might be able to tell, upon listening to it, how the PNG file will look like in a visual sense? In my view, this type of rationale is not applicable to our scenario. In the first case the literary work, that is, the ticket stamp, was an intermediary stage for the claimant to create an artistic work—a certain fabric pattern. Namely, when designing the fabric pattern the designer first recorded his design on the ticket stamp in the form of words and numbers rather than first making a drawing of the pattern. In our case the musical work embodied in the MP3 file is not an intermediary stage but the final product. The composer of the music does not create the sounds comprising the music in order to record his artistic copyright; the music is not an intermediary stage for creating an artistic work, but the end product in itself. Furthermore, in *Abraham Moon* the claimant invested artistic skill and labour in creating the ticket stamp (visualising the final article—the fabric that was an artistic work). It was therefore more straightforward to find such a ticket stamp, which recorded the design of an artistic work, to be an artistic work irrespective of it being represented by words and numerals, which are usually typical of literary works.[18] However, in the present case, the composer does not invest artistic skill and labour in creating the music,[19] as visual appearance is not likely to be contemplated at all by her or him. Overall, finding the work embodied in the MP3 file to be an artistic work, when the composer of the music did not contemplate visual elements of the work when the music was composed, would render the UK copyright division between different classes of works—meaningless.

Another significant factor proved to be that once the musical work in the MP3 file is turned into a visual representation recorded on the PNG file, it was no longer possible for members of the public to retransform it back to music. This was so since a lot of information was lost during the original transformation process from music to visual representation and could not be "uncovered" by retransforming the visual representation into music. Since the PNG file created by BeatWoven could not practically serve as a basis for recreating the original, it was more likely that it did not constitute a copy within the legal sense of the word.

In conclusion, we established that it was not likely that the PNG file was an infringing reproduction of the work embodied in the MP3 file. As explained above, where the PNG file is not infringing the copyright in the work embodied in the MP3 file, the Jpeg or Tiff files as well as the actual fabric article are also not likely to be infringing the musical copyright in the MP3 file.

Adaptation

As regards adaptation, an assessment of the legal position in the UK seems to weigh against infringement. S.21(1)(b) defines adaptation of a musical work as "an arrangement or transcription of the work." The PNG file is clearly neither.

Other Jurisdictions

It appears that the above conclusion was equally applicable to other major legal jurisdictions around the world.

For example, for reasons akin to those discussed above, the legal position in the USA should be similar as well. Furthermore, US law contains an immensely flexible judicial tool that is designed to enable the courts to engage in a balancing exercise of the competing interests in a given dispute: the Fair Use doctrine. Under this judicial mechanism, the fact that the use of the musical work is highly transformative,[20] and the fact that such use is unlikely to have a negative effect on the composer's market for musical works,[21] are likely to prove decisive in finding that the textile designer's use constitutes "fair use" and therefore does not amount to infringement.

An analysis under German copyright law is likely to lead to similar conclusions. One of the limitations on the scope of copyright under German law is to be found in S. 24(1) of the *Urheberrechtsgesetz* (UrhG); it is known as free use (*freie Benutzung*). For S.24 to apply, and for free use to be present, it must be shown that "*angesichts der Eigenart des neuen Werkes die Züge des geschützten Werkes verblassen.*" This means that the trait and characteristic features of the old work fade in the light of the peculiarity of the new work. In the case at issue, due to highly transformative nature of the use made by the textile designer, it is likely that there would be sufficient inner distance between the two works so as to establish that the characteristics of the musical work faded away[22] when compared to the shapes recorded on the PNG file.

RESEARCH IMPACT

The collaborative research described above, between a textile designer and the author of this chapter—an intellectual property lawyer, proved highly beneficial to both parties. I personally found the engagement with an industry partner to be illuminating. Rather than addressing legal issues or conflicts in abstract, I had an opportunity to examine an actual business model, look into a creative process while querying the designer about the various stages of the process and the essence of her contribution and produce conclusions that impacted the said business model. The industry partner also found the collaboration to be highly beneficial. Here is what Nadia-Anne Ricketts, the designer and proprietor of BeatWoven, had to say about the project:

> Noam and I were introduced to each other through Creativeworks London, as a result of a research and development funding application I was submitting to help answer many IP and copyright questions that had arisen as a result of an idea of fusing the patterns behind music with woven textiles. I was starting a woven textiles label called BeatWoven and had, to that point, had a great response to my work and idea. I did realise that music is under copyright law, and that it would be a shame to de-value the process of BeatWoven of literally translating and visualising the music rather into "inspired" by, and knowing this would be the basis if my business model; where will I stand with selling the woven product in a commercial setting? Would I need a license? Pay a royalty? If so, how much? Which licensing category would my work sit in if it does? How would I market the product using trademark music names such as bands/musicians or song names?
>
> There were many levels to my work, working with artists themselves, choosing music myself and designing them into collections for interior projects, or bespoke commissions. My vision for the brand has been varied seeing the fabrics being used in a variety of settings, from fashion to interior arts. I wanted to make sure I have laid all the foundations I needed to prevent, as much as I can, any legal complications in the future.
>
> Noam and I worked together sharing knowledge about each other's expertise, discussing my business model, plans for the future, technicalities of the software and my process, the language I use for marketing. With all of this, Noam went away and used his knowledge and researching techniques to collate together an outcome of where I stood legally, and then advised me accordingly. It helped me see what my options are, and to see I had a choice, and could start planning to move forward taking BeatWoven into the market place in a confident manner. In addition, the project gave me the tools to be able to answer any tricky questions and able to manage difficult discussions even with legal professionals such as lawyers.

In conclusion, the project provided all participating parties with a unique opportunity to engage with one another at a stage where the industry partner's business model still had sufficient flexibility to consider and be informed by the output of our engagement and exchange of ideas. As Nadia-Anne's above statement suggests, this engagement assisted her in developing her business model, which in turn contributed to the success of BeatWoven.

Notes

1. Another example might be the conversion of musical compositions to fragrances.
2. Parodies may serve as a good example, where existing works have been altered in such a manner as to convey a new original message—while still retaining a considerable amount of the original expression in order to conjure up the earlier work.
3. William M. Landes, "Copyright, Borrowed Images, and Appropriation Art: An Economic Approach," *George Mason Law Review* 9, no. 1 (2000): 2.
4. On economics-based justifications to intellectual property laws see Richard A. Posner, "Intellectual Property: The Law and Economics Approach," *Journal of Economic Perspectives* 19, No. 2 (2005): 57–73.
5. Such theories underpin copyright law in most civil law countries.
6. As is the case under the Lockean theory, see John Locke, *Two Treatises of Government*, ed. Peter Laslett (Cambridge: Cambridge University Press, 1960), 9.
7. As would be the case under a Kantian-based authorial right system. See Abraham Drassinower, "A Rights Based View of the Idea/Expression Dichotomy in Copyright Law," *Canadian Journal of Law and Jurisprudence* 16, no. 1 (2003): 3–21.
8. See, for example, the statement of the Australian High Court in Roadshow Films Pty Ltd v. iiNet Ltd, HCA 16 (20 April 2012): "the concept and the principles of the statutory tort of authorisation of copyright infringement are not readily suited to enforcing the rights of copyright owners in respect of widespread infringements occasioned by peer-to-peer file sharing, as occurs with the BitTorrent system."
9. It is the creative process as currently employed by BeatWoven, the industry partner in the Creativeworks London's collaborative research project that is discussed in this chapter.

10. Wikipedia defines "mood board" as "a type of collage consisting of images, text, and samples of objects in a composition. They may be physical or digital, and can be 'extremely effective' presentation tools," used by designers in order to illustrate the styles they wish to pursue. (https://en.wikipedia.org/wiki/Mood_board).
11. A graphic software application intended for concept sketching.
12. For example, Coleridge introduced into his translation of Schiller's "Wallenstein" lines of exquisite poetry, which could not be found in the original play.
13. Autospin (Oil Seals) Ltd v. Beehive Spinning, RPC 683 (1995).
14. Abraham Moon & Sons Ltd v. Thornber & Ors, EWPCC 37 (2012).
15. If the answer to this question is yes, the court will then proceed to assess whether there was "substantial taking" from the music embodied in the MP3 file, which may result in a finding of infringement.
16. Sawkins v. Hyperion Records Ltd, EWCA Civ 565; 1 WLR 3281; EMLR 688 (CA (Civ Div), 2005).
17. *Abraham Moon & Sons Ltd*, EWPCC 37.
18. A literary work being a separate category of copyright protected works.
19. Obviously, she did invest musical skill and labour in that process.
20. The transformation at issue is to such an extent that a member of the public, even a professional musicologist, is not likely to be able to identify the original musical work when examining the visual representation on the PNG file.
21. The textile designer's product is not competing with the musical work in the marketplace; on the contrary, such use can be argued to increase the popularity of the musical work by contributing to its iconic status.
22. Its characteristic features obviously relate to sounds and aural experience.

At Home with Collaboration: Building and Sustaining a Successful University–Museum Partnership

Alastair Owens, Eleanor John, and Alison Blunt

There are many similarities between museums and universities. Both are places where knowledge is made and disseminated; both employ creative people who are allowed considerable freedom to generate new ideas and pursue their own projects; at the same time, both are increasingly responsive to wider public agendas and commercial imperatives which require them to think strategically about how they are distinctive and to prove their worth in the context of shifting political priorities and economic pressures. This chapter is about a partnership between a university (Queen Mary University of London) and a museum (The Geffrye Museum of the Home), located just two miles apart from one another in East London. The partnership was formed out of a general recognition that universities and museums have much in common and would do well to work together, but it also arose because both Queen Mary and the Geffrye had strong expertise and interest in a common intellectual focus: domestic life and the home. But while universities and museums do have many things in common, it is also the differences and complementarities of their aims, missions and reach that provide opportunities for strong and mutually beneficial partnerships. Our goal in this chapter is to describe how our partnership—The Centre for Studies of Home—works, reflecting on the

---

A. Owens (✉) • E. John • A. Blunt
Queen Mary University of London, London, UK

© The Author(s) 2017
M. Shiach, Tarek Virani (eds.), *Cultural Policy, Innovation and the Creative Economy*, DOI 10.1057/978-1-349-95112-3_10

nature of collaboration, as well as to consider the benefits and challenges of working together.[1] As we shall describe, Creativeworks London has been one of the sources of support and funding that has enabled our partnership to thrive; it has also been significant in allowing us to take our collaboration in new directions, opening up fresh possibilities for the future.[2]

Coming Together: The Centre for Studies of Home

The Centre for Studies of Home was founded in 2011. While the origins of our collaborative partnership go back to a jointly supervised Economic and Social Research Council–funded PhD project on nineteenth-century domestic material culture which commenced in 2005, the Centre emerged from a detailed feasibility study commissioned and funded by Queen Mary University of London. Undertaken by Caron Lipman, this study investigated different models of collaboration, assessed the degree of interest and level of commitment to a partnership within both institutions, and scoped potential themes and topics for research and other joint activity, including identifying sources of funding.[3] Before tying the knot in early 2011, we had an intensive period of courtship where we sought to better understand the cultures, working practices and priorities of each institution, and to anticipate some of the potential obstacles to building and sustaining the partnership.

For the Geffrye, the formation of our partnership came at a moment of significant uncertainty and upheaval as a consequence of policy shifts linked to the election of the coalition government in 2010 and associated changes to the funding of museums. At the same time the museum was beginning to look to its future and to a major development project that would expand both its size and broaden its focus. The Geffrye is located in eighteenth-century almshouses on Kingsland Road in Shoreditch, East London. The almshouses were converted into a museum in 1914. Originally conceived of as a furniture and woodwork museum aiming to educate workers employed in the local furniture industry, in fact, when the museum opened, the displays showed a much wider variety of (mainly) domestic objects. Following the relocation of the furniture industry further out of London, the Geffrye's remit moved to educating children. Period rooms were installed to display the collections, and the museum gradually moved towards a focus on the domestic interior and more specifically on the domestic world of the London middle classes displaying a series of typical living rooms at certain key dates stretching from 1600 to the present day. While these period rooms are still the core of the museum, there was a strong desire for this not to be the sole focus and to move beyond the living spaces of the metropolitan middle class to consider home in a broader sense, in both historical and contemporary contexts. A significant extension to the museum completed in 1998, provided a new space for its twentieth-century period displays along with learning rooms and venues for temporary exhibitions. It is these latter spaces that have offered opportunities for the museum to extend the social, temporal and geographical scope of its interest in home through successful temporary exhibitions such as the "West Indian Front Room: Memories and Impressions of Black British Homes" (co-curated with Michael Mcmillan, 2005–06), "At Home with Japan: Beyond the Minimal House" (co-curated with Inge Daniels, 2011), and "Homes of the Homeless: Seeking Shelter in Victorian London" (co-curated with Jane Hamlett and Lesley Hoskins, 2015). One reason for this broadening of the museum's remit was that the locality within which the Geffrye is situated has changed profoundly over the course of the later twentieth century; migration has led to a more diverse population whose understanding and experiences of home are different to those of London's middle class. The museum's flagship learning programmes—its work with school groups and adult learners—has been at the forefront of understanding and engaging with these different senses of home that a diverse population brings, including the trauma and dislocation of leaving a dwelling place because of forced migration and the complex transnational forms of belonging and domestic identification that are a feature of growing up and living in a global city. A desire to enhance and develop the range of work that the museum does to engage with diverse audiences, as well as to reinterpret the period room displays, was an important consideration for the Geffrye in entering into a partnership with Queen Mary, which was also exploring new ways of engaging with the "superdiversity" of its own East London setting and student body.

In some ways it was a lucky coincidence that as a neighbour university of the Geffrye, Queen Mary had significant interest and expertise in researching home and domesticity. The idea of launching a centre for the study of domestic life was initially thought desirable by some of us at Queen Mary as a way of bringing together areas of research expertise and teaching activity *within* the university and especially between the Schools of Geography and History; the prospect of a partnership with a museum added a new and exciting dimension to the venture. As well as offering a way of linking research activity within Queen Mary with complementary expertise at the Geffrye, it was quickly recognised that such a partnership would feed into the university's desire to develop its public engagement activities and to provide it with pathways to securing the wider impact and benefit of its research activity. The latter issue of "research impact" has, in particular, become an important strategic focus of research-intensive universities as it now forms a central component of the periodic audit of the quality of UK research activity, the Research Excellence Framework. In other ways too, the partnership with the Geffrye seemed to align with the wider policy trajectory established for both museums and universities. As early as 2005 a report published by the Department for Culture, Media and Sport talked of enhancing the research culture of museums "through closer links with the Higher and Further Education sectors."[4] The agenda of developing partnerships, sharing expertise and being more creative and entrepreneurial has become a core feature of museum sector policy in recent years and our partnership could certainly be seen as aligning with these developments.

However, in narrating the story of our collaboration we would want to resist giving the impression that the formation of our partnership was instrumentalist, responding solely to neoliberal policy imperatives and guided by associated regimes of regulation and audit. The Centre is fundamentally rooted in shared intellectual concerns and emerged as a consequence of specific projects that came from the "ground up," rather than being driven from on high. That is not to say that we do not have ambition or that we dismiss wider strategic priorities, but we would emphasise first and foremost that the success of our collaboration stems from working together on enjoyable and intellectually stimulating projects to which individuals at both institutions are fully committed. The Centre provides a context and framework for our collaboration and defines our identity as a group of museum professionals and academics interested in "the home." This helps in terms of securing funding to support day-to-day costs as well as in making grant applications and similar bids for larger projects. Indeed, the Centre is purposely outward-looking, since the intention was that it would not only provide a means for individuals at the Geffrye and Queen Mary to work together, it would also offer a platform for drawing in others interested in home and domestic life, including different museums and universities, and organisations and individuals from beyond those sectors. Our aim is to serve as an international hub for research and learning on the theme of home (see Table 1 for a summary of the main activities of the Centre).

Table 1 Centre for Studies of Home: main activities

Develop, host and support funded research projects.
Host, supervise and mentor PhD projects, Research Fellowships and visiting researchers.
Provide training, support and networking opportunities for PhD students and Early Career Researchers, via an annual postgraduate study day and other events.
Develop content for exhibitions, gallery displays, learning and education programmes and other public engagement events within the museum.
Share knowledge and understanding among centre members across the museum and university via an annual "Research in Progress Day" and other events.
Serve as a national and international hub for research and learning on home via convening the "Studies of Home" Seminar Series (at the Institute of Historical Research, School of Advanced Study, University of London), hosting at least two conferences per year, having an annual public lecture and maintaining a "research register" of home "experts" on our website.

The centre operates under the leadership of two co-directors: one from Queen Mary (currently Alison Blunt) and one from the Geffrye Museum (currently Eleanor John). They chair the steering group which comprises academic colleagues from different schools at Queen Mary, along with PhD students and early career academic representatives, and individuals from different areas of the Geffrye Museum. The steering group receives and assesses project proposals but is also proactive in determining future areas of interest and developing applications for new activity. It is a forum where there is inclusive decision making; both museum and university perspectives are aired and consensus is reached through dialogue. Indeed, the principle of the Centre being a fully joint partnership, where both institutions equally lead and shape the projects that are pursued, lies at the heart of the collaborative culture we have tried to establish; our model is of two-way knowledge exchange, not one-way transfer. This involves a commitment to learning about and seeking to understand each other's working regimes, institutional priorities and constraints, and respecting the different professional traditions of research, learning and communication that are intrinsic to museums and universities. At a more practical level we spend a lot of time in each other's company working together and alternating between the Geffrye and Queen Mary for meetings and events. University staff attend and participate in exhibition launches and key events in the annual calendar at the Geffrye; museum staff visit Queen Mary for lectures, public engagement events and seminars. Ours is therefore an intensive model of collaboration involving substantial energy and commitment from both parties. However, we would argue that our approach is one that has been successful, enabling us to attract considerable external research funding for a range of projects which, five years on from the founding of the Centre, are starting to have a major impact on the work of the museum, the university, and our wider audiences and partners.

Working Together

Since it was set up in 2011 the Centre for the Studies of Home has attracted c. £1.1 million of external income for research projects and knowledge exchange activity. The majority of this funding has been used to support original academic research, but in each case, projects were designed so that they involved collaborations with the museum and included significant outputs that contributed to or extended the work of the Geffrye. Here it is worth emphasising that the Geffrye's involvement was not solely at the end of projects when the core outputs are typically produced. In the majority of cases museum staff worked with university colleagues to conceive and develop applications to funders and have been centrally involved in the supervision and management of projects. This has helped to deepen relationships and provided opportunities for mutual learning and for realising benefits from projects that were not originally envisaged.

Indeed, jointly conceived projects have been a hallmark of our partnership. The launch event for the Centre—attended by staff from across the Geffrye Museum and by academics, researchers and PhD students from many disciplines at Queen Mary—included a workshop session where participants were encouraged to discuss ideas for research projects. Two of the themes identified at this session—"home and work" and "religion and the home"—became the focus of applications to the Arts and Humanities Research Council's Collaborative (AHRC) Doctoral Award scheme. Both topics appealed to the Geffrye as they were themes that were felt to be under-represented in the museum's collections, displays and educational activity, while for Queen Mary these topics offered the potential for bringing colleagues from across different schools—Geography, History and English and Drama—together. Both applications—"Home-Work: Connections and Transitions in London from the Seventeenth Century to the Present" (which commenced in 2012) and "Home and Religion: Space, Practice and Community in London from the Seventeenth Century to the Present" (which commenced in 2015)—were ultimately successful and generated eight PhD projects (four were funded under each theme).

Obtaining funding for PhD studentships has been a particular area of success, but the Centre has also hosted major research projects, fellowships and a range of smaller and more specific collaborative ventures (see Table 2 for a list of projects 2011–16).

Table 2 Centre for Studies of Home–funded projects, 2011–16

Project title and start date	Funding source	Core outputs for Geffrye Museum
Living with the past at home: domestic pre-habitation and inheritance, 2011	AHRC, Standard Research Grant	Temporary exhibition, workshops with museum visitors
Home-Work: connections and transitions in London from the seventeenth century to the present, 2012	AHRC, Collaborative Doctoral Award, Extended Programme (4 studentships)	Major exhibition; new learning and education materials; engagement and outreach work with local Vietnamese community
Inside teenage bedrooms, 2012	ESRC studentship	Temporary exhibition; materials for archive
Masculine emotional geographies: home, ageing and later life, 2012	Queen Mary studentship	Materials for archive
The home making of the English working classes: home and power in late-Georgian England, c. 1790–1820	Queen Mary studentship	Contributions to seminars and conferences
Meanings of home, love, belonging and selfhood for women in relationships together, 1900–1960	Queen Mary studentship	Contributions to seminars and conferences
Home and inhabitation: a biography of the Aylesbury Estate, 2012	Leverhulme Early Career Fellowship	Temporary exhibition, materials for archive
Connected communities: diaspora and transnationality, 2013	AHRC Connected Communities Programme, Research Review	Workshop on home, migration and community
Documenting Homes, 2013	Arts Council England	Enhancement of major collections
Making the invisible visible: enabling audiences to "see" archive collections, 2014	AHRC Creativeworks London, Creative Voucher	Collections visualisation tool

(*continued*)

Table 2 (continued)

Project title and start date	Funding source	Core outputs for Geffrye Museum
Home futures: an exploration through photography and sculpture, 2014	AHRC Creativeworks London, Entrepreneur in Residence scheme	Art installation as part of temporary exhibition, community engagement work, symposium
The Aylesbury Estate as home	Centre for Public Engagement, Queen Mary University of London	Art installation as part of temporary exhibition, community engagement work, symposium
Research on display: a guide to collaborative exhibitions for academics, 2014	AHRC, Collaborative Skills Development Scheme; The Culture Capital Exchange	Workshop and production of collection of edited essays on translating academic research into exhibitions
Home and religion: space, practice and community in London from the seventeenth century to the present, 2015	AHRC, Collaborative Doctoral Award, Extended Programme (4 studentships)	Temporary exhibition, new learning and education materials, materials for archive
Globe: home and belonging in East London, 2016	Leverhulme Artist in Residence	Development of new methods of practice-based collaborative research
Swept under the carpet: servants in London households, 1600–2000, 2016	Queen Mary Humanities and Social Sciences Collaboration Fund	Major exhibition and related events programming

These projects have generated a range of outputs for the Geffrye. Perhaps one of the most significant impacts of the partnership has been the research that has provided the materials and understanding to support new exhibitions and displays. As a relatively small museum, the Geffrye does not have the capacity of some of the national institutions, which have large research departments, to undertake the depth of research and preparation required to curate specialist exhibitions. Moreover, as the museum's core focus is historical and centred on the middle-class home, expertise on other periods, locations or different social groups is more limited. The Centre has provided a way of broadening expertise and supplying material for a varied programme of exhibitions and displays, extending interest in home beyond this core historical focus. Here too, the creation of exhibitions is collaborative—researchers partner with curatorial staff, external designers and others to produce content, promote and launch the exhibition and to evaluate it. Particularly for PhD students and early career researchers, this experience of working in collaboration with museum staff develops skills that open up additional employment opportunities within the museum and wider heritage sector. Being embedded in a museum partnership exposes researchers to other key elements of the museum's activity including archiving and collections management, and learning and engagement (Table 3).

Table 3 Case study

Project: Home-Work: Connections and Transitions in London from the Seventeenth Century to the Present Funder: Arts and Humanities Research Council Tessa Chynoweth and Laura Humphreys completed PhDs as part of our "Home-Work" AHRC Collaborative Doctoral Award Extended Programme. Both projects focused on domestic labour: Tessa's examined "Domestic Service and Domestic Space in Eighteenth-Century." London' and Laura's investigated "Domestic Labour, Metropolitan Middle-Class Households and the Wider World, 1850–1914". In a variety of ways their research impacted on the work of the museum and its audiences.
After securing additional funding from the AHRC, Laura ran a series of workshops for PhD students and early-career researchers exploring how to turn academic research into an exhibition, resulting in the publication of an edited collection of essays. Both students worked with the museum's Learning and Engagement team to produce new national curriculum-aligned materials for use with schools. With additional funding from Queen Mary's Humanities and Social Sciences Collaboration Fund, Laura and Tessa also co-curated a major exhibition with Hannah Fleming at the Geffrye, "Swept under the Carpet: Servants in London Households, 1600–2000". Unlike other exhibitions and displays generated by research undertaken in the Centre, this project focused on the museum's core period rooms. It involved a series of interventions into these rooms (see Fig. 1) to mark the presence of servants and expose the traces of domestic work. The exhibition stands as a good example of where the collaboration has succeeded in enabling reinterpretation of the existing museum content to reveal other kinds of domestic experience. Associated with the exhibition was a number of talks, a one-day conference and a performance event. Tessa's research has also informed the museum's collections policy, leading to the purchase of a number of eighteenth-century domestic guides

Laura Humphreys, ed., Research on Display: A Guide to Collaborative Exhibitions for Academics (London: Queen Mary University of London, 2015), http://www.geog.qmul.ac.uk/docs/staff/147183.pdf.

Fig. 1 Period room "intervention," part of "Swept under the Carpet: Servants in London Households, 1600–2000," Geffrye Museum of the Home, 15 March to 4 September 2016 (Credit: © Geffrye Museum of the Home)

The majority of our projects to date have been two-way partnerships between university researchers and museum staff, based upon original academic research. Creativeworks London funded two initiatives which developed our collaboration in new and different ways. Given Creativeworks

London's particular interest in the city's digital industries and the Geffrye's location close to the media and digital technology hub in Shoreditch, a project that explored the potential for bringing new kinds of technology into the museum seemed like a worthwhile opportunity. Supported via a Creativeworks voucher under the Archives funding round, we undertook a pilot project to develop new ways of enabling museum visitors and researchers interested in its collections to visualise its holdings. A key aim was to enable a better understanding of the range and scope of the collection—its historical variability and geographical spread—as well as to make more accessible, at least in some form, the large volume of material that is not on display. The project differed from others not only because its focus was on the digital visualisation of collections data, but also because it involved a three-way collaboration between the museum (the former Collections Manager Ananda Rutherford undertook the main research activity), Queen Mary and an IT company. The project succeeded in developing a visual timeline of the collections that will be piloted in the twentieth-century galleries providing access via interactive tablets to the "documenting homes" archive collection showing a wide range of households around the date of each period room. This will be developed for further use in the galleries and new collections study room which will be created as part of the planned major redevelopment of the museum over the next few years. While the product that has been created requires further refinement and development, the Creativeworks London funding illustrated the value of partnering with external commercial organisations, where specialist expertise is required.

Creativeworks London also supported artist Nadège Mériau to take up an Entrepreneur-in-Residence position at Queen Mary in order that she could work with Richard Baxter, a Leverhulme Early Career Fellow based in the School of Geography and the Centre for Studies of Home. Richard's work explored modernist high-rise living in London through a focus on the Aylesbury Estate in Southwark. Concerned with questions of how people "make home" in vertical environments and, given the recent demolition of the original estate, how homes get "unmade" as a consequence of programmes of "renewal" and displacement, the project was of particular interest to the Geffrye due to the museum's desire to engage with a wider range of metropolitan domestic experience.[5] An exhibition was always a planned output of the research, but the involvement of Mériau enriched the project by adding a more creative element to the venture based on new forms of engagement, collaboration and community participation. The exhibition "The Aylesbury Estate as Home" (which ran from 5 April to 18 September 2016) focused on the history of the estate from the utopian visions that underpinned its origins, planning and design in the late 1960s through to the demolition of the estate in the early to mid-2010s. Alongside photographs, drawings, text and interviews with residents, two artworks—a sculpture made out of papier mâché blocks designed to invoke a dwelling-like structure and a metaphorical film about the demise of high-rise estates—provided provocative juxtapositions to the more conventional display materials. The blocks that formed the sculpture were co-produced with Aylesbury Estate residents and others in a series of workshops led by Mériau.[6] The film raised wider questions about the recent history of social housing from the faded hopes of post-war designers to the contemporary politics of housing shortage within cities like London. A linked symposium on "Home and the Housing Crisis" brought together community groups, estate residents and artists with policy makers and academics to consider the wider issues raised by the exhibition and underpinning research.

The inclusion of this more creative dimension to the Aylesbury Estate project has proved inspirational in highlighting to both museum and university partners how artist collaborations can not only shape the research questions we ask, but can also provide a means of engaging others in processes of research and communication and in stimulating responses and debate around research findings. This model has informed subsequent collaborations hosted by the Centre including Janetka Platun's Leverhulme-funded Artist-in-Residence project "Globe," which examines issues of home, belonging and migration in East London. It does so with the explicit goal of developing new forms of practice-based collaborative research, whereby creative practice becomes integral to all stages of a project's evolution, from design through to the articulation and dissemination of research findings.

Taking Stock and Looking to the Future

Five years into our partnership it still feels like a multitude of opportunities for collaborations lie ahead. Working together has been an important learning experience. Our two institutions have learned a good deal about each other and, as the examples of the Creativeworks-funded projects reveal, we also continue to learn about (and remain open to exploring) new ways of working together effectively. Aside from the wide range of outputs from specific projects hosted by the Centre, working intensively together has resulted in other benefits for the participating institutions. Key amongst these has been the development of the skills and capacities of people involved in the work of the Centre. For example, many staff from across the Geffrye have broadened their experience of research project supervision and management through co-supervising doctoral students (each of the 11 PhD students who have been associated with the Centre to date has 1 or 2 Geffrye supervisors who work alongside their academic supervisors). Academics and early career researchers at Queen Mary have not just learned from Geffrye staff about how to curate and put on exhibitions, work with education and engagement teams has also enabled them to better understand how to reach out to schools and audiences of different ages. Indeed, the Centre hosted a Creativeworks London event in the "Capturing London's audiences" strand, bringing together academics and museum learning specialists on "Young people and museums: engagement, co-curation and co-production with 14–24 year olds." The relevance of this theme to the work of universities like Queen Mary barely needs emphasising.

Of course, collaboration is not without challenges. Creating the capacity to develop and sustain projects has perhaps been the most significant of these in our case, especially because we have chosen to pursue a close and intensive working relationship that involves spending a good deal of time at each other's institutions. For example, while some staff at the Geffrye had supervised PhD projects in the past, managing the support of 11 doctoral students over the past five years has added significantly to workloads. Proposals for future projects and collaborations are carefully vetted in the context of existing commitments and workloads, although we have all enjoyed pushing ourselves into developing a partnership that has stretched us and led to many pleasurable experiences of working together. Linked to this, some parts of the university have been more willing to engage with the collaboration than others, in spite of ambitions to develop truly interdisciplinary programmes of work, projects that stretch beyond the humanities and social sciences have so far been limited.

Funding has also been a challenge, although never a barrier. Indeed, as a model, our Centre has been quite successful at levering resource into both the museum and the university. Having a range of "different sized" funding opportunities has been important. Large research grants and collaborative PhD programmes have been critical for completing significant pieces of research and collaboration, but smaller pots of money—such as the schemes offered by Creativeworks London—have been essential in developing more experimental ideas, piloting small projects, building capacity and networks (internally and externally), and for enriching the impact, and extending the reach, of larger projects. As the novelty of our partnership wears off, and as the landscapes of university research funding and museum finances shift, we hope that the range of resources for supporting collaborative working and knowledge transfer can be sustained.

Our partnership has been important in raising the profile of both Queen Mary and the Geffrye; the Centre is becoming known as an international hub for research and learning on home and domestic life. We have attracted a number of visiting researchers from overseas and the idea of building international partnerships with museums of domestic life and universities with shared interests in other countries is a logical next step and, at the time of writing, a core priority. Closer to home, a more immediate and significant priority is the £15 million "Unlocking the Geffrye" project, underpinned by a £11 million grant from the UK's Heritage Lottery Fund. This major initiative will involve significant change to the museum including the opening up of its lower ground and first floors (more than doubling current gallery and exhibition space), creating a new collections study room and collections stores, and building additional venues for learning and events. Indeed, while collaborative activity to date has resulted in a range of individual outputs specific to each project, a wider and longer-term outcome of all these projects is to provide the knowledge and understanding to underpin the significant programme of redisplay and new temporary and permanent galleries that will be at the heart of the "Unlocking the Geffrye" project. The recent work of the Centre was highlighted in the Geffrye's successful application to the Heritage Lottery Fund, illustrating the museum's capacity for research and demonstrating the depth of expertise it can call on to sustain a larger institution with a wider ranging intellectual remit. Looking ahead, opportunities for further collaboration therefore seem assured and we look forward to developing our partnership in new and creative ways.

Notes

1. The Centre for Studies of Home can be found at www.studiesofhome.qmul.ac.uk.
2. See Tarek Virani, "Mechanisms of Collaboration Between Creative Small, Medium and Micro-Sized Enterprises and Higher Education Institutions: Reflections on the Creativeworks London Creative Voucher Scheme" (Creativeworks London Working Paper No. 4, Creativeworks London/Queen Mary, University of London, 2014), https://qmro.qmul.ac.uk/xmlui/bitstream/handle/123456789/6542/PWK-Working-Paper-4-SEO.pdf?sequence=2.

3. Caron Lipman, *Geffrye Museum and Queen Mary University of London Partnership: Feasibility Study, Final Report* (London: Queen Mary University of London, 2010). Further discussion of the origins and development of the Centre can be found in Alison Blunt, Eleanor John, Caron Lipman and Alastair Owens, "Centre for Studies of Home: a partnership between Queen Mary, University of London and the Geffrye Museum of the Home," in *Collaborative Geographies: The Politics, Practicalities, and Promise of Working Together*, eds. Ruth Craggs, Hilary Geoghegan, and Innes M. Keighren (London: Historical Geography Research Group, 2013), 111–25.
4. Department for Culture, Media and Sport, *Understanding the Future: Museums and 21st-Century Life* (London: Department for Culture, Media and Sport, 2005), 12.
5. On this theme see Richard Baxter and Katherine Brickell, "For Home Unmaking," *Home Cultures* 11, no. 2 (2014): 133–43.
6. The collaboration and exhibition were also supported by an award from the Centre for Public Engagement at Queen Mary University of London.

Connections—Movements—Treasures: Unlocking the Potential of the June Givanni Pan African Cinema Archive

Emma Sandon and June Givanni

> *Historic moments in the development of Caribbean, Black-British, African-American and African cinema have played witness to significant movements that transcend geographical boundaries and give rise to a global dialogue. The JGPACA is born out of the passion that has driven these aesthetic, intellectual and socio-political positions within the diaspora experience.*

June Givanni, October 2014, quoted in *June Givanni Pan African Cinema Archive (JGPACA) Business Plan*, January 2016. Thanks to those at Creativeworks London, and all those collaborators, partners, advisors, volunteers mentioned by name in this chapter for their support for JGPACA; as well as Jemma Amarchee-Broad, Samantha Iwowo, Zuri Da Silva, Zoe Lambe, Miranda Quammie, Shanice Martin, volunteers in cataloguing and in the many and varied tasks necessary in supporting the events described above; specifically artist Benito Major for helping to install and take down the show at Chelsea College; and artist Junior Appau Boakye-Yiadom, for assisting with the JGPACA pop-up archive installation at the Creativeworks Festival in April 2016. Thanks also to Jacqueline Maingard for editing this chapter.

E. Sandon (✉)
Birkbeck, London, UK

J. Givanni
Pan African Cinema Archive, London, UK

© The Author(s) 2017
M. Shiach, Tarek Virani (eds.), *Cultural Policy, Innovation and the Creative Economy*, DOI 10.1057/978-1-349-95112-3_11

Connections

The call for projects on the theme of "Archives" put out by the Creativeworks London Voucher Scheme in Autumn 2013 prompted June Givanni, an independent film curator, to contact Emma Sandon, an academic at Birkbeck, with a view to collaboratively exploring the potential of the collection on Pan-African cinema that Givanni had accumulated over more than 30 years of curatorial work in African and African diaspora cinema, including African-American, Black British and Caribbean cinema. The archive was housed in two places: at the Stockwell Community Centre who had offered Givanni a free space in 2011, and a room in her house in Streatham, where it currently still remains. Givanni curated programmes for cinemas and exhibitions, as well as acting on panels and juries deciding on film awards, and as programme consultant and interviewer, for festivals all over the world. In 1995, when she was heading the African Caribbean Unit at the British Film Institute (BFI), Givanni and Gaylene Gould put together a collaborative pan-institute programme of 12 projects representing the film component of *Africa 95*,[1] a major festival of African arts, which was entitled *Screen Griots*.[2] She had collaborated with Sandon on a colonial archive project Sandon was researching for *Africa 95*. On an MA placement in the National Film Archive (NFA), Sandon was researching its holdings on colonial Africa, and approached Givanni for advice. In response Givanni set up a steering group, to which Sandon reported, which included herself, the Curator of the NFA, Clyde Jeavons, and filmmakers John Akomfrah and Imruh Bakari, who had been members of the Channel 4–funded black film workshops, Black Audio Film Collective and Ceddo Film and Video Workshop. One of Sandon's briefs from this group was to see if she could find evidence of the involvement of Africans in filmmaking in the British colonies in Africa before independence.[3]

When Givanni approached Sandon in 2013, the latter was therefore aware of Givanni's work and background and could appreciate the urgency of making the Pan-African cinema archive more widely available, with a funding strategy involving potential revenue-earning activities and the status to apply for public-sector grants.[4] The AHRC Creativeworks London call provided a unique opportunity to formalise a partnership between Givanni as an independent curator and Sandon, interested in Pan-African cinema and the film archive to explore the contemporary significance and value of the archival resource and develop ways of bringing it to the attention of academia—one of its significant potential client groups.[5] Sandon also brought the Birkbeck Institute of the Moving Image into the Birkbeck partnership, through the collaboration of its director, Professor Laura Mulvey:

> The project will develop a strong evidence-base for the Archive and the company by developing its database, making its materials more accessible and identifying potential stakeholders. The relationship with Birkbeck's Institute of Moving Image (BIMI), a research centre promoting film archive and history scholarship, will be crucial in presenting the collection to key potential stakeholder groups in the arts, academic and educational sectors. BIMI will provide the academic expertise and space to establish a research framework for the company's archival remit of preserving and exhibiting Pan African cinema collections by drawing out and presenting key connective themes.
>
> The project will organise two film screenings and an exhibition to engage stakeholders in formulating, presenting and debating the relevance and potential of the collection as a valuable resource for specialist research and the cultural exhibition of Pan African cinema. [6]

The Voucher Scheme bid was successful, bringing in funding of £15,000, which was split as £10,000 for the academic partner and £5000 for the Small and Medium Enterprise (SME). The academic funding paid for a research assistant, Nana Ocran, to work with Givanni in her archive, to sort out the tasks that needed doing, and to explore themes within the collection. The SME budget paid for a small proportion of Givanni's time as she began to work full-time on the project, and some of the archive's expenses. There began a period of a few months in which Givanni and Ocran worked together on the archive, and Sandon joined them for regular meetings and updates on the research assistant's findings. Out of the process of June articulating what the archive contained, explaining the context of photographs, films, audio recordings, publications and other materials, how different archive connected and spoke to each other and the historical value they held for Pan-African cinema, emerged various themes. The conversations and dialogue were an essential part of the project as it developed.

Givanni already had a wide and formidable network of filmmakers, producers, photographers, and black arts and cultural workers through her work as a curator both in the UK and internationally. She had three professional creative advisors to mentor her about developing her archive: David A. Bailey, MBE, photographer, writer, curator, lecturer and cultural facilitator, founder member, advisor and previously Senior Curator of Autograph, part of the Institute of International Visual Arts (INIVA) and co-curator with Sonia Boyce of the Black Arts Archive; Imruh Bakari, filmmaker and writer, founder member of Ceddo Film workshop, Director of the Zanzibar International Film Festival, and Programme Leader of film studies at the University of Winchester; and Gaylene Gould, arts consultant, broadcaster, and writer, formerly at the Arts Council England and who, together with Givanni, constituted the BFI's African Caribbean Unit, where they developed and published the *Black Film Bulletin:* Gould also staged *Black World* at the BFI in 2005. The Creativeworks London Voucher Scheme award ran for a six-month period, and Givanni and Sandon invited cultural historians and film studies academics at Birkbeck, Professor Laura Mulvey, Professor Ian Christie, Professor Annie Coombes, Dr Luis Trindade, Birkbeck's Impact Development officer Wendy Earle, Maureen Roberts from the Huntley Archive at the London Metropolitan Archive, Richard Paterson, Head of Research and Scholarship at the British Film Institute and Rebekah Polding, London Screen Heritage Manager at Film London onto the advisory group. The advisory group met three times during the project. Givanni also invited a number of people significant in the field of Pan-African cinema and black art, to become patrons (see JGPACA website), including the Haitian Director and Head of the FEMIS film school in France, Raoul Peck; and the French-based Martinique film director, Euzhan Palcy.[7]

The initial plan to produce a small exhibition at the Peltz gallery, Birkbeck and two screening events in the Birkbeck Gordon Square cinema in the summer of 2014, became difficult when it was not possible to co-ordinate the booking of the gallery at the same time as the cinema. This prompted a most fortuitous expansion of the project through a further collaborative partnership with the University of the Arts London. The team had begun looking for another cinema and gallery space. Givanni knew the artists and professors Sonia Boyce and Paul Goodwin, who jointly held the Chair of Black Art and Design at Chelsea College of Arts, the University of the Arts London. They were interested in collaborating and offered gallery space at Chelsea College of Arts, the Triangle Gallery as well as the Cookhouse Gallery. Givanni and Sandon decided that summer 2014 was too premature to mount the exhibition and the University of the Arts London event was proposed for October 2014.

Movements

The outcome of the collaboration with the University of the Arts London, was a major exhibition of the June Givanni Pan African Cinema Archive curated by Sonia Boyce, Paul Goodwin and June Givanni, at the Chelsea College of Arts, 16–27 October 2014 and a one-day international panel discussion between archivists, curators, filmmakers and scholars at the Birkbeck Gordon Square cinema on 18 October 2014. In addition to these events, there was a smaller exhibition at the Peltz gallery, Birkbeck and three further screenings in the Birkbeck Gordon Square cinema. The exhibition, *Movements: Selections from the June Givanni Pan-African Cinema Archive*, presented screenings in the Triangle Gallery of rarely seen films: features, shorts, and documentaries with filmmakers and curators present, as well as Givanni herself, introducing the films and hosting discussions with audiences.[8] In the adjacent Cookhouse Gallery, an accompanying exhibition also included film screenings, a poster exhibition, audio recordings with filmmakers, artists and writers, displays of books and publications, pamphlets, film scripts, festival catalogues and programmes, enlarged photographs—both production stills and snapshots, postcards, film and festival posters, publicity materials and other paper documents, artefacts and memorabilia. The gallery was bright and spacious and its windows afforded a lot of daylight on the objects displayed. Boyce worked with Givanni, who selected the archive for display and screening, drawing on the themes that the research assistant had compiled. Goodwin, designers and framers assisted the process of putting the exhibition together.[9] The curating took advantage of the gallery's four interconnected spaces, with books, publications and memorabilia displayed in glass vitrine display cabinets, photographs framed on the walls accompanied by interactive film and audio recordings, film and festival posters mounted with white frames in another room, and a further screening with headphones and seating set up in another space and a 1980s timeline of film titles and events in the archive, displayed along a shelf connecting the two rooms.[10] Volunteers staffed the exhibition. During the exhibition, Givanni ran sessions for the MA Curating and Collections at Chelsea College of Arts, taught by Course Director Dr David Dibosa, taking students around the exhibition and through the curating decisions; and conducting a seminar on one of the films in the archive: Abderrahmane Sissako's *October* (1993).

In the Gordon Square cinema, Birkbeck hosted the one-day international panel discussion, *Pan-African Cinema, Négritude and the Archive*. Panellists included Givanni herself; filmmaker and artist, John Akomfrah and scholar, Reece Auguiste, both from the former Black Audio Film Collective; Imruh Bakari, advisor to the archive mentioned earlier; Nadia Denton, producer and writer; Louis Massiah, documentary filmmaker, and founder of Scribe Video Center, Philadelphia and director of the film *WEB Dubois: A Biography in Four Voices* (shown in the Triangle programme), the filmmaker, Euzhan Palcy; and Birkbeck film scholar, Laura Mulvey. Two panel discussions and a screening of an extract of Palcy's film, *Aimé Césaire: Une Parole pour le XXième siècle/ A Voice for the 21st Century* (1994), provided a fertile space of reflection on the exhibition, Pan-African cinema archive and its political and transnational roots in ideas of Négritude. Panel one in the morning, "The Relevance of Pan-Africanism and Négritude" debated the contemporary relevance of the JGPACA:

> What interest does a Pan-African cinema archive collected within a key historical period of anti-colonial struggle and the emergence of African diaspora cinema hold for filmmakers and film scholars today?[11]

Panel two in the afternoon was devoted to "How can the *June Givanni Pan-Africa Cinema Archive* promote and make accessible its collection and its Pan-African legacy?" It explored the historical importance of the archive and how it could "respond to the diversity that defines this culture, whilst taking into account the challenges that exists for archiving film across the African continent and diaspora."[12] The small accompanying exhibition in the Peltz gallery, "Biography of an Archive: The June Givanni Pan African Cinema Archive," co-curated by Givanni, Coombes and Sandon, 10–24 October 2014, told the story of the collection, and three subsequent screenings of films at the Birkbeck Gordon Square cinema on the theme of Pan-African cinema and Négritude during October and early November, presented by Givanni and Professor Hakim Adi, University of Chichester, an African historian who specialises in Pan-Africanism and African diaspora, rounded up the season.[13]

Movements was a very successful outcome for the partnerships between June Givanni and Birkbeck, and with the University of the Arts, London. Once the ball was rolling from the Creativeworks London Voucher

Scheme, it became easier to attract additional funding for specific aspects of the activities. Both university partners had been able to raise further funds within their colleges to supplement the Voucher Scheme monies to support the activities of JGPACA. Chelsea College of Arts had paid for some of the exhibition and design costs, beyond what had been originally budgeted and further funds raised within Birkbeck from the Higher Education Innovation Fund (HEIF), £3000, helped to pay for volunteers' expenses and for volunteers to work on cataloguing the collection and for website redesign for the *June Givanni Pan African Cinema Archive* online presence.[14]

The impact of this series of exhibitions, panel discussions and screenings raised the profile of the Pan-African cinema archive, asserted the importance of black archives and histories, engaged public interest and gained media coverage. The public events and their exposure also generated new contacts, networks, invitations and more work for Givanni. CSM offered her a "practitioner in residence" post in the Fine Art department during 2015–2016. The events and exposure also helped to identify stakeholders in public organisations, in the arts and cultural sector and educational institutions. After the successes achieved with the Creativeworks London Voucher Scheme in 2014, Givanni began to look into the possibility of applying for a National Heritage Lottery grant. This had been one of the suggestions from her advisory board. Other sources of funding were also being considered by Givanni and Sandon, including BFI regional funding for touring some of the exhibition, plus support from cultural and arts organisations and universities in the regions. It was at this point, at the beginning of 2015 that Creativeworks London announced that they were launching a new programme, BOOST, for follow-up funding for those projects that had already been funded which would run twice in 2015. This was a very welcome development and Givanni and Sandon agreed to continue their collaboration to compete for this further Creativeworks funding. BOOST had a competitive process involving an initial application to secure selection for the next round, and then a pitch for a new stage of the project to a panel of experts in creative entrepreneurship to win the award. Givanni and Sandon decided to compete for the second round in May and June.

The partnership proposed this time to work on a model for the archive, and a business, IP and digitisation plan. It was clear that the archive's development as a business enterprise needed the input of a lawyer and a business consultant to set the archive up as a business enterprise. However these were not the kind of services that an academic partner could provide—certainly the Birkbeck School of Law and Department of Management did not employ practitioners. So Givanni and Sandon discussed how to shape the collaboration with academic partners in ways that could benefit the project in terms of feeding into a business plan. The knowledge base they identified that the partnership could draw on and academic expertise that could contribute to strengthening the archive's sustainability plans was in arts management.

Treasures

The pitch for BOOST Givanni and Sandon created was entitled *Treasures: Unlocking the Potential of the June Givanni Pan African Cinema Archive*. Their proposal was based on the idea that the primary importance of the archive was in its cultural, historical and pedagogical value. There were two aspects to the next stage of the project, which needed addressing: location and space for the archive, including storage; and long-term funding. In terms of location and space, it had become clear during the process of the Creativeworks Voucher Scheme how important it was in the project's development to keep the JGPACA's independence, and if the archive were placed with an institution, "access" for Givanni would have to be very clearly defined. They also were keen to emphasise that it was important not to split the collection. They were familiar with the trends and funding priorities of institutions and that libraries were often known to glean collections for what is considered valuable or popular whilst the rest—the value of which they may not know—is stored or placed elsewhere or disregarded. They had heard some problematic stories about collections being donated to university libraries, which were not properly stored or cared for and eventually ignored as staff "champions" of it moved on. The next stage of the project, they argued in the pitch, therefore was to research how other archives operated, and to investigate similar collections of the size and complexity of the JGPACA, and the conditions in which these were developed or kept.

In terms of long-term funding, they understood that the JGPACA's potential to generate revenue through commercial activities was limited. For most of the films on video formats in the archive, the IP belonged to the filmmakers, and they required IP agreements and copyright clearance from the owners to screen them. Screening the films for exhibition purposes would often also involve actual film-hire costs of the original.

Givanni had some copies of films that were no longer available, and those urgently needed digitisation. Some of the Cuban silk screen film posters that Givanni had bought in Havana in the 1980s, had commercial value, but valuing them was difficult as there was a sizable market for Cuban film posters on the Internet with a wide range of prices for collectors. The pitch therefore became focused on developing a new model for a business, IP and digitisation plan for a small independent archive within the current funding climate that acknowledged the need for a mixed economy of public funding and private sponsorship.

Another element that had become clear throughout the Creativeworks Voucher Scheme was that the archive, as a personal collection, depended on Givanni's knowledge of its contents as well as the contexts which the documents, images and artefacts related to and in which they could be used. The next stage of the project therefore needed to create mechanisms for knowledge transfer. Cataloguing was one of these priorities, and a certain amount had been already achieved by volunteers since 2011 and was on-going, however other forms of knowledge transfer needed to be put in place. Digitisation is a key process to the cataloguing and online presence of the archive. Givanni, herself, wished to organise the collection in the long term so that someone else could take over and manage it as an archive.

To develop this model through a process of research required a team that included arts management expertise. For the BOOST programme, Givanni and Sandon factored in formally from the outset of the project the creative and artistic talents of colleagues at the University of the Arts, London. Sonia Boyce, meanwhile, had won a major AHRC award for a three-year project on *Black Artists and Modernism*, and was not available as a partner for this next phase. Givanni found new collaborators in the University of the Arts, London, this time in Central Saint Martins (CSM), in the Museum and Study Collection. Givanni had been invited to provide materials for the MA Culture, Criticism and Curation programme at CSM after her successful engagement with students at the Chelsea College of Arts during the *Movements* exhibition. Judy Willcocks, the Head of the Museum and Study Collection and Steven Ball, Research Fellow and artist, both had expertise in working with collections and arts and cultural institutions.[15] Sandon also invited Ben Cranfield, another highly experienced colleague working in Arts Management at Birkbeck to join her in the partnership with Givanni. Cranfield had already worked with Willcocks on other cultural projects and both were very well connected within the community arts sector, particularly in London. The budget of

£25,000 this time was split between the academic allocation of £15,000, split between Birkbeck and University of the Arts London, CSM mainly for academic buy-out of a small amount of time for each of the academics and £10,000 for the SME. Givanni used her allocation to bring in David A. Bailey, with business consultancy and arts archiving expertise and GianMaria Givanni, her son (who knows well the genesis of the archive), an experienced architect and designer, who would address issues of space and location and would assist in the project management of BOOST. As Creativeworks London described in their publicity: "The project team expanded from the original pairing into a dynamic and creative group of SME and academic partners."[16]

The pitch the partnership presented to the selection panel in the Whitechapel gallery, won the *June Givanni Pan African Cinema Archive* the BOOST funding. This led to the next creative and innovative stage of the project, which began in August 2015. Members of the team Ball, Cranfield and Willcocks, who had not visited the JGPACA before, went to Stockwell Community Centre to see the collection. The outcome of this visit was that Willcocks contacted the National Archives, as a result of which Kate Wheeler, in charge of Archiving the Arts, and Philip Gale, Senior Advisor for Independent Archives, visited JGPACA at the beginning of September 2015 and made a number of immediately useful recommendations. The National Archives had recently taken responsibility for archives nationally and had a role in regional programming. Interestingly Givanni had been in touch with the National Archives earlier in the year and whilst she had been given some advice, she had not solicited a proactive result. This suggests that collaboration with academic institutions for SMEs not only can provide important expertise, but also wider contacts, networks and credibility.

The freshly constituted grouping of seven members made up a strong team with important skills and contacts. They met on a regular basis and came up with a plan to visit relevant small to medium archives, collections and museums and conduct semi-structured interviews with the directors and curators.[17] Reports coming out of the visits formed the basis of recommendations for the archive model. They found out that the publicly funded institutions would split a collection like the JGPACA, putting the films and videos into a film archive and the paper, documents, ephemera into another archive. The emerging finalised model that they came up with is for an independent archive with an alternative structure and operation to those of existing archives, collections and museums. It is based on the idea of a decentralised and flexible archive, which can be involved in various partnerships and where the different functions of the archive are split into storage and preservation on the one hand, and activities and outreach on the other.

The *Academic Report and Recommendations* that the four academics produced, found that in order for the JGPACA to become sustainable, the archive would need to be registered as a charity, with an appropriate structure of governance. This would qualify Givanni to be able to engage in a series of public funding bids. Willcocks came up with an inspired plan of action that Givanni apply for funding in stages to formally set up the archive. This could be achieved through first targeting the Heritage Lottery Fund Start-Up Grant, and then Heritage Lottery Fund Young Roots and Transitional Grants, before bidding ultimately for a large Heritage Lottery Grant. In that way Givanni was advised she would have more possibilities of eventually gaining a larger, more strategic grant from the Heritage Lottery Fund. There was also other funding she could apply for from the Arts Council, the British Film Institute and AHRC funding schemes for targeted activities. She would need to establish appropriate partnerships with public and private institutions and collaborations that would enhance the public visibility of JGPACA. Meanwhile Ball's assessment of the archive was that the immediate vulnerable sections of the archive—particularly the audio-visual material on video, both VHS and Umatic—needed immediate conservation action. The location of appropriate storage for the archive for both immediate access and long-term holdings was also necessary. One of the key ideas however was that JGPACA "decouple" the storage from the working archive and utilise a pop-up approach to exhibiting the archive and a strategy of working in partnerships with both academic and public-sector stakeholders.[18] The *Academic Report and Recommendations* fed into the *JGPACA Business Plan* written by David. A Bailey, and the *JGPACA Spatial Strategy* prepared by GianMaria Givanni.

The *JGPACA Business Plan* suggests a ten-year plan for the archive. Phase One in the first two years would see JGPACA establish a board structure, register JGPACA as a charity, and formalise partnerships with public and private institutions. It would also include formalising copyright and IP agreements with the artists who own films or other materials. These activities would require start-up grants and fundraising for staff. Phase Two in year three of the plan for the following two years would see JGPACA concentrate on securing staff, and researching and implementing the programme funding focusing on space. It would also include implementing the cataloguing and digitisation programme for an online digital catalogue. Aside from these foundational activities, JGPACA would also do outreach both nationally and internationally through a two-year artistic programme cycle. Phase Three in years six to eight would continue the development of the archive in a new home and the online digital catalogue in order to be able to launch JGPACA in Phase Four in the ninth and tenth year.[19]

JGPACA Spatial Strategy reviewed the current storage situation for the archive. There are now plans for redevelopment of the Stockwell Community Centre, where the JGPACA has been partially housed, as part of the larger estate upgrade. There is a commitment to house the JGPACA in the new Centre, however at present it is unclear what this will entail and whether the space would be suitable for the archive as yet. The academic partners located in Central London are not presently able to offer space to JGPACA as a special collection in their library holdings. The proposal therefore is for JGPACA to consider partnerships within existing Community Hubs to provide a spatial resource. Yet whilst academic partners and community groups seem to offer the best way forward for JGPACA to create partnerships, there are also advantages to collaborating with commercial businesses especially as the funding trends are that local and community groups are being increasingly encouraged to be self-sustaining businesses. GianMaria Givanni notes therefore that community organisations seem to be increasingly adopting collaborations with commercial businesses, a process of what he describes as commercial hybridisation:

> The best combination for JGPACA would be to seek a partner who itself has already begun this process of commercial hybridization, see the Nettlefold Hall/Picturehouse; or the Curzon/Goldsmiths development. Entering into a potential tri-party Partnership where there is access to non/commercial groups and commercial groups might provide a wide range of possibilities, in particular if the commercial organisation is film or media related.[20]

Another recommendation in the spatial strategy is that it would be beneficial to JGPACA, in the event that Stockwell Community Centre was not able to continue to provide a suitable space, to find another space and new partnerships within Lambeth, a local authority sympathetic to black cultural initiatives, and already housing the Black Cultural Archives.[21]

Lambeth offers a number of Community Hubs, which could provide affordable space for JGPACA. The idea would be to find a partner in Lambeth to share space with, whilst locating an off-site storage space for some of the archives, if necessary in another part of London or beyond, a practice in keeping with the National Film and Television Archive and the British Library.

The second phase of the JGPACA project funded by the BOOST programme came to its end in February 2016. Creativeworks London ran a festival showcasing its funded projects on 29 April 2016, which gave Givanni a chance to trial the pop-up archive model. In the Anatomy Museum at Kings College, as part of the day-long festival, Givanni set up a three-screen installation which formed three walls to a desk in the centre with an archivist working on the cataloguing. A box of archive materials was available for people to browse or to enter on the catalogue system, assisted by the archivist. The screens show different elements of the archive materials: a screen showing posters, another screen displaying photographs with audio captions and a further screen with clips from films and documentaries. People visited, dropping by to engage with the materials and to discuss the archive with the archivist, curator and volunteers. On the ground floor the archive was also showcased in the digital installation curated by Dr Alda Terracciano, including a world map indicating the various locations of film festivals around the world, that are featured in the archive. This was coupled with audio recordings of interviews conducted by Givanni and others, at some of those festivals during the last 33 years. The JGPACA had moved into its next phase where the possibility of realising the independence of the archive as a self-sustaining business was now in sight.

Conclusion

Givanni's passion and commitment to creating an archive from her collection of Pan-African cinema has been the main driving force behind the success of this project. The collaborative pairing of Givanni and her cinema archive with Birkbeck, and then further partnerships with the University of the Arts, London, achieved through the funding schemes of Creativeworks London, enabled Givanni to benefit from a wide range of advisors, collaborators and volunteers to build a model for the JGPACA archive adapted to present-day public funding and institutional environments. The two consecutive Creativeworks London awards, the Voucher Scheme followed by the BOOST programme, allowed Givanni's collaborators precious time and space to consider ways of promoting JGPACA. First the project ran a series of events, exhibitions and screenings, exposing the archive to a wide range of public stakeholders. It then built a model and business plan to establish the archive spatially and virtually with a sustainable funding strategy. The project overall enabled an environment in which Givanni could talk to and with advisors, partners and stakeholders about the significance of her archive and build her case for support. The process was one in which a deep dialogical engagement, exchange and conversation were embedded. The politics of archive was key to how these conversations were shaped. Givanni with her partners created a space for the dissemination and appreciation of Pan-African cinema through the archive. The JGPACA's importance as a Pan-African cinema archive cannot be underestimated. It is a fragile and vulnerable archive covering a marginalised field of cinema. The project also involved researching and writing a business plan, IP, digitisation and spatial strategy for the archive, which resulted in an innovative model for sustainability, based on further collaboration and partnerships, and a ten-year plan to set up the online access and actual archive in a dedicated space. The next stage is for Givanni to secure sufficient funding from a number of sources to allow her to build this original and valuable cinema archive as a public resource.

Notes

1. Kobena Mercer, "Art of Africa," *Artists' Newsletter*, December 1995, 28–30; Nancy van Leyden, "Africa95: A Critical Assessment of the Exhibition at the Royal Academy," *Cahiers d'Études Africaines* 36, no. 141 (1996): 237–241.
2. "Screen Griots: The Art and Imagination of African Cinema" (British Film Institute programme, August–December 1995). The programme involved: African Classics Film Season, Haile Gerima Film Season, Haile Gerima Visiting Fellowship, TV on the Southbank Season, Mystery Melodrama and Comedy Season, Africa and the History of Cinematic Ideas Conference, BFI African Film and Video Releases, Teaching Pack with Workshops on African Cinema, Sight & Sound Supplement *African Conversations*, *An African Cinema Reader*, Mbye Cham and Imruh Bakari, *Symbolic Narratives: African Cinema*, and June Givanni.

3. The report of Sandon's research did not lead to a programme of films or conference for *Africa 95*, but it alerted the National Film Archive to the potential of its colonial holdings and resulted ultimately in the "Colonial Film: Moving Images of the British Empire" project, http://www.colonialfilm.org.uk/.
4. The recognition of the importance of private archives was registered by UNESCO as early as 1984. See Rosemary E. Seton, *The Preservation and Administration of Private Archives. A RAMP study* (Paris: Record and Archives Management Programme and UNESCO, 1984).
5. Givanni had had an early presentation of the archive in a collective show as part of the *Underground Railroad* group of black artists (set up by Gaylene Gould), held at the Royal Society of Arts in 2011.
6. Creativeworks Voucher Scheme application by June Givanni, 5 December 2013.
7. Filmography: Raoul Peck: *Haitian Corner* (1988), *Lumumba, Death of a Prophet* (1990), *The Man by the Shore* (1993), *Sometimes in April* (2005), *The Villemin Case* (2006), *Moloch Tropical* (2009), *Fatal Assistance* (2013), *Murder in Pacot* (2014). Euzhan Palcy: *Rue Cases Nègres* (Sugar Cane Alley) (1983), *A Dry White Season* (1989), *Siméon* (1992), *Aimé Césaire: A Voice for History* (1994), reissued as *Aimé Césaire: A Voice for the 21 Century* (2006), *Ruby Bridges* (1998), *The Killing Yard* (2002), *The Journey of the Dissidents* (2006), *The Brides of Bourbon Island* (2007), *Saving Nadine* (2014), *My Chat with Nelson Mandela* (2015). See http://www.euzhanpalcy.net/.
8. Seventeen titles including *Black Girl*, directed by Ousmane Sembène (1966), *Twilight City*, directed by Reece Auguiste (1989), *October*, directed by Abderrahmane Sissako (1993), *Pressure*, directed by Horace Ove (1976), *Home Away From Home*, directed by Maureen Blackwood (1994), *Badou Boy*, directed by Djibril Diop Mambéty (1970), *Contras City*, directed by Djibril Diop Mambéty (1968). See "Movements: Selections from the June Givanni Pan-African Cinema Archive" (Chelsea College of Arts and Birkbeck Institute of the Moving Image, exhibition catalogue, 16–27 October 2014), http://www.creativeworkslondon.org.uk/wp-content/uploads/2014/10/Movements-

programme-web.pdf; June Givanni Pan-African Cinema Archive website, http://www.junegivannifilmarchive.com/.
9. Louise Leonard, photos and audio; Will Brady, graphic design; Fola Odumosu, JGPACA website; Roy Richards, framing.
10. "Movements."
11. Ibid. See also the podcast for the day, http://www.bbk.ac.uk/arts/research/birkbeck-institute-for-the-moving-image/podcasts-and-videos/podcast-pan-african-cinema-negritude-and-the-archive.
12. See http://www.bbk.ac.uk/arts/research/birkbeck-institute-for-the-moving-image/podcasts-and-videos/podcast-pan-african-cinema-negritude-and-the-archive.
13. *Cuba, an African Odyssey*, directed by Jihan El-Tahri (Paris: Temps Noir, 2007).
14. See http://www.junegivannifilmarchive.com.
15. Ball was instrumental with David Curtis in setting up the British Artists' Film and Video Study Collection, of artists' moving image works on video, related publications, paper documents and still images, mainly British, with additional European and US examples, between 1960 and 2000.
16. "Unlocking an Archive," in *Creativeworks London: A Knowledge Exchange Hub for the Creative Economy, 2012–2016* (London, Creativeworks London, 2016), 53.
17. Interviews were conducted with partnerships: Huntley Archive at London Metropolitan Archive; Women's Art Library at Goldsmiths College; British Artists' Film and Video Study Collection at Central Saint Martins; Bill Douglas Cinema Museum at Exeter University; Stephen Dwoskin Archive at University of Reading; and with Independent Archives: George Padmore Institute; Black Cultural Archives; Cinema Museum, London.
18. GianMaria Givanni, "JGPACA Spatial Strategy" (June Givanni Pan African Cinema Archive, document, January 2016), 15.
19. David A. Bailey, "JGPACA Business Plan" (June Givanni Pan African Cinema Archive, document, January 2016), 3.
20. Givanni, "JGPACA Spatial Strategy," 18.
21. Black Cultural Archives, http://bcaheritage.org.uk/.

Process as Outcome: Research Across Borders

Caspar Melville

If there is a clearly defined boundary between academia and "industry"—something there is reason to doubt—it is one that is routinely crossed, at least in the corner of academia in which I work. Academics like me, who spend their time researching, teaching and writing about popular music and the creative economies through which its circulates, not only spend a lot of time thinking about issues associated with "the industry," but often spend time working in industry too. Popular music scholars are usually trained in academic disciplines like sociology, political economy and cultural studies, but following in the footsteps of the pioneers of pop music studies Simon Frith and Dave Laing, many started as music journalists and continue their academic careers with one foot, or at least a toe, in the world of music outside the university, working as journalists, running music organisations and festivals or working as musicians and DJs.[1] One of my colleagues in the Music department at SOAS, Lucy Duran, has combined an academic career with that of a prolific record producer and broadcaster, and she is not the only one.

I have criss-crossed this unmarked border numerous times in my own career. Following my undergraduate degree I worked for a decade as a freelance music journalist and promoter, before returning to academia

---

C. Melville (✉)
School of Oriental and African Studies, London, UK

© The Author(s) 2017
M. Shiach, Tarek Virani (eds.), *Cultural Policy, Innovation and the Creative Economy*, DOI 10.1057/978-1-349-95112-3_12

to complete an MA and PhD, then veering back to work as a journalist, magazine editor and CEO of an educational charity. I did not get my first full-time academic post until the age of 46. I have written previously about what it means to conduct research from outside the academy.[2] Thus I may be somewhat atypical of the academics involved in the Creativeworks London Voucher schemes and my access to the world outside academia did not have the full force of novelty that it might have for others. Yet this also felt like an advantage, since as Virani argues, prior experience of cross-border collaboration is one of the major indicators of likely success of a Creative Voucher project.[3]

I was hired in 2013 by SOAS, University of London, to teach a new MA in "Global Creative & Cultural Industries" in the School of Arts, a new field of enquiry for the school and a sign of the recognition that arts and humanities research needs to upgrade its textual and aesthetic focus by taking seriously the emergence of new kinds of cultural economy. It was thought that this would boost recruitment by providing humanities students with "skillsets" and career pathways into what is now routinely called "the creative industries." While this is evidently to be welcomed it was also clear that a course like this represented part of a reorientation of the university away from notions of "pure" research and the development of abstract theory towards a more pragmatic emphasis on impact, measurable outcome and collaboration with industry that could provide governments and their proxy funding bodies clear evidence of a return on their investment. The growing emphasis on "impact" within the Research Excellent Framework remains one of the key drivers here.

For many in academia such a trend forms a worrying part of the general neoliberalisation of education, and the emergence of what Andrew Ross calls University Inc.; the culmination of government policy initiatives designed to ensure that universities pay their way by making measurable contributions to economic value, which risk making universities, in Terry Eagleton's memorable phrase, "service station[s] for neocapitalism."[4] Within this model, the subsumation of the arts, humanities and media under the newly minted umbrella term "Creative Industries" risked, in the view of many humanities scholars, reducing the meaning and value of art and culture solely to an instrumental idea of its economic value.[5]

Though much of this went unspoken at my university, except at Union meetings, the wariness with which my arts and humanities colleagues greeted such new initiatives could be felt. Everyone, from scholars of Indian classical music to Islamic art professors, voiced enthusiasm for the idea of teaching cultural industries and building links with industry, yet there was reluctance to engage in the detail, suggesting an unwillingness to sully pure research agendas with the grubby vocabulary of capitalism, with its profane talk of markets, consumers, intellectual property and employment contracts. The concrete result of these unspoken worries was that once I was hired I found everything which smacked of business or industry plopping onto my desk—from a proposal from Nokia to collaborate in producing world music ringtones, to organising a seminar on careers in the cultural sector, joining a "Knowledge Quarter" working group and fielding queries about copyright for SOAS marketing, I found myself the one-stop for "enterprise" related projects, as my colleagues planned their next round of fieldwork. Which is why I found myself invited to a Creativeworks London ideas pool, where I first heard about the Creative Voucher scheme.

The SOAS-Carthage Research

The meeting with my eventual research partner—Catherine Steinmann from the music publisher Carthage Music—who I met at the first ideas pool, felt serendipitous but was in fact a result of pre-existing networks. She already knew my SOAS colleague Lucy Duran from their work together on world music projects and it was Lucy who had suggested that we collaborate. In fact an even deeper network connection revealed itself when, after meeting a few times, Catherine and I realised that we had mutual friends. This is not such a coincidence as it might appear given the importance of music in the cultural lives of the social networks we occupy, which has led us, as many of our contemporaries, into careers involved with music.

The urgency of the Voucher application cycle encouraged us to think fast and after two useful ideas sessions hosted by Creativeworks London, Catherine and I hatched a plan to investigate how the copyright system works when applied to traditional global repertoires. The rules of the Voucher system are that the research question must originate from the SME partner. As a specialist music publisher representing many repertoires from outside the Western world, with a particular expertise in the catalogues of the griot musicians of West Africa, including Kassé Mady Diabaté who is widely regarded as one of Africa's finest traditional singers, a need to understand how copyright worked, and could be made to work better, for these traditional repertoires, was a clear business imperative. But this was also a research subject that fitted well with my own desire to develop a research profile focusing on copyright—the core source of economic value in the cultural economy—and to build upon my knowledge of a region of the world that falls within the geographical areas of SOAS expertise.

We crafted a proposal called "Valuing Tradition: Making ethical use of music publishing and copyright to sustain musical tradition and nurture music careers," which passed successfully through the streamlined and swift application and decision-making process.

The Creative Economy Lexicon

At the various Creativeworks London meetings and workshops, we were introduced to a new research vocabulary that has emerged from contemporary "creative industries" thinking. While my SME partner and myself had little trouble finding a common language with which to communicate with each other and report our findings, this creative enterprise lingo of "fusing," "igniting," "catapults," "incubators" and "knowledge brokers" could feel a little alienating, with its strong whiff of the late-1990s Blairite project to "rebadge" Britain as the centre of the Creative Industries based on innovation and entrepreneurship, a project which has been successfully exported globally but widely and justifiably criticised for embodying a reductionist view of art and culture.[6] Innovation Voucher schemes themselves are an artefact of this period.[7]

Allied with this was the strong steer we got from the start to try to develop innovative research methods—using if possible digital tools and big data sets—which might generate not just findings but also proprietary intellectual property. We were introduced to some of the previous voucher projects which had developed impressive and innovative ways to gather and present data, and bespoke digital programmes to render it in novel ways, including as cloth. But in discussion with my SME partner it become clear that we both considered ourselves to be involved in what you might term more "old school" methods of cultural and academic production—Carthage Music is a small independent publisher which relies on strong interpersonal relationships and straightforward contracts to claim royalties for the writers they represent; my preferred research method, based on the Chicago School sociology of C. Wright Mills and Howard Becker, is the long-form open-ended interview, hanging around with people in whatever scene is the subject of enquiry and doing a lot of reading. It was clear from the start that we were going to stick to what we know rather than trying to develop an innovative, copywritable research methodology.

At the heart of the research were 26 interviews I conducted between June 2014 and January 2015. Several were conducted over email, a couple on the phone, the rest were face to face. I also attended three concerts by relevant performers. We held a public meeting at SOAS as part of the research attended by around 50 people—featuring a performance by Kassé Mady—and I did a radio interview with SOAS radio.

Process as Outcome

Fitting with the old school character of our project the agreed outcome came in the form of a single authored report, which outlined the main findings, discussed case studies and made recommendations about future activities for the independent publishing sector. The report will sit on the Carthage website and be linked to, circulated and discussed by the independent music sector via Carthage Music's networks. However both partners agree that perhaps a more significant outcome than the report was the process of the research itself. The fact of spending time investigating the ecosystem in which Carthage operates—the specialist global repertoires represented by Carthage Music represent a small segment of the music market defined by a network of relationships between musicians, publishers, promoters, producers, small labels and the copyright collection agencies in territories across the world who manage royalty payments—and the chance to objectify their own practice provided a valuable space for Carthage in which to make visible what is usually unspoken and swept aside by the urgency of the everyday. The research created space for institutional reflexivity that is all too rare in business, a process which allowed Carthage to consider what it was they knew and why they did what they did. Here we can see a clear benefit from collaboration with academia where such reflexivity is part of our everyday teaching, researching and thinking practice.[8]

Beyond this Catherine Steinmann emphasised to me how hearing the research interviews with musicians, fellow publishers and other actors in the terrain deepened her own understanding of the issues her company faced, and in particular led her to realise the great knowledge and experience embedded in her own business: in the interviews with her two partners Joe Boyd and Guy Morris she was able to see how, despite the everyday pressures of keeping afloat in a competitive business environment and the ever-present sense that the economics of the music business were collapsing under the "digital tsunami," her team had the right combination of knowledge, experience and commitment to weather the storm and continue doing a worthwhile job representing the interest of their clients. Interviews with some of the African composers and musicians Carthage represents had similarly given her the sense that though, from certain politicised angles, the relationship between traditional musicians and European publishers can look like a form of neocolonial exploitation (one of the issues explored in the report), from the perspective of musicians trying to make a living, feed their families and preserve and extend an ancient tradition, the royalty revenues Carthage is committed to extracting for them comprised one of the most important and reliable income streams available to them, especially in the light of Mali's recent political and economic instability which followed in the wake of 2012's coup and Islamist insurgency.

From the academic perspective the great opportunity afforded by such collaboration is the chance to road test academic assumptions and theory in a real world context, and transfer knowledge about how issues are viewed within academia to those outside; the interview is always a two-way process, it is always dialogic. I went into the field armed with a weight of ethnomusicological argument about how copyright was Eurocentric, incompatible with the conventions of traditional music's production and consumption, and risked commodifying traditional culture.[9] It was intriguing how many of those involved in the administration of copyright—label bosses, publishers, managers—were prepared to concede the fundamental weaknesses of copyright law and the potential for exploitation the system might allow. However there emerged from interviews a fascinating re-reading of the notion of exploitation—Carthage partner Guy Morris insisted that the job of a publisher was precisely to exploit the potential of their client's music as much as possible, that is extract the maximum value from it in terms of royalties, and return them to the composer (minus a percentage). Here we had a clear example of the clash between academic and business lexicons, and a revealing way in which the abstract theorising of academia comes into contact with, and is modified by, the pragmatics of everyday business, where copyright is considered in the words of Carthage's Joe Boyd, to be a bit like democracy, that is "the least worst system."

But such research collaborations also raise the clear ethical issue which is inherent in the Voucher process by which academic researchers are recruited by SMEs, to research an issue which they believe will enhance the value of their business. When the issue raised, as in our research, includes such questions as "should that SME actually be doing the business they are doing?" what is the scope for the researcher to go against the interest of the SME? In my case, I reached what I consider to be a properly thought-out and supported conclusion that Carthage and other independent publishers were doing an effective and ethical job providing much needed revenue to often struggling traditional musicians, but I was aware both of the potential difficulties of presenting research findings to the contrary and of the way in which the research outcomes might be greeted by my, professionally critical, academic peers: "[N]ew research led by independent publisher finds that independent publishers are doing a good job." Well it would, wouldn't it?

One way in which the research sought to address such concerns was in considering how the independent publishing sector might be able to contribute to the development of more robust collection processes in developing countries such as Mali, that would lead in the future to a new relationship between traditional arts and Western companies, which is not necessarily any more headquartered in the capital cities of Europe or America. Indeed during the project Carthage sponsored, through a trusted intermediary in Bamako (who was also a research informant), a meeting of the Malian collection agency BuMDA, and continues to support, knowledge transfer to African musicians to ensure they are fully versed in the intricacies of the copyright system. Within this emergent Malian network, those artists who have worked with London-based publishers and labels and established solid working relationships with companies such as Carthage Music and World Circuit who work at the coalface, have taken a leading role as their international success has secured local prestige, and the transparent reporting practices of the European publishers have allowed Malian musicians to begin to build an understanding of how the apparently mysterious and circuitous copyright system works.

Perhaps the other most important lesson both partners learned is that £15,000 is not a lot of money—there was so much more we would have liked to do which our budget would not allow.

A Sort of Conclusion

To finish I want to return to the question of what a university is for and how this is changing. As I indicated above there is a lot of anxiety within academia about the neoliberalisation of the university, how what was once a space dedicated to the pursuit of knowledge for its own sake, and the production of "abstract" as opposed to applied research, has become a business in itself, delivering knowledge to student-consumers, and expected to justify its existence by the economic contribution it can make to overall GDP.

Whatever your politics it certainly seems clear that the role of the university is changing, and in particular the idea that universities have, or should have some kind of privileged access to knowledge, or is the only place that can produce knowledge, is no longer tenable. As the anthropologist Ruth Finnegan writes "we have to entertain the notion of a plurality of co-creating participants in knowledges, 'local,' situated, and diversely defined rather than always monolithic or officially sanctioned—and open furthermore, to change and dispute."[10] Collaborations between academic and SME actors, such as provided by the Voucher schemes, are a good way to reinforce this.

However, we do need to recognise that universities are distinct and valuable in ways that are beyond their immediate contribution to the balance sheet. In his discussion of relations between academia and the world of research "outside the walls" educationalist Frank Webster notes that despite the lip service played to the idea that University research is a vital driver of business innovation, given the fact that research is routinely undertaken across the science, technology and creative industries, "it seems dubious to claim that university research is vital for economic success."[11] This is not to say that the university is not valuable, but that what we value about the university needs to be what academia does best, the kinds of "pure" research that aspires to generate theoretical knowledge, which is by nature abstract, generalisable and formulated, as opposed to the ends-driven forms of applied research typical outside academia. We need to value this form of knowledge, Webster says, precisely because of its distance from the everyday cut and thrust of business

> If we extend the notion of research in the direction of its popular definition as "finding out," collating facts and investigating subjects, then we might, within this more encompassing conception, include an ability to understand and absorb knowledge, to apply what is known to novel situations and come up with innovative answers to problems, and to have developed capacities to explore and to critically assess phenomena.[12]

The key aspect of this form of knowledge generation is that it draws on what universities have that industry generally does not—"autonomy, resources and the values of free enquiry." In the end the aspirations of such research are both modest and practical and, it seems to me, self-evidently important: "helping people come to terms with a world, our world, in constant and accelerating change."[13]

This is what I hope my research did for Carthage—and also what doing the research did for me—and is, no matter the cavils, in itself a vindication of the creative collaboration between academia and industry.

Notes

1. Examples include Professor Andrew Dubber and Professor Jeremy Gilbert who DJs at hip London club Beauty and the Beats. It goes both ways as well, as the work of music journalists such as Simon Reynolds is widely taught within university Popular music courses.
2. Melville, Caspar, "Building Knowledge through Debate: openDemocracy on the Internet," in *Participating in the Knowledge Society: Researchers Beyond the University Walls*, ed. Ruth Finnegan (Basingstoke: Palgrave Macmillan, 2005), 198–212.
3. Tarek Virani, "Mechanisms of Collaboration Between Creative Small, Medium and Micro-Sized Enterprises and Higher Education Institutions: Reflections on the Creativeworks London Creative Voucher Scheme" (Creativeworks London Working Paper No. 4, Creativeworks London/Queen Mary, University of London, 2014), https://qmro.qmul.ac.uk/xmlui/bitstream/handle/123456789/6542/PWK-Working-Paper-4-SEO.pdf?sequence=2.
4. See Stuart Hall, "The Neo-Liberal Revolution," *Cultural Studies* 25, no. 6: 705–728; Andrew Ross, *Nice Work If You Can Get It: Life and Labor in Precarious Time* (New York: New York University Press, 2010); Morag Shiach, Jana Riedel and Jasmina Bolfek-Radovani, "Fusing and Creating: A Comparative Analysis of the Knowledge Exchange Methodologies Underpinning Creativeworks London's Creative Vouchers and London Creative and Digital Fusion's Collaborative Awards" (Creativeworks London Working Paper No. 25, Creativeworks London/Queen Mary, University of London, 2014), 8, https://qmro.qmul.ac.uk/xmlui/bitstream/handle/123456789/11413/Shiach%20Fusing%20and%20Creating%202014%20Published.pdf?sequence=1; Terry Eagleton, "The Slow Death of the University," *Chronicle of Higher Education*, 6 April 2015.

5. Justin O'Connor, "Surrender to the Void Life after Creative Industries," *Cultural Studies Review* 18, no. 3 (2012): 388–410; Angela McRobbie, *Be Creative: Making a Living in the New Culture Industries* (Cambridge: Polity Press, 2016).
6. Robert Hewison, *Cultural Capital: The Rise and Fall of Creative Britain* (London: Verso, 2014). Cf. Justin O'Conner and Kate Oakley, "The Cultural Industries: An Introduction," in *The Routledge Companion to the Cultural Industries*, eds. Justin O'Conner and Kate Oakley (London: Routledge, 2015), 1–33.
7. Shiach, Riedel and Bolfek-Radovani, "Fusing and Creating."
8. Frank Webster, "Research, Universities and the Knowledge Society," in Finnegan, *Participating in the Knowledge Society*, 245–63.
9. Anthony Seeger, "Ethnomusicology and Music Law," in "Music and the Public Interest," special issue, *Ethnomusicology* 36, no. 3 (1992): 345–59; Anthony McCann, "All That is Not Given is Lost: Irish Traditional Music, Copyright, and Common Property," *Ethnomusicology* 45, no. 1 (2001): 89–106; Steven Feld, "A Sweet Lullaby for World Music," *Public Culture* 12, no. 1 (2000): 145–171.
10. Ruth Finnegan, ed. *Participating in the Knowledge Economy: Researchers Beyond the Walls,* (Basingstoke: Palgrave Macmillan, 2005).
11. Webster, "Research, Universities and the Knowledge Society," 246.
12. Ibid. 258.
13. Ibid. 259.

Social Art Map: Reflections on a Creative Collaboration

Emily Druiff and Sophie Hope

The Social Art Map acts as a starting point and resource for people interested in social art practice, including those engaged in producing, commissioning, curating, collaborating and participating.[1] By using the contested term "social art" we refer to contexts where artists work with people in the co-creation of a public outcome. The thinking behind the Social Art Map has evolved over ten years of conversations between Emily Druiff and Sophie Hope about socially engaged art practice, its place in society, how it is organized, supported and critiqued. Having both studied MAs in curating at Goldsmiths (Sophie in 1999–2000 and Emily in 2003–4), we have ended up working in areas that continue to sustain our curiosity and enable us to enact forms of socially engaged practice—Emily as a curator and director of Peckham Platform and Sophie as a practice-based researcher and teacher at Birkbeck, University of London.

Over a six-month period in 2015 the research partnership between Emily and Sophie supported by funding from Creativeworks London, mapped the commissioning processes of social artworks across five

E. Druiff
Peckham Platform, London, UK

S. Hope (✉)
Birkbeck, London, UK

different organizations in London: AIR, CREATE London, Chisenhale, Peckham Platform and The Showroom. This has created an in-depth study of five art commissions from the three different perspectives of (again contested categories) artist, commissioner and participant resulting in a printed Social Art Map.

When asked to consider the theme "Creative Collaborations" for this publication we wanted to look at the challenges we faced in our collaborative relationship as well as the potential future developments that are emerging from it. The format of this text is a way for us to write collaboratively, where we both answer the same set of questions about our motivations for developing the Social Art Map revealing potentially separate intentions and motivations that made this project a joy to work on.

The change in sociopolitical environment over recent years has had a significant impact on the cultural landscape. Unprecedented cuts to the arts at both the national and the local level have put cultural organizations in an increasingly competitive financial climate. These changes have not only impacted the cultural sector but also other public services including: youth provision; secondary and higher education; libraries and mental health services. It is in this increasingly challenging financial climate that we are looking at the critical role of creative collaborations. This context sets a very definite opportunity if not demand for cross-sector partnerships. Through our research in the Social Art Map we have been able to explore how organizations and artistic practitioners work in partnership with public services through a socially engaged artistic model. The opportunity to have these discussions has been a collaborative process in and of itself and the sharing and dissemination of it we hope will foster further cross sector conversations.

From the start of the project, there has been an interesting tussle between the instrumental mission of Creativeworks London to assist businesses and contribute to London's creative economy and the input and role of academic research. The funding from Creativeworks London was underpinned with the agenda of contributing to London's creative economy. The economic rationale for funding the arts is often linked to its contribution to cultural regeneration and employment. The assumption that these reasons are purely positive needs questioning as regeneration can lead to gentrification and employment in the arts can be precarious, inequitable and unsustainable. What kind of creative economies are creative collaborations between arts organizations and universities promoting and perpetuating? For universities the economic argument for justifying research agendas is also increasingly placed on its impact on the wider economy. Where is the critical practice and research that asks difficult questions of this process? We approached this project with these underlying questions to try and work through, together and with others, ways of exploring the impacts of austerity politics, cuts to public resources and services and an increasing emphasis of having to justify carrying out art and research on economic terms. We had to find a balance between the project being beneficial to Peckham Platform's mission to promote social arts practice and increase sector understanding as outlined in their business plan and how the project worked in terms of research. As research, for example, the project might question the underlying assumptions about *why* social art practices are worth supporting and the expectation that they should or could contribute to the creative economy in London. These are sometimes uncomfortable conversations, but they happen because of the trust built up between us and the commitment we both have to exploring the complexities of these practices.

It is these complexities we wanted to focus on in our mapping of social art practices in London (geographically restricted to the capital due to the funding criteria of Creativeworks London). We decided to investigate five specific projects organized by five small-scale arts organizations that worked with visual artists and had a history of curating work beyond the gallery. We then mapped these projects in detail with the artist, curator and/or commissioner and collaborator or participant of each project. This mapping took the form of timelines on long pieces of paper, with everyone telling the story from their different perspectives of how and why things began, evolved and came to an end. Within the projects, narratives varied of beginnings, middles and ends as the individual experiences merged and departed at different points along the way. The narratives of beginnings often opened up before the official "start" of a project and endings were prolonged by stories that continued long after the "completion" of a project.

By sitting down together to do the mapping, there were perhaps things that were not said, but also by listening to each other's stories, there was a heightened awareness of each other's experiences, responsibilities and understandings of what occurred. The maps revealed the intricacies of the processes; the inner mechanisms, shared stories and refined nuances that make up the practice. We tried to keep as much of this messiness as possible in the final printed map. This editing process was tricky in itself as inevitably there were interpretations of the material along the way. The individuals involved in the mapping decided to be named which then made it important they had an input into this process, meaning further layers of editing. This was a necessary process, but also one that led to further modification of what was said, particularly as organizations are presented publicly.

One of the reasons for doing this project was to find ways to be transparent and honest about the issues, problems and relational aspects of the processes of making social art practices happen. We were interested in the language used to justify and explain these practices and the chance to explore different, perhaps conflicting narratives of these experiences. The issue of course, is when the guts of a project are made public there are repercussions for the field. As budgets are becoming even more restrained and as partner organizations are having to close their doors or reduce staff and budgets, the tendency might be to become more isolated and protective of what remains and more competitive for funds. Another option is for organizations to expose the labour involved in their work, the realities of the lives of those participating (artists, curators, collaborators) and the means by which things happen and occur. To reveal the cogs makes these projects solid, visceral objects in the world and perhaps harder to ignore.

With the launch of the map on 2 December 2015 we brought together people to explore ways of continuing this work as a growing network of organizations and individuals. We started to identify what is needed in terms of research and resources and how we can work together to support, in critical and practical ways, the ever evolving and morphing field of social art practices. For example, how can we bring our understandings of histories and futures of social art practices together to articulate our present positions? Sharing these processes together, coming out of the corners of galleries and communities and baring all, is a brave gesture of solidarity with other practitioners and is hopefully where trust and understanding can grow. The Social Art Map project is where difficult conversations can be held which contest the demand for narratives of slick, polished and productive projects and allows for the necessary messiness of these processes to be valued and explored.

WHAT INSPIRED YOU TO COLLABORATE ON SOCIAL ART MAP?

ED: For some time, I have had a nagging feeling that what has come to be called social artwork remains one of the more misunderstood genres of contemporary art. With such a broad church of approaches that resist definition, numerous attempts to pinpoint, define or shape this genre seem muted by its state of constant flux. With increased mainstream attention on this art form in recent years accelerated by revered academics, gallerists and curators; one might be right in thinking that social art is having something of a renaissance. However, this renaissance seems tainted by the need to meaningfully reveal the complex multiple voices, politics and ethics behind these practices. More often than not behind the glossy public facade of contemporary social art lies more interesting narratives that reveal an array of intentions from the artist, commissioner and participant. These multiple narratives offer insights that are loaded with meaning and motivations which we can learn from. Ultimately it was the need for a better insight into these dynamics that drew me to want to explore the journeys of social artworks further.

I have been active within this field since art school, firstly as an artist and then as a commissioner. During this time I have experienced the practice from two different sides of the fence; one where I was seeking the right context and support to self-produce my own work as an artist and secondly where I was seeking the right context and support to help support someone else's, as a commissioner. As this transitional journey from artist to commissioner unfolded, I came to understand that working on both sides of this fence was really very similar; it was about process. From that point, my concern with the processes at play behind social art became more focused and I sought out opportunities to explore this further. Social Art Map has been a great start to expanding these interests in more depth.

SH: The inspiration to develop what became the Social Art Map came from an ongoing fascination with the underlying motives and meanings of why people work together, develop projects and attempt to interact with, intervene into and question the worlds they operate in. I try and do this myself and am interested in how other people manage it. My research and practice over the past 15 years has more or less been asking the same questions: about what it means to be critical and political, the limits of this and the issues of being paid or expected to be critical and socially engaged in some way. I wanted to find out more about the micro-politics of the commissioning process—what happens, under what conditions, how and why. There is a tendency and political and economic pressure to evaluate processes and outcomes in ways that focus on the success stories. Rarely are the criteria of success questioned and it seems difficult to have honest, public conversations that unpick the details of why and how something is happening in a way that brings in and builds on knowledge and understanding of previous practices. There is an emphasis on demonstrating positive outcomes so as to justify money has been well spent. But what if it hasn't? What if it was more complicated than that?

I was also interested in exploring the language people use to describe what they do—how they justify and defend decisions and reflect on the experiences they have had. This was an opportunity to dig deeper into specific cases in a collective manner and hopefully lead to a way of sharing practices, problems and experiences from the perspectives of artists, curators/commissioners and community partners/participants/collaborators. The timing of this was also relevant in that I was interested in how the people involved in projects that have been funded and commissioned relate to the current political climate of austerity and funding cuts.

What Did You Learn from Collaborating on Social Art Map?

ED: Working on the Social Art Map has taught me a lot. For some time I wanted to step back from the immediacy of commissioning social artworks and look at how a range of other projects were produced and supported in their realization. I felt like this would not only enable my broader and in-depth understanding of the sector, which would help me evolve my practice, but also provide the opportunity to share my approach with others. The positive knock-on effect of that being that there would be a resource that others could utilize for their own purposes and research. One of the most exciting ways of doing this was for us as an arts organization to work with an academic partner and established researcher with a specialism within the field of social arts practice.

The opportunity to work with Sophie Hope came up through the innovative funding stream titled Creative Voucher from Creativeworks London which took place over a number of years and focused on different themes each time. The ambition of the fund was to bring together small and medium size enterprises (SMEs), in this case Peckham Platform, with higher education institutions (HEIs), in this case Birkbeck, University of London to deliver collaborative research towards a joint outcome. The fund was the perfect opportunity to have this cross-sector collaboration and when Sophie and I started talking about our ideas in light of this opportunity, our existing relationship and interests generated a lot of similarities on the topic of social art research. On a personal level one of the more valuable things that I learnt was how to structure a research methodology around an idea and how best to facilitate an outcome from a wide-ranging group of people in a clear and inclusive way. I also learnt how important the art of listening is within a professional context. When we visited each organization to listen to their commissioning journey I was playing a very different role to my normal work environment which was really useful and challenging.

SH: I think this aspect of listening is really significant in the research process. I feel that being as open-eyed and open-eared as possible in the research process is really important, and something I had to consciously learn during my PhD. It is something I always have to practice! It involves listening out for things you do not want to hear. In the space of collaboration I think this active listening is also crucial—how do we come together and genuinely hear what each other need or expect? Then, how do we combine that with our own objectives and expectations to create something new? In any collaboration, I think you have to be aware of the differences as well as the possible overlaps. For us, I think the overlaps were a shared long-standing curiosity about the relationships between artists and non-artists, social change and the politics and ethics of commissioning this work. The distinctions between us might be the fact that Emily has the practical pressures of keeping an arts organization afloat whereas I am framing my work as practice-based research—which means the work I do has to have underlying research questions and enquiry at its heart. These differing contexts in which we work mean we might have different motives and expectations of the collaboration. Acknowledging these differences early on, however, meant we were able to make use of each other. I am interested in making sure my research is grounded in practice and is useful to the practices I am involved in so collaborating with Peckham Platform was a way to do that, and I hope the critical distance that academic research can provide has been useful for Emily/Peckham Platform to position her/itself in the field.

The collaboration involved working with each other in devising and carrying out the research. There were also collaborative moments in the process between us and the other partners, but what does collaboration mean in this context? It is an over-used term for all sorts of relationships, partnerships and exchanges. It involves a push and pull between those involved in the process. While we were generating material about the five projects from the people we invited to the table, the act of reflecting and mapping was also of potential benefit to those involved as this sort of conversation is not often given time and space. This is something I think we will pick up in the future of SAM.

WHAT WERE THE CHALLENGES PRESENTED/OVERCOME DURING THE PROJECT?

ED: As ever the challenges for many projects are about allowing a creative process to happen and creating structures and boundaries, both for those managing it and for those participating in it, so there is a joint understanding of aims and outcomes. As the project built momentum Sophie and I were delighted with the demand for increased learning in this area from a range of practitioners that we spoke to. In fact it confirmed my suspicion that access points into the field of social arts were lacking, despite being in demand. Therefore one of the largest challenges presented during this project were its restrictions. How could we consider these longer-term and wider visions whilst having only six months and restricted income to deliver the first stage of what was becoming a much larger idea? For example we wanted to extend the project outside of London and possibly the UK in order to gain a wider perspective of practices nationally and internationally, but this simply was not possible given our resources. We wanted to increase the links with the project to existing learning on social arts practice and embed it into curricula, even set up a permanent resource with resident researchers. As we progressed, we realized that the potential of this project to expand to a much larger one is very real and very exciting but one that needs resourcing, planning and time to fulfil.

Increasingly, I became concerned with how we would restrict the amount of unpaid time that we were both spending on the project, whilst ensuring that we had enough time with people involved to deliver what we set out to do. Ultimately, I think we gave a lot of in-kind time and resources to the project which have paid off in that we have established firm partnerships and dialogues with practitioners and potential funders for the future, despite this resource not factored into the starting budget.

SH: The limited time and budget meant we had to focus on five projects and hold two- to three-hour sessions with the artists, curators/commissioners and participants/collaborators of each project around one table to map the different trajectories. This provided a useful framework that was focused and tangible, but also presented some problems. We wanted to select organizations that had comparable aspects with Peckham Platform but also had distinct characteristics (for example, two did not have permanent gallery sites, three did). This meant that there were many organizations in London and beyond that we could not engage with. Also, by having to select just three to four people to map each project, we were aware there were plenty of people who were instrumental to the projects that we did not hear from.

How does sitting around the table with others prompt self-censorship—how could we generate conversation and reflection that is as honest and open as possible? Inevitably there are things that go unsaid when the people you have worked with are in the room. There has also been the issue of editing the material for publication and in the process flattening the rich, complex stories that emerge through reflecting on the practice. While we tried to keep as much of the detail as possible, this was a design challenge. Due to the open nature of our editing process, and wanting the partners to have a say due to the projects not being anonymous, this meant the design stage was lengthy. There is always a compromise when individuals and organizations are being named in the research, as they have to approve their words before going public. It is also a challenge to retain mixed, conflicting agendas that occur in the process of reflection. We wanted to keep these transparent and not have to move towards consensus of opinion. Hopefully this comes across in the printed SAM.

WHAT ARE YOUR HOPES AND ASPIRATIONS FOR THE FUTURE OF THE PROJECT?

ED: There are so many potential outcomes from this project that the challenge is to know where to start and how to build critical elements at each step of the way. I am really interested in how such a collaboration could evolve to realize a more permanent learning resource, increasing access points and wider understanding of this practice. For example what would a Social Art Library look like? Does the sector need a more permanent resource for those wanting to learn more about the field of socially engaged art? If so what would this look like? How could it allow a range of different voices to publish research findings and convene to lead debate? My preconceptions of what this could be changed through the project from some of the brilliant conversations that we had especially at the round table launch in December 2015. The shape that we agreed that this could take is a Social Art Network with future funding, which would then feed into the development of a more permeant resource such as a Social Art Library.

SH: I have been using the material generated during this research towards a chapter I am writing for a book. I am also reflecting on how this process connects to my overall research planning—this involves continuing to explore ways of understanding histories of art and politics, exploring the role of the unfamiliar, the uncertain and the affect of strangeness in processes of socially engaged practice and the (gendered) labour involved in holding safe spaces for such uncertainty to be experienced and understood. I am adapting the method of timeline mapping for another series of projects I am researching, which will hopefully contribute to the SAM and have also been developing a card game (called Cards on the Table) which aims to prompt conversations between artists, curators and community partners/participants to bring out differences in expectations and understandings of working together. The SAM process has also triggered interest in developing a network of practitioners across the country, which Emily and I are exploring further.

Conclusions

What has it meant to develop a creative collaboration? Methodologically this has meant us developing research questions together and for the questions to be formed and adapted through the conversations with others in the process of the project. There are precedents for this (Participatory Action Research for example), and while we did not prescribe this methodology to the Social Art Map process we took an approach that was framed by us and then those around the table shaped the content. We brought our skills together to carry out the project, which led to practical divisions of labour, for example, Emily worked on administrating and marketing the project and Sophie worked through and analysed the audio recordings, extracted themes and compiled edited versions for the map. We both worked towards finalizing the edits for the designer and discussed how the final Social Art Map should look and how it can be distributed. What was important was that we both devised the content and structure of the project together and both facilitated the workshops, all of which took time and listening to do properly.

At the public launch of the Social Art Map in December 2015, at the Keynes Library, Birkbeck College we led a round table of interested practitioners from across the UK. This energized conversation allowed us to establish key concerns for the future development of the work. With this initial group we looked at identifying current resources available as well as the gaps that we realistically think we could address through the development of the work. At this round table there were many opinions expressed including the need for the network to exist both within and outside of the institution so that there is the room for critical voices to be expressed and not co-opted or consumed by larger agendas. The need for the network to allow for conflictual ideas and differing practices was really key. The future of the network should not be one that has a single voice or representative but should be multifaceted and allow for the full range of practices to emerge rather than a homogenous "good practice" that all should follow. It was agreed that if this was allowed to happen then it would facilitate the articulation of a more political agenda and individual value to the practice. The idea of an archive or library was challenged as it could become too singular, but something that was alive as a resource would enable the development of debate and forge new ideas for the sector.

What is clear is that funding is needed to develop future collaborations and that partnership working involves extra resources and costs on top of existing workloads and budgets. Our project has demonstrated a demand for sharing experiences, learning from each other's practices and developing a strong body of knowledge. This sort of activity asks critical questions of art and research's relationship to the creative economy and involves a more nuanced funder to understand the demand, value and worth within the activity. Certainly the opportunity to monetize, professionalize and marketize one's activity is something the Social Art Network would like to explore further. The future of the collaborations required to facilitate this need to be cross-disciplinary and involve SMEs and HEIs as well as other independent voices that are not formerly constituted as such. The idea of having a multicentred facility was key to increasing access points to this learning resource. It is these findings that are informing the expansion of the project to the next stage where we seek funding to support a range of outcomes including a research network and more permanent resource for social art practices.

Note

1. To find out more about the project and download the map, visit www.socialartmap.org.uk. We hope you will use this document to inform your work, challenge assumptions and invite further critical conversations with practitioners, collaborators, researchers and educators.

Making Friends: Childhood, the Cultural Economy and Creative Collaboration Through Technology

Tessa Whitehouse and Emilie Giles

"Making Friends" was a pilot project developed in collaboration between Tessa Whitehouse of Queen Mary University of London (QMUL) and Emilie Giles of Codasign.[1] It sought to explore historically informed research questions about childhood friendships and technology through hands-on electronics-based creative activities with children. The methodology we have developed is a participatory one involving children from Stoke Newington School and their teachers, other academic researchers, and museum, gallery, education, technology and charity-sector professionals. To draw together and build on the expertise of this wide range of participants we structured the project through workshops. Our aim was to create open spaces for idea-sharing and activity development which were informed by our original intellectual and methodological questions. The children participated in three workshops and a presentation afternoon while the adults were invited to two sessions that we called "Idea Forum" workshops.

The core principles of "Making Friends" informed the structure of our creative collaboration as a whole and each of the specific activities within

---

T. Whitehouse (✉)
Queen Mary University of London, London, UK

E. Giles
Codasign, London, UK

© The Author(s) 2017
M. Shiach, Tarek Virani (eds.), *Cultural Policy, Innovation and the Creative Economy*, DOI 10.1057/978-1-349-95112-3_14

it. The first principle was commitment to a participatory practice that was as open and democratic as possible within the confines of a project that had named project leads. The second principle was that technology should be treated as both an object of investigation and a tool for creative engagement by all project participants: this characterised the collaboration between Codasign and QMUL which itself acted as an incubator for further collaborative activities. "Making" was both therefore conceptualised by the project's aims and enacted in each project activity. The constructivist, creative and polyvocal character of the resulting project accorded with the topic we were researching: how friendships are formed, sustained and understood. Supporting this was a second area of investigation: how does friendship among children today relate to the ways in which children experienced friendship in the past? This chapter will first explain the intellectual underpinnings of our project, explaining why collaboration with creative enterprises was essential. It will then proceed to outline the range of creative collaborations that took place across the duration of "Making Friends" before reflecting on the challenges and opportunities of collaborative work.

CHILDHOOD AND FRIENDSHIP: THE INTELLECTUAL BACKGROUND

The reasons for investigating the past and present conditions of childhood friendship relate to several forms of historiographical occlusion. Historians of childhood and of friendship respectively have struggled to identify and analyse the friendship experiences of historical children. This is a specific instance of a well-recognised "problem" of childhood studies generally: that evidence is lacking. David Oswell highlights a reason for the particular difficulty of finding evidence of children's interpersonal and peer relationships:

> Historical evidence of children often points to them being addressed…in the singular (i.e. as a son or daughter, or as a child learning). Children's horizontal affections or experiences with other children are not by and large the focus of attention.[2]

Though on one hand the difficulty originates in the past we are studying, in that we are restricted to what the historical record has kept for us to see, it is compounded by a second difficulty that lies in the expectations of adult researchers in the present. Andrea Immel expresses the conundrum elegantly:

> [C]hildren have always suffered from being too intelligible to those who wish to understand their condition. It is assumed that since everyone has once been a child, therefore anyone can intuitively grasp the nature of childhood experience.[3]

As a counterweight to this rather negative framing of the problems of studying children and childhood, it should be emphasised that we wanted to build on the positive disposition of childhood studies which values participation and shapes praxis around an ethics of dispersed authority.[4] The involvement of Codasign was central to achieving this.

Codasign is an education company that teaches people how to be creative with technology through workshops led by tutors who are experts in their field. All tutors specialise in a variety of areas, including electronic textiles (e-textiles), physical computing, game design and digital music. Since its foundation in 2011, Codasign has been at the forefront of co-produced and cascaded models of project design through creative technology workshops for young people and adults. Codasign's leadership in this area meant that the research questions of (1) how the children's experiences of their worlds of childhood (particularly their emotional worlds and worlds mediated through technology) can be presented in the children's own terms while being accessible to researchers,[5] and (2) how the children's expertise in those worlds can shape the evolving questions of the project as a whole, informed workshop structure and activity aims. Therefore we were able to challenge any assumptions we might have had (both explicit and latent) that as adults we intuitively understand the experience of childhood by listening to children's own articulations of their experience as the project progressed and devising activities which allowed children to experiment rather than reaching a predetermined endpoint.[6]

The project's research goal was to enable children to make objects that expressed perceptions and experiences of friendship. This was pursued with reference to debates in the new sociology of childhood and material culture studies. Differentiating the material culture of childhood from all the objects in the world at large is, observes Carla Pascoe, "a vexed process." Today, as in the past:

> the objects used by children are often created or gifted by adults. Can we argue that the teddy bear, cot and sandals used by children adequately

represent children's cultural heritage? Or do these artefacts tell us much more about adult perceptions and expectations of children than those of children themselves?[7]

While acknowledging that the answer to Pascoe's final question is often "yes," "Making Friends" sought to resolve the issue (at least in part, and for the present) by placing the construction of objects of childhood friendship in the hands, literally, of children themselves. Among the outcomes of the project were tangible items: visual and aural stories produced by groups of friends using circuits and sound recordings and inspired by the surroundings of the historic property Sutton House; e-textile patches (designed and stitched by the children using conductive thread to incorporate LEDs) which the children chose to give to someone special; video interviews recorded by the children themselves. These are unusual outcomes of a literary-historical research project. Children's creative engagement with the topic, site and items under investigation produced material objects that bear traces of the process of research as well as capturing the children's own views in forms that are meaningful to them.[8]

These outcomes brought with them the further challenge of evaluating these objects and incorporating the evidence they provide into our analysis of the project as a whole. This requires language and approaches beyond the remit of traditional scholarship.[9] It is one of the many areas of the project that benefited from the collaboration between academics and creative technologies partners: we were able to share novel approaches to complex research questions and their outcomes, as the following account of the workshops will show.

What Happened: Collaboration in Practice

The workshop element of the project was delivered over three sessions with students from Stoke Newington School. These took place between December 2014 and February 2015 at the school itself and Sutton House in Hackney, concluding with a showcase of their work in the school library in May 2015. We centred the workshops around creating small collaborative projects using technology and incorporated activities to encourage the young people to get to know each other through games and conversation. Tools which we used during these sessions included photos brought in by the children, iPads provided by the school for research tasks, e-textile materials designed by Codasign which the children used to make light-up patches and capacitive sensing circuit boards by Bare Conductive to trigger sound files recorded by the young people. We also set the students the task of documenting their lives using disposable cameras, the results of which were used in small interactive installations which they created together in our final workshop. Along with the tasks we set during the workshops, the young people also discussed their work with each other using an interview methodology developed by Lamees Al Mubarak (the project research assistant) which gave them the opportunity to reflect on their creations but also gave us an insight into their thoughts around the process. It demonstrated the potential which they saw for their handmade objects such as sharing photographs via social media or giving them to their parents as presents.

The showcase at the school library was scheduled so that the young people could share with their peers and friends what they had produced during their participation in the project. This event was valuable for us to observe as researchers and educators as it gave us the opportunity to experience the project from the perspective of the young people. It was also an opportunity for the young people to conduct further interviews with each other, which generated feedback such as "I really enjoyed the project because I was able to learn new things and meet new people that I didn't talk [to] before." Overall, the young people appeared to be very positive about their experience of participating, noting particularly the social and creative aspects of the project.

In tandem with the creative technologies workshops, we led two Idea Forum sessions for adults. The first was scheduled to take place after the introductory workshop but before the two making-based sessions, and the second at the end of the work with children. The two Idea Forum afternoons were designed to capitalise on and develop Codasign's position as a thought-leading company in the field of digital making and participation within cultural institutions while positioning the "Making Friends" collaborators as guides to the intersection of digital making with emerging research methodologies in the humanities. We curated the events with two goals in mind: firstly, to hear feedback on our developing project and secondly, to foster a network of expertise in different aspects of participatory creative and research work with children in cultural institutions with the potential for future collaboration. To fulfil these goals we sought a diverse range of attendees. We welcomed educators, policy makers, researchers and cultural industries professionals including museum and gallery staff working in the fields of education, outreach, curation and digital programming. All the participants were concerned with the engagement and participation of young people (Table 1).

The first Idea Forum took place in January 2015. It was planned and coordinated by the project leads and facilitated by Katy Beale from Caper. We introduced "Making Friends" (including research questions and an

Table 1 Participants in the "Making Friends" Idea Forum

Name	Role	Organisation/Institution
Oliver Benjamin	Programme Associate	A New Direction
Katy Beale	Director of Caper and Facilitator of Making Friends Forum 1	Caper
Linda Cockburn	Facilitator of Making Friends Forum 2	Caper
Emilie Giles	Head of Outreach and Participation and Project Lead for Making Friends	Codasign
Liat Wassershtrom	Lead Children's Workshop Instructor	Codasign
Catherine Ritman-Smith	Head of Programmes—Learning	Design Museum
Dawn Ingleson	Head of Learning	Discover Children's Story Centre
Claire Cooke	Outreach Officer	Ealing Council
Tempe Nell	Takeover Team Project Assistant	Kids in Museums
Alexzandra Jackson	Education Manager	Phoenix
Chris Tyrer	Digital Arts Manager	Phoenix
Lamees Al Mubarak	PhD Candidate	QMUL
Dr Mariza Dima	Creativeworks London Postdoctoral Research Assistant	QMUL
Brigid Howarth	Senior Partnership and Business Development Manager	QMUL
Eithne Nightingale	PhD Candidate	QMUL
Dr Kiera Vaclavik	Senior Lecturer in French and Comparative Literature	QMUL
Dr Tessa Whitehouse	Lecturer in English Literature and Project Lead for Making Friends	QMUL
Tom Furber	Heritage Educator	Valence House
Alex Flowers	Leader of Digital Programmes	V&A Museum
Andrea Cunningham	Head of Learning	V&A Museum of Childhood
Teresa Hare Duke	Community Development Officer	V&A Museum of Childhood
Chas Mollet	Inclusive Technician	Wac Arts
Kate Watson	Interactive Project Coordinator	Wac Arts
Dr Stephen Willey	Co-Founder	Watadd

outline of what Codasign does) and a summary of the first workshop with Stoke Newington School including a video. We felt it was important to do this as it was an effective way to incorporate the voices of the children into the forum meeting for adults. We then asked participants to respond to the following prompts in small groups:

- What does participation mean to you?
- How is friendship valued and supported in your workplace?
- How is technology changing the way you work in participatory contexts and/or with children?

These discussion points generated a number of different focus areas including:

- The relationships between professional aims and personal interests
- The role of friendship and friendliness in workplaces, with colleagues, among other stakeholders including children
- Levels of participation
- The need for flexibility and openness
- The extent to which workplaces identify friendship as an aim or hope in their work (rarely!)
- Incorporating children's voices in an authentic way: children's forums, youth forums, youth trustees
- Connections between making and creativity on one side, and personal interaction and friendship on the other
- The exclusions that increasing reliance of technology can create

The first forum was deliberately open-ended and acted primarily as a platform for idea generation and the sharing of experiences while the second forum was more focused on particular examples of collaboration with children and young people. This took place in June 2015 and was again planned and coordinated by the project leads. This time the facilitator was Linda Cockburn.

We decided to factor in some hands-on making time with an activity similar to the one we had done with the young people from Stoke Newington School of making tactile interactive objects to trigger sounds files. It enabled the participants to better understand what Codasign does and acted as a great grounding for everyone in the room to think about working with young people and how digital hands-on making activities can be used to expand engagement with the themes of friendship and collaboration. It also helped participants get a sense of the children's experience of working together in their "Making Friends" workshops.

The making session was followed by four case studies intended to prompt discussion and reflection on two themes: "Young People's Voices" and "Planning Digital Programmes." The case studies were presented by participants from Kids in Museums, A New Direction, the V&A and Phoenix Leicester. To further ground the discussion in practical examples we had tasked all attendees to consider the following questions in advance:

- How could you incorporate the theme of friendship in the design of new programmes?
- For existing programmes, how could friendship be incorporated? How this might influence how people learn/ participate?

These questions worked well in sparking ideas in the attendees with discussions revolving around:

- Peer mentoring
- Questioning what friendship is
- Creating together
- Museums as a social space
- Capturing the child's voice
- Managing expectations for mixed groups
- Social skills for friendship
- Limitations/risks of social media

The second forum ended with participants saying that they were inspired by each other's case studies and experiences to design original programmes to foster creative participation and engagement with collections. The range of knowledge brought into the room by the attendees was invaluable, opening up potential opportunities for ongoing conversations and further creative collaborations. Participants exchanged contact details and also voiced a desire for similar forum sessions in the future.

The informality of the relationships between children and adults and across the different groups of adults involved (including teachers, Codasign, QMUL researchers, Idea Forum participants) was an important element of our methodology. This was in keeping with the principle of dispersed authority and was supported by elements of the project design, such as having a professional facilitator for the Idea Forum meetings. This choice located practical and organisational aspects of the afternoons away from the members of the "Making Friends" team and meant that the project leads could participate in the activities and discussions on equal terms with everyone else.

Effective Collaboration 1: The Benefits of a Shared Ethos

The guiding ethos of Codasign, that creative play can be educative and that learning can be fun, resonated strongly with the researcher's wish to trial alternative methods of investigating the constitution of friendship in childhood. The academic background of both sides of the project team meant that attentiveness to the definition of terms and observing the complexity of apparently simple processes led us to the shared decision to emphasise "making" as a methodology that incorporated ideas, imagination and skills development. Agreement that the meaning of "Making Friends" would be instantiated through interpersonal relations, manual and intellectual processes and awareness of historical circumstances that could be explained verbally as well as felt in our material surroundings (for example, of Sutton House) allowed us to test out a variety of ideas for practical activities rather than following a predetermined programme. Though we approached the objective of developing workshops for children and adults to explore ideas about friendship and technology from different intellectual and practical starting points, both project leads shared the desire to take an exploratory approach.

This flexibility was central to the evolving nature of the project. Our respective prior experiences had underscored the novelty of the methodology we were developing. Research into childhood histories rarely invites the participation of children (let alone through working with electronics) while museum and gallery-based creative technologies workshops, though often inspired by the museum's setting or by certain collection objects, rarely have research questions informing the design of their workshops. It would be hard to overstate the point that the innovative aspect of "Making Friends" was the unique combination of historically grounded, participation-oriented research questions and innovative, bespoke, hands-on activities that our collaboration enabled. We feel extremely fortunate that our mutually reinforcing skills and prior knowledge, coupled with our shared goal of producing intellectually rigorous participatory activities that provided fresh insights into long-standing scholarly problems could be incubated and supported via Creativeworks London.

Our collaboration was enabled in a number of practical ways. First and foremost, the funding allowed both sides to develop existing strengths into new directions. For example, most of Codasign's workshops are programmed as single events that take place in cultural organisations. Key benefits to working on the "Making Friends" project were:

- Achieving greater self-reflexivity in planning workshop content while creating a unique offering which could be repeated with new partner institutions
- Trialling the use of academic methodologies in analysing the impact of the workshops in order to measure their outcomes in ways which would not usually happen in the commercial sector
- The opportunity to network and find potential new partners for collaborations in museums and galleries

The Codasign founders, directors and many of its tutors have PhDs in engineering or postgraduate training and research expertise in e-textiles as tools for accessibility, long distance networks and metamaterials. Due to their own academic interests, Codasign welcomed the opportunity to deliver a set of workshops with more rigorous methodologies in place than would normally be possible at their public events. To be able to explore the impact of the content on the participants seemed worthwhile too. Two further motivations for collaborating with an academic partner were the opportunity to engage with participants' perceptions of the workshops Codasign delivers, and to explore the research potential of Codasign's work in a pilot that could inform future programming. The opportunity to partner on a project with more longevity than usual was a unique opportunity to build a more substantial and theorised body of work.

For the academic partner, the benefits of "Making Friends" were also very clear. It made it possible to pursue research methods that are impossible to implement alone and especially to access Codasign's expertise in workshop design, electronics principles, and giving abstract concepts a material and processural presence. The research lead gained skills in working in new settings, with new materials, and in new formations (such as researching with children and non-academics) and developed new professional networks via Creativeworks London, Codasign and the Idea Forum meetings.

As well as a clear sense of the benefits we hoped to receive, the project leads shared a commitment to a key principle that helped the smooth running of our collaboration. We both agreed that the participants in the project should be able to benefit from joining us (these benefits are explained elsewhere in the chapter). Having articulated the benefits for partners and participants from the outset and therefore being able to work towards these and to monitor whether they were being achieved were crucial elements within the positive experience of the collaboration.

Effective Collaboration 2: The Benefits of Powerful Resourcing

Without funding, the project would have been impossible and the wide range of people that it brought together would probably never have met, let alone been able to work together for over six months. The method by which the funding was distributed to Codasign allowed for materials and preparation costs for the workshops to be covered from the start, for 50 per cent of the grant was awarded before the project began and 50 per cent at the end. This mitigated against the cash flow issues which beset creative SMEs and which might have curtailed Codasign's ability to deliver "Making Friends." It also offset the risk Codasign took on in committing time and materials to a long-running project. The funding for Codasign was allocated to project planning and management, tutor facilitation time, the creation of learning materials, physical materials for the sessions, Codasign director strategy time and forum participation. Having the costs of materials and planning time covered was critical to building Codasign's capacity to participate in a research-led project. Each workshop with the young people was unique, requiring more planning than a standard workshop. Creating original materials is labour-, time- and cost-intensive. For these reasons, the grant was essential to cover the Codasign team's time sufficiently to allow "Making Friends" to be tailored to the overall research needs.

Time was the most valuable element of the voucher award for the academic lead too. The funding allowed the lead researcher to appoint a research assistant with expertise in workshop-based childhood research whose time was spent sharing methods for child-led interviewing, observing the workshops and participating in the Idea Forum. The voucher funding also afforded half a day per week to manage the project (in addition to research time) and this provided the flexibility to travel around

East London for meetings at Stoke Newington School, Sutton House and at Codasign. The voucher funding covered the acquisition of data collection equipment and material. It also paid for the two Idea Forum meetings, which was particularly valuable in enabling non-academic stakeholders to attend the sessions and in some cases to travel from outside London to share their projects. Finally it allowed us to be able to afford to hold two of the school sessions off campus. Codasign has a strong track record of delivering workshops that connect the technology activities they teach to the surroundings in which the sessions are taking place, and this meant that we had been thinking about suitable locations for the workshops from the outset. The funding we received enabled us to move outside the school environment and to pay for a year's schools membership to the National Trust so that we could meet at Sutton House in Homerton. Thanks to the membership arrangement, all the students of Stoke Newington School (not just the few who participated in Making Friends) can visit Sutton House and National Trust properties, thus bringing wider benefits to the school community in terms of opportunities for experiential learning about history and culture.

Effective Collaboration 3: Meeting Complex Challenges Together

Almost all of the challenges we faced derived from the unusual nature of the methodology we were trialling. For the academic, "Making Friends" was the first attempt at devising a new kind of research process, and it proved to be one that required far more leadership than the traditional model of a lone scholar working in an archive. Some of this was expected, such as presenting aims of the research crisply for non-specialists; participating in a variety of group sessions; building awareness and enthusiasm for the project as a whole among constituencies within and beyond the academic community. But the scale and kind of leadership were both more significant than expected. The project involved far more people than just the two project leads: by the end of the grant, we had worked with ten children, two teachers and a librarian from Stoke Newington School; a research assistant from QMUL; a Codasign tutor; two contacts at Sutton House; and fifteen professional participants in the Idea Forum. It was deeply enriching in intellectual and experiential terms to build such a large and diverse community around our idea, and doing so meant that the Making Friends methodology had begun to inform programme development at other institutions already, such as Leicester Phoenix. But it also necessitated a considerable amount of time being spent on the logistics of communications and event planning, which took time away from data analysis. The challenge is one of personnel: is it useful to devote funding to the appointment of a dedicated project manager? Is it beneficial to divide up practicalities from research when timetabling a project? How much time buy-out should be costed into a funding application? These are questions that all creative collaborations must work through from early on. The answers will depend on the duration and scale of the project, the nature of the deliverables and the resources available.

For Codasign, being a very small company in an emerging field while committing to a novel research agenda accounted for the challenges of participating in the project. Working on "Making Friends" meant recalibrating Codasign's usual approach, for example by taking more time to plan activities and devoting energy to critical reflection during the design process in order to help fulfil the research needs. Balancing this with producing learning materials and workshops that could not only run as part of this project but have longevity and be delivered as a package afterwards was a positive challenge. It was also necessary to monitor how this could inform the planning and curation of the two Idea Forum meetings which in themselves required a great deal of work. The practical challenges of how a small company could deliver a project of this duration were also significant. Codasign is very fortunate to have a strong team of eleven tutors who all teach regularly and have complementary areas of expertise. This is advantageous as it makes the company nimble and diverse in what it can deliver. All the tutors have other time commitments so it is rare to schedule one person to teach all workshops in a given area. However, the research project element of "Making Friends" had a specific timespan and required consistency in delivery. Through careful planning and with the support of the Codasign directors, the same team was able to deliver all the workshops for the Making Friends project.

Given that the challenges we faced were due to the innovative nature of the project, we found that trust between the project leads, as well as from the other organisations involved, was very important in overcoming these challenges. For example QMUL supported this risky research through ethics committee approval, provision of resources and facilities, and research support; while Stoke Newington School did so agreeing to participate, hosting two events, making time to build a strong relationship with us early on and offering feedback on our workshop plans.

Creativeworks London were hands-on funders and their support enabled us to anticipate and overcome potential challenges. This began even before the funding application was submitted, for we were required to conceptualise our project in idea pool sessions. This meant our collaboration was well-developed in theoretical, social and creative terms before we started gathering data. Both partners knew what we were doing together, and the aims, strengths and limitations of the other. Post-award, the regular roundtable meetings hosted by Creativeworks London were informative about other awardees' projects and an opportunity to exchange knowledge and experience around various case studies. Sharing the progress of our project and its findings as we went along in a supportive environment was beneficial from a reconsolidation perspective. The invitation to write blog posts and present at the Creativeworks London event "Women in Digital Culture and Economy" at the V&A helped raise the profile of Codasign and "Making Friends" and incorporate new voices into follow-up activities.

Conclusion

We believe that the positive experience of our collaboration was enabled in practical terms by having focused timescales, clear aims and manageable research questions. Overarching this, we think the three key concepts grounding our project enabled its success. "Making Friends" worked:

- By sharing expertise: this was fundamental to all areas of the workshop design and research process, especially in observation practices
- Discursively: we asked "what do we know about friendship?" of ourselves and all the participants. We posed follow-up questions to the children at their workshops and to the professionals at their Idea Forum sessions. These questions were guided by our project but were open-ended, ensuring that opportunities for voices to be heard were built into every element of "Making Friends"
- Recursively, in that the design of component activities were not fixed. Because we observed each activity and sought feedback we could adapt elements and introduce new ones as needed

Finally, we wish to emphasise that we do not see the set of workshops and forum meetings that constituted "Making Friends" as self-contained or finished but as the first phase of an ongoing collaboration between humanities researchers, creative technologists, children and museums that we are very excited to be pursuing. We see the project as having longevity, having the capacity to be accessed by many more people and having the potential to carry on the conversation about how childhood friendships in the past, present and future can be explored through hands-on electronics-based creative activities.

NOTES

1. We would like to thank Adam Stark for bringing us together and his help in formulating "Making Friends" in the early stages of the project.
2. David Oswell, *The Agency of Children: From Family to Global Human Rights* (Cambridge: Cambridge University Press, 2013), 21.
3. Andrea Immel and Michael Whitmore, "Introduction," in *Childhood and Children's Books in Early Modern Europe, 1550–1800*, ed. Andrea Immel and Michael Whitmore (Abingdon: Routledge, 2006), 6.
4. Jonathon Sargeant and Deborah Harcourt, *Doing Ethical Research with Children* (Maidenhead: Open University Press, 2012), 28–31.
5. Berry Mayall, *Towards a Sociology of Childhood: Thinking from Children's Lives* (Buckingham: Open University Press, 2002), 121.
6. Alan Prout, *The Future of Childhood: Towards an Interdisciplinary Study of Children* (Abingdon: Routledge, 2005), 34.
7. Carla Pascoe, "Putting Away the Things of Childhood: Museum Representations of Children's Cultural Heritage," in *Designing Modern Childhoods: History, Space, and the Material Culture of Children*, eds. Marta Gutman and Ning de Coninck-Smith (New Brunswick: Rutgers University Press, 2008), 209.
8. Mary Kellett, "Children and Young People's Voice," in *Children and Young People's Worlds: Developing Frameworks for Integrated Practice*, eds. Heather Montgomery and Mary Kellett (Bristol: The Policy Press, 2009), 239–41.
9. Elizabeth Wood and Kiersten F. Latham, *The Objects of Experience: Transforming Visitor-Object Encounters in Museums* (Walnut Creek: Left Coast Press, 2014).

Outside the Voucher: Evaluating the Creative Voucher Scheme

Andy Pratt, Helen Matheson-Pollock, and Tarek Virani

This chapter seeks to elaborate on what one might have expected to be the straightforward task of delivering and evaluating Creativeworks London's (CWL) Creative Voucher scheme.[1] What made the project difficult was that the notion of the "creative" voucher has not been used before; it was not a policy developed from a direct evidence base. Moreover, the Creativeworks London project was premised on the delivery of three funding streams of which the vouchers were one; indeed something approaching half of these funds were targeted to resource creative vouchers.

This chapter offers a discussion of how we implemented the creative vouchers, the products of which make up most of this volume. It also raises the question of what and how one might evaluate vouchers; something, we argue, that does not gain from a reduction to a limited set of quantitative indicators. Indeed, our reflections on the process projected us into a far more exploratory and nuanced narrative account of the vouchers; hence the chapters of this book which represent a range of different facets and experiences of the Creative Voucher scheme.

A. Pratt
City University, London, UK

H. Matheson-Pollock • Tarek Virani (✉)
Queen Mary University of London, London, UK

© The Author(s) 2017
M. Shiach, Tarek Virani (eds.), *Cultural Policy, Innovation and the Creative Economy*, DOI 10.1057/978-1-349-95112-3_15

Traditional evaluations of innovation and knowledge transfer are based upon simplistic mono-causal models whereby the dominant notion is that knowledge will naturally diffuse from high concentrations to low concentrations: like a gas; this of course is a social physics model. The failure to diffuse evenly, it is normally hypothesized, must be due to some "blockage" or "barrier." In keeping with mechanical analogies, much policy action is focused on "fixing the plumbing," that is, the leaky knowledge pipelines. The challenge is that the logic behind knowledge transfer, let alone policies such as vouchers, are seldom explicitly stated, but rather assumed as common sense.

As we experience the transformation from mass production economies to those based on what are variously termed service economies, knowledge economies, or even cultural economies the physical movement of goods, innovation and ideas materialized as "solutions" (as "technology" has commonly been) has been replaced by weightless or virtual goods: ideas. Physicalist analogies might have been helpful in an old manufacturing economy; it is clear that they are less helpful in either dematerialized production, or the realm of ideas exclusively.

Moreover, the Creativeworks London project was explicitly funded by the Arts and Humanities Research Council (AHRC) with a view to demonstrating the role of what the arts and humanities can contribute to the processes of knowledge transfer between universities and the creative economy (see chapter "Introduction"). It is obvious that the arts and humanities favor different approaches to knowledge than that of the sciences; in particular the humanities focus on the nature of human experience and ideas—one might argue that it is the ideal type of knowledge transfer. The humanities has a rather more nuanced and relational perspective on knowledge and human experience than the sciences, focused as they often are on physical processes and outcomes. We thus saw it as our task to explore and reflect on creative vouchers and meanings.

Whereas the individual voucher stories provide a rich narrative of what the knowledge exchange process "looks like" and at times what it might "feel like," and what meanings it produces for those involved, this chapter attempts to examine a linked story across the voucher process. It is not seeking to generalize or summarize, rather it explores the voucher process. In this sense we resist the traditional notion of evaluation, arguing that it is necessary to understand the process before we can possibly evaluate it against objectives, personal, institutional or political.

Unpicking and Interpreting the Idea

The notion of knowledge transfer, and/or knowledge exchange, has become a fashionable one in policy circles of late. It is based on the paradigm suggesting that "knowledge intensive" industries will replace manufacturing, and be driven by a highly educated workforce, with high wages, producing high value and high return products. This notion has been expressed by many, but Peter Drucker and Daniel Bell have sketched out the social as well as economic dimensions of the "knowledge society." UK government policy has been redirected to this aim since the 1980s, such that it has become part of the common sense of industrial and education policy. However, how to turn big ideas and brave prescriptions into concrete actions has been a challenge. On one hand we have had many analyses showing that industry has been less innovative due to a lack of investment in research and development. On the other we have had the expansion of higher education and more skilled workers. However, somehow the boosting of investment, and training—or universities cross-subsidizing employers' training—has not had the desired effect.

Other approaches have noted the outsourcing, or disinvestment in research and development by business, and encouraged universities to take up the slack. The notion that physical proximity to universities was important to science- and innovation-hungry industries, or that universities could generate their own "spin offs" were strong ideas underpinning the policy of science parks. In effect it was assumed that sharing the research scientists, their laboratories and their seminars would diffuse ideas and generate growth. Related ideas of the benefits of co-location in competitive and collaborative skills and part-finished products were derived from the impacts of the Italian New Industrial Districts, and given significant support by the UK government in the Business Clusters idea—all of this is well documented in the literature. Interestingly, the same notion was applied to high-tech clusters as to cultural or creative clusters: culture was just another industry that would benefit from co-location and seed knowledge transfer via diffusion (although with a little help).

A third wave of knowledge policies has emerged through a number of initiatives in the EU, and these are based less on diffusion than on a market in ideas; here knowledge exchange is figured as a market. Diffusion is replaced by the market allocation system of supply and demand. However, there is a problem as the market in ideas seems to be stuck. The idea that has emerged of how to "help" the market is to incentivize the transaction, to create a "voucher" that gives both parties a financial prize for their knowledge exchange practice. These initial vouchers were focused on technology industries, and inter-industry collaboration. The idea was then transposed to the UK and a pilot scheme set up with "creative credits" which was run by NESTA (see chapter "Cultural Policy, Collaboration and Knowledge Exchange"). The origin for the Creative Hubs voucher program was this experiment, which at the time of commissioning the Creativeworks London project had not been completed, nor evaluated.[2]

As we were faced with a project that required us to deliver £1 million worth of creative vouchers over four years we did due diligence on the notion, and its assumptions and how it had been evaluated. As just noted, the NESTA evaluation was not complete,[3] and in any case the scheme was different.[4] In our project, it was to be university–creative industry vouchers, not creative industry–creative industry vouchers (which was the innovation voucher model). We tracked the notion back to the EU innovation vouchers and were surprised to find that many of the schemes had not been evaluated either. It was seemingly considered as self-evidently a "good thing."

Looked at another way, one might consider a valid evaluation tool to be the "take up" of vouchers: the voucher award is ipso facto a case of collaboration and exchange. We think that this common sense notion of a voucher "empowers" the practitioner to seek collaboration, which is probably what underpins the popularity of vouchers (and, as a footnote, we can see that vouchers are a common currency in neoliberal states: be they school-place vouchers, training vouchers, etc.). If we accept this (albeit) superficial model then it points to a rather oversimplified model of knowledge and its transfer. It is a contact form of transmission—like diffusion. Human agency, reflection and values do not enter into it. There is now a substantial body of academic work that has examined the notion of knowledge and its transfer, and simplistic and mechanistic notions, such as those implied above have been on the whole rejected and displaced in favor of relational and generative notions of knowledge.[5] As part of our contribution to a "meta-knowledge transfer" we regarded it as critical that we shared this knowledge in our understanding of the voucher process.

Additionally, academic work on innovation has rejected the linear and atomistic notion of the lone genius—current debate concerns the social, economic and cultural environment that can enable, or constrain, knowledge production and transfer.[6] A body of research has concerned itself with the ways in which institutions frame and enable or block the transfer of knowledge, and this suggests that a knowledge market does not simply exist. Instead it has to be made and operated, and regulated. Reflecting on this we can reinterpret the creative voucher as a spur to construct such institutions. This is rather a bizarre way of going about things, but perhaps reflects a reality. We had to deliver a policy instrument (the voucher) into a mis-functioning market in knowledge, assuming that a financial incentive would "free up" this market. In order to achieve this effect we had to create a knowledge market, and build institutions and an exchange mechanism, as well as a system for the dispensation and auditing of vouchers. In short we had to build a world in which the creative voucher made sense, and thus would be successful. The rest of this chapter discusses how we built the voucher system.

Making Vouchers

It is self-evident that for a voucher system to work one needs a pool of potential "awardees" from which to choose the best candidates; moreover one has to decide what criteria will be used for selection. A basic element of any voucher scheme will rely on the quality of the "gene pool" for eligible businesses and academics, as well as the skill and ability to match them up, and then manage the voucher process. This sounds logical and straightforward, but in practice it is difficult. There is no single or current register of creative industry SMEs in London (or anywhere else), thus the first job is to construct a list. This was achieved initially through the pre-existing resources of the partners, in particular The Culture Capital Exchange (TCCE), who have been acting as cultural intermediaries for many years, and thus have a database of contacts.

A related difficulty is that the creative economy is a very fluid and fast-changing field; thus, databases become quickly out of date. A structural and organizational characteristic of the creative economy is that much of the work is based on teams combining for short life projects, and on completion dismantling (and wrapping up the firm); then, creating a new firm or network when the next project comes along. This organizational form is not generally that of "firms," but of freelancers, artists and networks, what some have termed a cultural economy "ecosystem." Most creative businesses are not SMEs (which can be between 10–250 employees), but micro-enterprises (below ten employees), or sole operators. There is then, not a ready "population" from which a sample, or selection can be made. Nobody knows how many "firms" exist, and there is no register. Hence,

TCCE's contacts were vital; however, they were simply a starting point and much work had to be done to generate a reasonable directory; a task that took all four years of the project to develop, and tragically, risks being lost as the project dissolves.

While it is normally assumed that a population of firms can be identified, apparently no careful consideration had been given to the partner component of the vouchers: the academics. Universities do not all maintain a database of academic interests and their staff's willingness to engage with creative enterprises. Moreover, due to the innovative focus of this project, only a small proportion of "matches" would be skill- or interest-based, as in a skill swap. It is likely that if this demand had existed, it would already have been satisfied.[7] Thus, the Creativeworks London team faced a considerable challenge to "find" academics. In the course of the project Creativeworks London engaged 21 higher education institutions or independent research organizations and a further 22 creative economy partner organizations (private firms) in delivery of the project, the knowledge exchange program and research strands. This is a massive enterprise, which discloses a substantial networking and organizational infrastructure that had to be created and sustained. By the end of the project a total of 92 academics from partner organizations collaborated on projects across all funding schemes, with over 40 further research assistants contributing to the program. Together, this represented a combined investment in knowledge exchange projects of £1.6 million from Arts and Humanities Research Council (AHRC) and European Regional Development Fund (ERDF) and over 26,000 hours of collaborative research.

Creativeworks London has built a network between its partner organizations, SMEs and awardees and the wider public in a bid to increase awareness of the program and its activities. Four key elements of the dissemination strategy were: (1) the blog "Widening the Register" launched in 2014 which features articles and posts by members of the hub core team as well as invited pieces by researchers and awardees and (2) the monthly newsletter sent out by the knowledge exchange team featuring items, articles and event listings relating to hub activity and that relating to awardees and partners. Figures relating to the newsletter highlight the strength and size of the network and evidence of wide public engagement. As at January 2016, the total recipients of the newsletter were 4072 per month. The average open rate between February 2015 and January 2016 was 25.1 percent, meaning on average one in four people opened the newsletter, approximately 1022 people. The click-through rate across the same period was on average 19.4 percent or around one in five, which equates to approximately 790 people per month engaging with news items, events and articles circulated by the hub. A benchmark email-open rate is 24.9 percent, which is broadly equal to Creativeworks London's rate; significantly, however, the average click-through rate is 3.42 percent, meaning that Creativeworks London's click-through rate—that is, actual engagement with information contained within the newsletter—is almost six times higher than the benchmark figure.[8] Creativeworks London has a database of a network totaling 1966 SMEs and researchers who have actively engaged with the hub.

Third, further partnership activity also took the form of workshops and events for academics and businesses, who offered wider opportunities for knowledge exchange and network building. These were successful and well attended by hundreds of individuals and businesses. New formats to promote knowledge exchange specifically to digital creative companies, such as "culture hacks," modeled on software "hackathons," were experimented with; and a blog, "Widening the Register," offers a repository of articles, reports and updates from Creativeworks London's people, partners, awardees and wider community. In a sense, this is all "hidden work" before the first voucher can be advertised, let alone awarded.

The fourth and final element was the voucher process, which was not only an advertising and award process, but an active and cumulative growing of the network of academics and creative businesses. The voucher process was organized around five phases of activity. First, a call for applicants, this was an educational and informational dimension (as nobody knew what a creative voucher was, or who was eligible). Second, an invitation to all those interested to an "ideas pool"; in effect this was the research-informed "dating agency" to match up academics and creative businesses. Third, a proposal-writing event where those who were keen to apply were helped with the application process and the refinement of the proposal. Fourth, the applications were reviewed and winners selected by a panel of the CWL team. Fifth, an awardees' roundtable was held, and contracts were awarded.

Of course the process did not end there, post-award, a lot of work had to be put in by the CWL team to liaise with individual universities[9] and their business support teams and finance offices to actually issue contracts (and deal with issues such as IPR, and processing of payments). In a sample of cases—as part of an evaluation process—voucher holders were invited back to share their experiences with one another and the CWL team. The outcome of all vouchers was documented, and some were selected for "showcasing" as exemplars to promote the program. It can be seen from the light description above that the organizational effort to establish a framework and process, as well as to disseminate information and expertise, as well as raising awareness in the creative community, was considerable. This is the "market making" side of the vouchers.

The process described above was repeated for each "round" of vouchers: over the period of the award, seven rounds were held. Each round had a theme; it was quickly realized that an open call for a voucher would not be as effective as both academics and creative businesses had to be drawn in with an idea, one that was general enough to be inclusive and provocative, but not too obscure to marginalize. Experience demonstrated that academic and research expertise was most helpful in setting the agenda of these sessions, in that way it was possible to engage particular academic expertise (not necessarily drawn on a disciplinary, but a topic, basis). This strategy made the task of recruiting academics easier, as well as then presenting an "offer" to creative businesses. Again, this active and intensive "curation" process was critical in getting participants "to the table": the market/community needed to be constructed step by step (see Table 1).

The team found recruiting academics particularly difficult whereas creative businesses were in search of an idea, or a solution; academics already had a full-time job with a more than full task specification. In many respects this was an extracurricular activity. In the high pressure, output-orientated modern academic world, it is remarkable that we managed to draw in as many academics as we did. This highlighted a rather naive conception among many policy makers and politicians about academics and their research. Academics who did cooperate were very committed to outreach, and often had to battle with their managers to get time to participate, or

Table 1 Proportion of attendees, to applicants, to awards

Creative Voucher round	Attendance at ideas pool	Number of voucher applications	Vouchers awarded
Round 1 Mobile Cultures	61	14	7
Round 2 Co-creation	49	20	5
Round 3 Localities	59	17	7
Round 4 Open	68	32	7
Round 5 Archives	71	28	8
Round 6 Demonstrating value	69	29	10
Round 7 Networks	65	30	7

get the value of the work acknowledged. Again, the project in this sense was an ongoing and cumulative task.

Approaches to an Evaluation

The process described above clearly indicates a learning process itself. The CWL team had to actively develop and redesign the delivery and modalities of voucher awards throughout the period as the methods were refined. Again, this was a learning process, and one that was based on a recursive process of discussing with participants and awardees what was working best; and, the growing population of the network. Moreover, the network although curated and mobilized by the ideas pools, other networking events and the newsletters, began to take on a life of its own as creative business began to use it as a networking space. The important point here is that business did not have the autonomous capacity to arrange such networking events; again, this was a community benefit that CWL added, that did not exist, had to be created and may disappear post-project.

There are many ways to evaluate the vouchers. One way that we are illustrating here is in a minimal sense, a descriptive one. This is purposefully provocative, in the comments that we are making about the process and the organization, we are stressing what is not recorded in the descriptive data; moreover, the whole of this book is testament to the diverse meanings and knowledge and learning experiences that participants traversed.

One measure of the success of the knowledge exchange program can be seen in the data gathered through a survey of all awardees across the funding schemes. Overall, 43 percent of partnerships across the three main funding schemes—creative vouchers, creative entrepreneurs in residence and researchers in residence—were formed through activity such as ideas pools for the vouchers, and information and match events for the residencies. A further 42 percent of collaborations were pre-existing, and 6.6 percent were formed through participants' existing contacts, mentioned in the survey as affecting the extent to which participants felt part of a "Creativeworks family."

In the survey, awardees were asked what the key value of Creativeworks London was to them and the responses highlight the broad appeal and worth of the program. Sixty-six percent of respondents highlighted access to CWL's network and networking events as a core value. Unsurprisingly the brokerage provided by the knowledge exchange team was acknowledged by 50.9 percent of respondents—the ideas pools for the Creative Voucher schemes were particularly praised as was the "light touch" approach of the application, balanced by a responsive and supportive delivery team. Highlighting the recognized value of knowledge and expertise, 47.2 percent of respondents recorded the value of access to specialist research and methodologies (relating to the research strands) and 34 percent valued access to a specialist creative and cultural skillset. Perhaps most significant given the program's stated aims, 64.2 percent highlighted the worth of validation of ideas through an external funder, 66 percent acknowledged the space for cross-sector experimentation and seeding of ideas not otherwise possible and 60.4 percent valued the fundamental access to exchange of knowledge made possible by the program. A significant 63 percent of awardees surveyed felt that the outcomes of their projects and their continuing work would have an impact on London's creative economy.

Overall, from the final reports and data gathered from the survey, 48 types of outputs were provisionally counted from the Creative Voucher projects. These included publications—academic or other including journal articles, internal or public facing reports, conference papers, blogs; tools—websites, apps, prototypes, methodologies or processes; visual outputs—films, artworks; events—exhibitions, workshops, conferences (local or international); and other—business plans, "new knowledge," "new networks," projects extending beyond CWL and so on. A provisional count of the data has recorded 420 outputs in total from the 109 projects, an average of 3.85 recorded outputs per project.

The impacts of the Creative Voucher scheme can be seen in four broad spheres—academic, business, creative and social/environmental. Some of the impacts are as expected—academic research outputs (published or work in progress, increased research capacity etc.), and sometimes increased business turnover. Some impacts are joint, for example, leveraged funding benefiting both the academic partner and the SME—for much of which the seed funding provided by the voucher scheme provided the catalyst. Unintended impacts might include a number of SME partners or creative entrepreneurs seeing the collaboration with an academic partner as a catalyst to pursue research for a higher degree themselves.

The majority of the successful projects (more than 95 percent) produced academic impact through their published outputs and events; a number engaged students—from undergraduate to doctoral level—with frequent mentions of engagement with an SME affecting a researcher's teaching practice. Projects such as "Making Friends" (Round 7) engaged with school children in another example of educational impact. Business impacts are hard to quantify in any commercial sense with such small investments and over a brief time period, but resolutions to business problems provided by knowledge exchange, collaborative research and researchers' expertise can clearly be seen to have an effect on business practice moving forward, in, for example, BeatWoven and June Givanni's Pan-African Cinema Archive. Projects that claimed new design approaches along with other creative outputs such as showcase films feed directly into and have an impact on London's creative economy as these approaches are further explored and subsequently adopted. Social and environmental impacts of the Creative Voucher scheme can also be seen in a range of examples, including Vital Arts, which sought to transform Royal London's Renal Unit through art and design intervention, and Heidi Hinder's Money No Object, which used an adaptable interactive technology to explore financial transactions and donations and redefine value at the Victoria and Albert Museum.

The scale of projects pitched for the creative vouchers, as opposed to the CWL residencies, aimed for more significant, "weightier" outputs, for example, book chapters and journal articles for the researchers, or business practice or methodology for the SME partner. The voucher scheme had generated by early 2016 191 outputs, an average of 3.75 per project with the most commonly recorded being internal facing research or project reports. There were ten journal articles and eleven new processes, four apps, eight prototypes but no recorded "new marketable products," although this may be a reflection of the timing of the evaluation and the length of the program.

One thing that has become clear from the evaluation is that despite prolific publication and dissemination of the strands' research through various events, there has been minimal engagement with the core hub research from the perspective of the awardees, particularly not the entrepreneurs and researchers in residence schemes which were not directly connected to the research strands in the way that the creative vouchers were. Recipients of creative vouchers were generally broadly aware of the research associated with the strand that governed their award's round and may have attended additional events but there was very little engagement with working papers or other publications by awardees.

Reflections on the Creative Voucher

The Creative Voucher experiment is an interesting and provocative one. It provides us an interesting snapshot of the ways that policies find their way into programs, and then how programs have to invent them, and a process, as they go along. The case of creative vouchers was striking in that it seems to be based upon a "common sense" notion of knowledge and knowledge exchange that primarily exists in text books for the manufacturing industry. Moreover, the notion of the voucher as prize that will activate knowledge transfer is astonishingly naive. It works with a non-socialized account of society, as if it was mechanical, and one that is devoid of collective action, networks and institutions; the sort of assumptions that one expects to find in a GCSE level text on neoclassical economics. These do not apply to the real economy, let alone to the creative economy. The creative economy, in fact like all economies but more so, is driven by passions and a desire to make things and engage with audiences and users. Accordingly, while the evidence of the voucher scheme is firmly that of a success (in whichever value dimension that one chooses), it did not work because of the voucher scheme. It would be completely inappropriate to interpret the results as validating the scheme. What the evaluation shows is the inventiveness and ingenuity of the many cultural intermediaries—that CWL grew into—that was able to orchestrate this range of creatives, academics, institutions and the voucher scheme and turn it into something that was meaningful and useful to participants. As we can see in the other chapters presented in this book: how that happened was quite a different story, but one that needs to be told.

Notes

1. See Tarek Virani, "Do voucher schemes matter in the long run? A brief comparison of Nesta's Creative Credits and Creativeworks London's Creative Voucher schemes" "Creativeworks London Working Paper No. 10, Creativeworks London/Queen Mary, University of London, 2015), https://qmro.qmul.ac.uk/xmlui/bitstream/handle/123456789/6693/Working%20Paper%2010.pdf?sequence=2.
2. For more details, see chapter "Cultural Policy, Collaboration and Knowledge Exchange".
3. It was completed in 2013.

4. See Virani, "Do voucher schemes matter in the long run?".
5. See Andy C. Pratt, "Innovation: From Transfer to Translation. Illuminating the Cultural Economy," in *The Elgar Companion to Innovation and Knowledge Creation: A Multi-Disciplinary Approach*, ed. H. Bathelt, P. Cohendet, S. Henn, and L. Simon (Cheltenham: Edward Elgar, in press); Tarek Virani and and Andy C. Pratt, "Intermediaries and the Knowledge Exchange Process," in *Higher Education and the Creative Economy: Beyond the Campus*, eds. Roberta Comunian and Abigail Gilmore (Abingdon: Routledge, 2016), 41–58; Andy C. Pratt, "Resilience, Locality and the Cultural Economy," *City, Culture and Society* 6, no. 3 (2015): 61–67; Andy C. Pratt, "Creative Cities: Tensions within and between Social, Cultural and Economic Development. A Critical Reading of the UK Experience," *City, Culture and Society* 1, no. 1 (2010): 13–20; Andy C. Pratt and Paul Jeffcutt, eds., *Creativity, Innovation and the Cultural Economy* (London: Routledge, 2009); Andy C. Pratt, "Do Economists Make Innovation; Do Artists Make Creativity? The Case for an Alternative Perspective on Innovation and Creativity," *Journal of Business Anthropology* 4, no. 2 (2015): 235–244.
6. Pratt, "Innovation."
7. Except in the case where creative enterprises, or academics, did not know how to "find" a partner. The matchmaking element of CWL did do this; however, as noted above this simple matchmaking was a small proportion of the partnerships. Indeed, a really creative exchange would be based on partnerships that could not have been anticipated.
8. See https://www.signupto.com/wp-content/uploads/2016/01/email-benchmark-2016.pdf.
9. A characteristic of the scheme was that payments were made by CWL to universities, academics and creative SMEs.

Creative Collaborations: The Role of Networks, Power and Policy

Roberta Comunian

CREATIVE COLLABORATIONS: FROM THE MARGINS TO THE MAINSTREAM

Creative collaborations are not exactly new in the agenda of academics and the creative economy (CE).[1] They have been part of the historical fabric of both academia and creative practices for many decades. It is easy to see how universities have historically engaged with arts and cultural activities, themselves often patrons or commissioners of art pieces as well as hosts of artists—from poets and writers to architects and musicians—sharing their knowledge through teaching and practice.[2] Similarly, arts organisations and creatives have historically benefited from the knowledge and research developed within academia, from academic articles in arts catalogues to architects benefiting from new materials technologies.[3]

So why are collaborations—in this last decade—becoming so important and central both to higher education policy and practice and to the workings and functioning of the CE? Ironically, the new centrality of creative collaborations has not been actively promoted or campaigned for by the individuals involved in these collaborations—whether academics or artists. This is because while creative collaborations before were not supported or

R. Comunian (✉)
Kings College London, London, UK

© The Author(s) 2017
M. Shiach, Tarek Virani (eds.), *Cultural Policy, Innovation and the Creative Economy*, DOI 10.1057/978-1-349-95112-3_16

promoted, they were still always possible and accessible. The key promoters of creative collaborations have been a range of policy bodies, both at the level of higher education policy as well as the level of economic policy and cultural policy. Their agendas seem to have met in the emergence of creative collaborations for three key reasons: funding cuts (both to higher education and the arts); the emergence of new relational and instrumental arguments about value; and the increase in the importance of justification and impact for funding and policy interventions.

The first reason needs to be reconnected to the (recent) economic crisis (2007–2008) and following recession. This saw also the transition from a decade of New Labour policy, which had been very supportive towards the CE as well as regional investment, to a Conservative age of austerity.[4] The economic crisis had been the trigger for a wider range of funding cuts with the arts and creative activities being particularly affected, but it also reshaped and changed the funding structure of higher education, with particular impact for Arts & Humanities departments.[5] Furthermore, the introduction of full fees for English students to undertake their studies put particular pressure on departments to deliver "value for money" and, in particular, for Arts & Humanities to demonstrate employability and opportunities for their graduates.[6] Overall, the funding cuts and austerity measures from both sides of the creative collaboration spectrum highlighted the opportunity for each side to consider maximising funding via collaborations and in-kind exchanges, as well as thinking about what other (or new) funding opportunities could be accessed via partners that was not thought as important before.

The second reason, which is certainly connected also to pressure of funding, is the increased importance for the CE and arts and humanities to articulate their value in society.[7] While arguments for the value of both have long been there and have centred on their intrinsic value in aesthetic and knowledge terms, funding increasingly became attached to a demonstration of the wider impact and value of arts activities as well as university research in arts and humanities. In the field of arts and culture, the debate had emerged earlier on, specifically with increased emphasis during the New Labour government on funding the arts for their instrumental value and the benefit they bring to places and people, improving social and economic conditions.[8] In a similar fashion, placed within economic frameworks and measures usually applied to science and technology departments, arts and humanities were increasingly questioned about their value and impact in socio-economic terms.[9] Similarly, it is argued that increased emphasis was placed also on the instrumental value of teaching and the importance of employability and careers in connection to local labour markets.[10] While both sides were similarly and independently pressurised towards showing wider impact and value—with the influence of policy and advocacy also bringing them closer[11]—what emerged, I would argue, is the importance of presenting value in a relational way and using creative collaborations as a way to show value reciprocally[12] as well as place value in the social and cultural capital developed through connecting across academia and the creative sector; in many ways, value is articulated as social capital; that is, because it involves so many and functions beyond the restricted sphere of either academia or the arts, then it must be valuable. From this consideration academia—specifically arts and humanities—and the CE emerge as needing each other and being valuable to each other a priori (even before knowledge exchange actually happens).

Finally, connected to both the issue of funding cuts and limited availability of funding as well as an increased push for accountability and value for money in the public policy sphere[13] we see an increased importance and centrality for public policy (here including cultural policy, economic policy and higher education policy) to invest in collaborations and build funding infrastructures around encouraging collaborations and partnerships.[14] It makes sense of course, for example, for the institutions that are training the next generation of creative workers to be talking with companies and individuals developing new products and ideas in the CE; it makes sense that if funding is invested in academic research, this research should not be left solely in inaccessible books but also disseminated and applied as much as possible by practitioners.[15] It also makes sense that when funding is limited, one should use the funding, rather than targeting one sector and activities—which might be hard to justify and might prove risky in reference to demonstrating value for money and impact—to target networks, collaboration, "meeting points" of a range of activities (education, research, cultural expression, markets...), which will therefore have the potential to benefit more people (and be less open to criticism) because of their nature of being already multi-stakeholders and placing value on their relational capital.

After this brief introduction to the emergence of creative collaborations, the chapter is structured in three parts. The first highlights the importance of networks and their nature but also the dynamics of inclusion and exclusion they might generate. The second considers issues of power, which are connected to networks but also to institutional frameworks and the range of organisations which are called to collaborate in this new age of creativity. The third part concludes by reflecting on the role of policy—with specific emphasis on its importance in creating and facilitating networks as well as its impact on power relations and collaboration.

THE IMPORTANCE OF NETWORKS: CONNECTING AND DISCONNECTING KNOWLEDGE

Many academics studying the CE have highlighted the importance that networks—from local connections[16] to global links play[17] in the development of new knowledge, products and audiences. In reference to research, for many years the focus has been on the networks that develop amongst creative workers, industries and practitioners,[18] whether in relation to supply chain, product innovations or access to specific markets. From this, the attention has moved towards the role played by policy (local, national and international) in supporting and facilitating the development of creative industries and their production system[19] or in building an infrastructure around the CE.[20] However, until very recently, the role of higher education had not come to the forefront. A recent literature review[21] highlights the new centrality of higher education in academic research and policy reports. It is argued that universities—via academics and graduates or alumni—have long been present in local and regional creative networks, shaping often its direction and development.[22] Nonetheless, more recently developing collaborative networks—which span across the creative industries and academia, has been something of a new imperative and it is important to reflect on the nature of these networks as well as their potential in connecting but also disconnecting projects and opportunities.

Comunian, using the case of Newcastle-Gateshead, highlighted the strategic importance of networks for creative economy practitioners.[23] While that paper does not consider the value of the same networks in relation to academia, it offers an opportunity or framework to allow us to reflect more broadly on how this might apply. The first element considers the *interaction between networks and labour markets within the creative economy*. This is certainly very important from the employment perspective of creative practitioners. However, higher education certainly plays an important role in developing these networks too. Academia offers the first opportunity for students to both establish networks amongst themselves—that they will develop when graduates, but also to exchange and collaborative with researchers, academics as well as other professionals who might be involved in the courses.[24] Comunian and Gilmore highlight how the connections amongst students and alumni create a strong bond and how alumni and graduates remain often connected to their courses, via talks, internships and other collaborative work.[25] Higher education has an interest in developing networks which might facilitate the retention of students to the *locale*[26] but also that facilitate job and employment opportunities for incoming new cohorts.[27]

Networks developed within the university but also transitioning towards graduation are really important to create *marketing and branding opportunity (access to market)* for graduates as well as institutions. Graduates use the opportunity of degree shows and portfolios of practice that they develop within academia to establish future opportunities and audience. Similarly, the success of certain alumni in developing and expanding brands and business opportunities is often used by universities in their own marketing materials as they have to compete for criteria like employability, business start-ups and in general successful alumni.[28] Another important element of the networks that gets established within and beyond the campus is their role in providing *knowledge support and professional development*;[29] the presence of CE practitioners—whether alumni or not—in the locale or beyond can allow higher education institutions to bring in special forms of expertise and professional development support for their current students. Similarly, alumni who remain in the locale are often able to tap into the expertise of academic or knowledge infrastructure of the university to develop further their creative potential. While there is an informal permeability of networks on an often informal basis, there are more formalised opportunities, such as residencies that can provide a framework for this knowledge to travel and develop. Finally, as mentioned in the introduction, more recently these networks have also become a new way to access a range of *new funding opportunities or bodies*. The AHRC Knowledge Exchange Hubs for the Creative Economy initiative (launched in 2011) can be considered an example of the kind of *funding* that practitioners have been able to access recently through collaborative work, which had not been present before.

All of these motivations make networks really important in this knowledge ecosystem both for the CE practitioners and for the development of higher education. However—as we will discuss also in the following section—while there is a tendency to see networks as something positive and inclusive which facilitate creative collaborations, this is not always the case.[30] It is often the case that networks that might be easily accessible to some—often via accumulated social or cultural capital—might not be accessible to all. Furthermore, gender, ethnicity and social class are still considered strong barriers to creative work and creative careers progression[31] and a better reflection of how this might reflect in access to knowledge and opportunities within higher education is needed.[32]

Power Relations: Size and Knowledge Matters

So while it is easy to positively acknowledge the importance of networks and collaborations between CE and higher education,[33] it is also important to acknowledge the barrier that might hinder or block creative collaborations.

One of the key elements to consider is the balance of power which often characterises creative collaborations and also how power might also influence access and opportunities for further development. Power can be understood from a variety of perspectives and can have different impacts in the development of the process of collaboration.[34]

At the first level, there is an element of power in relation to *size and financial operation*.

On one side, universities tend to be large structures, with access to space, knowledge and funding. On the other side, the creative economy is mostly composed of small organisations which often lack cash flow and space or infrastructure. While collaborations are established, it might seem obvious that academic institutions will lead the agenda and that they will be able to set the terms and conditions and framework for the collaboration. This can become a source of contention or an obstacle for small creative economy organisations, which might not have the personnel or resources to commit or the experience to be able to frame conditions and objectives. Therefore, from the very initial steps, making sure that there is a balance of voices and a level playing field is important for the development of genuine collaborations. Small creative companies or individuals might struggle to set the terms and research agenda because of the lack of time or resources to set aside for initial meetings and agreements. However, if universities are engaging in collaboration with larger cultural institutions or multinational corporations in the creative economy, the power balance might be different, more equal, or even see academic institutions able to bend their programmes or frameworks in order to be able to use key cultural partners within their teaching or research marketing materials. Here, we can see that power at play reflects not only the size or financial capacity of organisations but also their brand and institutional power. Larger cultural institutions and commercial partners might bring cultural capital or status to a course or institution and this might be reflected in the kind of partnership that is established. Power relations are particularly relevant not only in setting the agenda and framework for collaboration, but also in determining access to these opportunities, and this highlights the importance of brokerage and networks.[35]

THE ROLE OF POLICY AND HEIS IN ENGINEERING (LOCAL) CREATIVITY

There are a wider range of roles that policy can play in supporting creative collaborations across the CE and HEIs.[36] Following the approach of Comunian, Chapain and Clifton, there are four key areas that have seen interventions and investments and provide a framework for supporting collaborations: physical shared infrastructure; soft knowledge infrastructure; markets and governance.[37]

If we focus *on physical infrastructure*, it is easy to see the role that policy can play in developing further interconnections between CE and higher education institutions. This is particularly important for small independent producers and sole traders as they often do not have access to infrastructure or space to develop their business ideas or projects. It is therefore easy to see how certain higher education institutions—with policy investment and guidance—have focused on providing their graduates or associated companies with cheap or free space to work and create.[38] Whether space is created through local council direct investment or within higher education estate development, there is a strong common agenda for local policy and higher education policy to work together to provide the right space, business advice and opportunities for the development of local creative companies or cultural initiatives. There are opportunities that go beyond space, for example, in the case of academic subjects which require expensive and specialised equipment for their students and research—for example, recording studios or laser-cutting equipment—the chance of having outside companies to pay rent or share costs of some of the equipment might be a lifeline. In a period of funding cuts, both to arts funding and local council budgets as well as to investment in arts and creative disciplines, the opportunity to think about shared infrastructures is an important policy framework that bridges across partners and opportunities.

While investment in physical infrastructure can be strategic, it requires usually a large amount of funding. Therefore, it is much more common to see investment by policy initiatives—both in higher education policy and local economic policy, towards the empowering or development of *soft infrastructure* opportunities. This covers a range of activities such as networking, knowledge sharing and training. These interventions are often bottom-up—by individuals in higher education or the CE sector and might benefit from small investment to enable greater engagement of partners and facilitate further exchanges. While many of these activities develop spontaneously, in the last decade, there has been also a push towards engineering collaboration and providing funding or frameworks (such as voucher schemes) to broker relationship and to empower collaborations that were not there before.

While less emphasis is placed on supporting *markets* for CE practitioners, universities and policy play an important role in engaging also with the distribution of and access to cultural and creative products. However, local graduate retention and the ability to support the co-location of a range of creative activities in a locale, rely on the development of markets and a sophisticated demand. Universities have a role to play in educating audiences—via exhibitions, fairs, open days or degree shows, they are therefore important also to bridge the gap between a creative product—developed with or across academia and the CE—who might not yet have an audience or market and new opportunities.[39] While higher education seems to have embraced this commercial agenda strongly within the science and technology field, this has not yet been the case in the field of creativity.[40]

Finally, policy seems to have often taken the lead in supporting creative collaborations via new funding frameworks but has been less active in thinking about governance interventions. If the financial climate and the reduced level of resources in public policy called for more collaborative actions—for example, the emphasis of the Arts Council of England on "grand partnerships"[41]—then more emphasis needs to be placed on *governance*. Universities often have capacity and ability to establish connections between local policy for industry and urban development as well as industry, local communities and other third-sector players (for example, galleries, museums, festivals, etc.). Despite their recent neoliberal turn,[42] they are still considered by many local policy makers as neutral agents or intermediaries. They are not seen as being driven by private interest but the greater (local) good and, therefore, are considered the ideal intermediaries and brokers for local development.[43] However, while academia can play such an important role, policy needs to consider that often interventions might benefit certain parts of the society and not all local stakeholders equally.[44] So while academia might be driving broader positive externalities for local contexts, it might still be disconnected from certain areas of society or specific communities of interests.[45]

Conclusions

The chapter has tried to highlight not only the symbiosis between higher education and the CE but also the recent pressure and policy interventions that have placed creative collaborations high on the agenda of both academics and practitioners in the CE. While the investment of funding bodies—such as the AHRC—to support creative collaborations has provided incentives and opportunities for further engagement, issues of sustainability and the importance of considering barriers and shortcomings of creative collaborations are also important for a better understanding of their development and future. In particular, while the grassroots networks and intertwined activities across higher education and the CE are unlikely to disappear or stop, it is also important to make sure there is an equal and ethical approach towards these interactions. The pressure, coming from funding cuts and new funding sources might in fact push each side to use the other instrumentally and undervalue the motivations and intrinsic values of each other's work in favour of the practicalities of the next grant and the next collaboration. Similarly, critical thinking—which is at the core of both academia and artist practice—should not be abandoned in favour of feel-good reports and advocacy towards more creative collaborations.

Notes

1. I use the term creative economy (CE) throughout the chapter as Comunian and Gilmore define it, as an umbrella term that has two core components the *creative industries* and the (publically funded) *arts and cultural sector*. See Roberta Comunian and Abigail Gilmore, "Beyond the Creative Campus: Reflections on the Evolving Relationship between Higher Education and the Creative Economy" (King's College London, 2015), 8, fig. 1, www.creative-campus.org.uk.

2. Marjorie Garber, *Patronizing the Arts: The University as Patron* (Princeton: Princeton University Press, 2008).
3. Elizabeth Bullen, Simon Robb, and Jane Kenway, "'Creative Destruction': Knowledge Economy Policy and the Future of the Arts and Humanities in the Academy," *Journal of Education Policy* 19, no. 1 (2004): 3–22.
4. David Hesmondhalgh, Kate Oakley, David Lee, and Melissa Nisbett, "New Labour, Culture and Creativity," in *Culture, Economy and Politics: The Case of New Labour*, ed. David Hesmondhalgh, Kate Oakley, David Lee, and Melissa Nisbett (Basingstoke: Palgrave Macmillan, 2015), 36–69.
5. Deborah Bull, "Culture in a Cold Climate," *Cultural Trends* 24, no. 1 (2015): 46–50.
6. Roberta Comunian, Alessandra Faggian, and Sarah Jewell, "Embedding Arts and Humanities in the Creative Economy: the Role of Graduates in the UK," *Environment and Planning C: Government and Policy* 32, no. 3 (2014): 426–450.
7. Department for Culture, Media and Sport, *Government and the Value of Culture* (London: Department for Culture, Media and Sport, 2004); Kylie Budge, "A Question of Values: Why We Need Art and Design in Higher Education," *Art, Design & Communication in Higher Education* 11, no. 1 (2012): 5–16.
8. Eleonora Belfiore, "Art as a Means of Alleviating Social Exclusion: Does it Really Work? A Critique of Instrumental Cultural Policies and Social Impact Studies in the UK," *International Journal of Cultural Policy* 8, no. 1 (2002): 91–106.
9. Eleonora Belfiore, "'Impact', 'Value' and 'Bad Economics': Making Sense of the Problem of Value in the Arts and Humanities," *Arts and Humanities in Higher Education* 14, no. 1 (2014): 95–110; Paul Benneworth and Ben W. Jongbloed, "Who Matters to Universities? A Stakeholder Perspective on Humanities, Arts and Social Sciences Valorisation," *Higher Education* 59, no. 5 (2010): 567–588.
10. Phil Ramsey and Andrew White, "Art for Art's Sake? A Critique of the Instrumentalist Turn in the Teaching of Media and Communications in UK Universities," *International Journal of Cultural Policy* 21, no. 1 (2015):78–96; Roberta Comunian and Alessandra Faggian, "Higher Education and the Creative City," in *Handbook on Cities and Creativity*, eds. David Emanuel Andersson,

Åke E. Andersson, and Charlotta Mellander (London: Edward Elgar 2011), 187–207.
11. Arts Council England, *The Cultural Knowledge Ecology. A Discussion Paper on Partnerships between HEIs and Cultural Organisations*, ed. Sarah Fisher (London: Arts Council England, 2012); Jane Dawson, and Abigail Gilmore, "Shared Interest: Developing Collaboration, Partnerships and Research Relationships between Higher Education, Museums, Galleries and Visual Arts Organisations in the North West" (Joint Consultancy Research Project commissioned by Renaissance North West, Arts Council England North West and the North West Universities Association, 2009); J. Taylor, "Unweaving the Rainbow: Research, Innovation and Risk in a Creative Economy" (AHRC Discussion Paper, Arts and Humanities Research Council, London, 2005).
12. Jean M. Bartunek, "Academic-Practitioner Collaboration Need not Require Joint or Relevant Research: Toward a Relational Scholarship of Integration," *Academy of Management Journal* 50, no. 6 (2007): 1323–1333; Elena P. Antonacopoulou, "Impact and Scholarship: Unlearning and Practising to Co-create Actionable Knowledge," *Management Learning* 40, no. 4 (2009): 421–430.
13. Christopher Humphrey, Peter Miller, and Robert W Scapens, "Accountability and Accountable Management in the UK Public Sector," *Accounting, Auditing & Accountability Journal* 6, no. 3 (1993): 7–29.
14. Judith E. Innes and David E. Booher, *Planning with Complexity: An Introduction to Collaborative Rationality for Public Policy* (London: Routledge, 2010).
15. Geoffrey Crossick, "Knowledge transfer without widgets: The challenge of the creative economy" (Lecture, Royal Society of Arts, Goldsmiths University of London, 2006), http://www.london.ac.uk/fileadmin/documents/about/vicechancellor/Knowledge_transfer_without_widgets.pdf.
16. Roberta, Comunian, "Exploring the Role of Networks in the Creative Economy of North East England: Economic and Cultural Dynamics," in *Encounters and Engagements between Economic and Cultural Geography*, ed. Barney Warf (Dordrecht: Springer, 2012), 143–157; Louise Crewe, "Material Culture: Embedded Firms, Organizational Networks and the Local Economic Development of a Fashion Quarter," *Regional Studies: The Journal of the Regional Studies Association* 30, no. 3 (1996): 257–272.

17. Allen J. Scott, "Cultural-Products Industries and Urban Economic Development: Prospects for Growth and Market Contestation in Global Context," *Urban Affairs Review* 39, no. 4 (2004): 461–490; Andrés Solimano, "The International Mobility of Talent and its Impact on Global Development: An Overview" (Discussion Paper No. 2006/08, UNU World Institute for Development Economics Research (UNU-WIDER), Helsinki, 2006), https://www.wider.unu.edu/sites/default/files/dp2006-08.pdf.
18. Gernot Grabher, "Cool Projects, Boring Institutions: Temporary Collaboration in Social Context," *Regional Studies* 36, no. 3 (2002): 205–214; Bas van Heur, "The Clustering of Creative Networks: Between Myth and Reality," *Urban Studies* 46, no. 8 (2009): 1531–1552.
19. Kate Oakley, "Include Us Out: Economic Development and Social Policy in the Creative Industries," *Cultural Trends* 15, no. 4 (2006): 255–273; Mirjam Gollmitzer and Catherine Murray, "From Economy to Ecology: A Policy Framework for Creative Labour" (Report for the Canadian Conference of the Arts, 2008), http://www.sfu.ca/cmns/faculty/murray_c/assets/documents/From-economy-to-ecology.pdf.
20. Roberta Comunian and Oliver Mould, "The Weakest Link: Creative Industries, Flagship Cultural Projects and Regeneration," *City, Culture and Society* 5, no. 2 (2014): 65–74.
21. Roberta Comunian, Abigail Gilmore, and Silvie Jacobi, "Higher Education and the Creative Economy: Creative Graduates, Knowledge Transfer and Regional Impact Debates," *Geography Compass* 9, no. 7 (2015): 371–383.
22. Comunian and Gilmore, "Beyond the Creative Campus."
23. Comunian, "Exploring the Role of Networks."
24. Daniel Ashton, "Cultural Workers In-the-Making," *European Journal of Cultural Studies* 16, no. 4 (2013): 368–388.
25. Comunian and Gilmore, "Beyond the Creative Campus."
26. Paul Chatterton and John Goddard, "The Response of Higher Education Institutions to Regional Needs," *European Journal of Education* 35, no. 4 (2000): 475–496.
27. Roberta Comunian and Alessandra Faggian, "Creative Graduates and Creative Cities: Exploring the Geography of Creative Education in the UK," *International Journal of Cultural and Creative Industries* 1, no. 2 (2014): 19–34.

28. Heiner Gembris, "A New Approach to Pursuing the Professional Development of Recent Graduates from German Music Academies: The Alumni Project," in *The Music Practitioner: Research for the Music Performer, Teacher and Listener*, ed. J. W. Davidson (Aldershot: Ashgate, 2004), 309–18.
29. Nerys Fuller-Love, "Formal and Informal Networks in Small Businesses in the Media Industry," *International Entrepreneurship and Management Journal*, 5, no. 3 (2009): 271–284; Gordon MacLeod, "The Learning Region in an Age of Austerity: Capitalizing on Knowledge, Entrepreneurialism, and Reflexive Capitalism," *Geoforum* 31, no. 2 (2000): 219–236.
30. Tim Vorley, Oli Mould, and Richard Courtney, "My Networking Is Not Working! Conceptualizing the Latent and Dysfunctional Dimensions of the Network Paradigm," *Economic Geography* 88, no. 1 (2012): 77–96.
31. Roberta Comunian and B. Conor, "Making Cultural Work Visible in Cultural Policy," in *The Routledge Companion to Cultural Policy*, ed. Victoria Durrer, Toby Miller, and Dave O'Brien (London: Routledge, 2017).
32. Mark Banks and Kate Oakley, "The Dance Goes on Forever? Art Schools, Class and UK Higher Education," *International Journal of Cultural Policy*, 22, no. 1 (2016): 45–57.
33. Comunian, Gilmore, and Jacobi, "Higher Education and the Creative Economy"; Comunian and Gilmore, "Beyond the Creative Campus."
34. Roberta Comunian, Calvin Taylor, and David N. Smith, "The Role of Universities in the Regional Creative Economies of the UK: Hidden Protagonists and the Challenge of Knowledge Transfer," *European Planning Studies* 22, no. 12 (2013): 2456–2476.
35. Comunian and Gilmore, "Beyond the Creative Campus."
36. Nick Clifton, Roberta Comunian, and Caroline Chapain, "Creative Regions in Europe: Challenges and Opportunities for Policy," *European Planning Studies* 23, no. 12 (2015): 2331–2335.
37. Roberta Comunian, Caroline Chapain, and Nick Clifton, "Creative Industries and Creative Policies: A European perspective?" *City, Culture and Society* 5, no. 2 (2014): 51–53.
38. Ashton, "Cultural Workers In-the-Making."

39. Jason Potts, S. Cunningham, John Hartley, and P. Ormerod, "Social Network Markets: A New Definition of the Creative Industries," *Journal of Cultural Economics*, 32, no. 3 (2008): 167–185.
40. See Jerry G. Thursby, Richard Jensen, and Marie C. Thursby, "Objectives, Characteristics and Outcomes of University Licensing: A Survey of Major U.S. Universities," *Journal of Technology Transfer* 26, no. 26 (2001): 59–72; Michelle Gittelman and Bruce Kogut, "Does Good Science Lead to Valuable Knowledge? Biotechnology Firms and the Evolutionary Logic of Citation Patterns," *Management Science* 49, no. 4 (2003): 366–382.
41. Peter Bazalgette, "Sir Peter Bazalgette's Inaugural Lecture as Chair" (Lecture, Royal Society of the Arts, London, 20 March 2013).
42. Joyce E. Canaan and Wesley Shumar, *Structure and Agency in the Neoliberal University* (London: Routledge, 2008).
43. John Goddard and Paul Vallance, *The University and the City* (London: Routledge, 2013).
44. Benneworth and Jongbloed, "Who Matters to Universities?"
45. Comunian and Mould, "The Weakest Link."

BIBLIOGRAPHY

INTERNET RESOURCES

Alan Dix. http://alandix.com
Beyond the Campus. http://www.creative-campus.org.uk
Black Cultural Archives. http://bcaheritage.org.uk
Centre for Studies of Home. http://www.studiesofhome.qmul.ac.uk
Colonial Film Database. http://www.colonialfilm.org.uk
Creativeworks London. http://www.creativeworkslondon.org.uk
Everyday Heroes of Postman's Park. http://www.postmanspark.org.uk
Fish Police. http://www.thefishpolice.com
Friends of the Watts Memorial. http://www.wattsmemorial.org.uk
Future Cemetery. http://futurecemetery.org
Heart N Soul. http://www.heartnsoul.co.uk
June Givanni Pan African Cinema Archive. http://www.junegivannifilmarchive.com
Make Your SoundLab. http://www.makeyoursoundlab.org
National Audit Office. https://www.nao.org.uk
OpenCV. http://opencv.org
Peckham Platform. http://www.peckhamplatform.com
Pervasive Intelligence. http://www.pervasive-intelligence.co.uk/projects
Prossimo Ventures. http://www.prossimo-ventures.co.uk
Royal Academy of Engineering. http://www.raeng.org.uk
Social Art Map. www.socialartmap.org.uk
Tate & Lyle. http://tateandlyle.com
WildlifeKate. http://www.wildlifekate.co.uk
Zooniverse. https://www.zooniverse.org

© The Author(s) 2017
M. Shiach, Tarek Virani (eds.), *Cultural Policy, Innovation and the Creative Economy*, DOI 10.1057/978-1-349-95112-3

All Other Sources

A Family Affair. 1959. Directed by Michael Johns. London: Robert Angell in partnership with Puritan Films. Film, 40min.

Aitken, Ian (ed.). 1990. *Film and reform: John Grierson and the documentary film movement.* London: Routledge.

Aitken, Ian (ed.). 1998. *The documentary film movement: An anthology.* Edinburgh: Edinburgh University Press.

Antonacopoulou, Elena P. 2009. Impact and scholarship: Unlearning and practising to co-create actionable knowledge. *Management Learning* 40(4): 421–430.

Arts Council England. 2012. In *The cultural knowledge ecology. A discussion paper on partnerships between HEIs and cultural organisations*, ed. Sarah Fisher. London: Arts Council England.

Ashton, Daniel. 2013. Cultural workers in-the-making. *European Journal of Cultural Studies* 16(4): 368–388.

Attitudes. 1972–76. Directed by Michael Radford. London: James Archibald for Tate & Lyle, c. Film, 33min.

Bailey, David A. 2016. "JGPACA Business Plan." June Givanni Pan African Cinema Archive, document, January 2016.

Bakhshi, Hasan, Eric McVittie, and James Simmie. 2008. *Creating innovation: Do the creative industries support innovation in the wider economy?* London: NESTA.

Bakhshi, Hasan, Eric McVittie, James Simmie, John Edwards, Stephen Roper, Judy Scully, Duncan Shaw, Lorraine Morley, and Nicola Rathbone. 2013. *Creative credits: A randomized controlled industrial policy experiment.* London: Nesta.

Banks, Mark, and Kate Oakley. 2016. The dance goes on forever? Art schools, class and UK higher education. *International Journal of Cultural Policy* 22(1): 45–57.

Barclay, Craig P. 2009. Heroes of peace: The royal humane society and the award of medals in Britain, 1774–1914. PhD diss., University of York.

Bartunek, Jean M, 2007. Academic-practitioner collaboration need not require joint or relevant research: Toward a relational scholarship of integration. *Academy of Management Journal* 50(6): 1323–1333.

Baxter, Richard, and Katherine Brickell. 2014. For home unmaking. *Home Cultures* 11(2): 133–143.

Bazalgette, Peter. 2013. Sir Peter Bazalgette's Inaugural Lecture as Chair. Lecture, Royal Society of the Arts, London, 20 March 2013.

Belfiore, Eleonora. 2002. Art as a means of alleviating social exclusion: Does it really work? A critique of instrumental cultural policies and social impact studies in the UK. *International Journal of Cultural Policy* 8(1): 91–106.

Belfiore, Eleonora. 2014. 'Impact', 'value' and 'bad economics': Making sense of the problem of value in the arts and humanities. *Arts and Humanities in Higher Education* 14(1): 95–110.
Benjamin, Walter. 2008. *The work of art in the age of mechanical reproduction*. Trans. J. A. Underwood. London: Penguin.
Benneworth, Paul, and Ben W. Jongbloed. 2010. Who matters to universities? A stakeholder perspective on humanities, arts and social sciences valorisation. *Higher Education* 59(5): 567–588.
Bernabei, R., and L. Power. 2012. Differentiating co-design and mass customization from a user-completion model within the realm of product design. The 2nd international conference on design creativity, 18–20 September 2012, Glasgow, pp. 227–233. https://www.designsociety.org/publication/32515/differentiating_co-design_and_mass_customisation_from_a_user-completion_within_the_realm_of_product_design
Bishop, Claire. 2012. *Artificial hells: Participatory art and the politics of spectatorship*. London: Verso.
Blunt, Alison, Eleanor John, Caron Lipman, and Alastair Owens. 2013. Centre for studies of home: A partnership between Queen Mary, University of London and the Geffrye Museum of the Home. In *Collaborative geographies: The politics, practicalities, and promise of working together*, ed. Ruth Craggs, Hilary Geoghegan, and Innes M. Keighren, 111–125. London: Historical Geography Research Group.
Brickwood, Cathy, Bronac Ferran, David Garcia, and Tim Putnam (eds.). 2007. *(Un)Common ground: Creative encounters across sectors and disciplines*. Amsterdam: BIS Publishing.
British Refined. 1960. Directed by William J. Bassett. London: Thames Refinery Film Unit. Film, 33min.
Bruneel, Johan, Pablo d'Este, and Ammon Salter. 2010. Investigating the factors that diminish the barriers to university–industry collaboration. *Research Policy* 39(7): 858–868.
Budge, Kylie. 2012. A question of values: Why we need art and design in higher education. *Art, Design & Communication in Higher Education* 11(1): 5–16.
Bull, Deborah. 2015. Culture in a cold climate. *Cultural Trends* 24(1): 46–50.
Bullen, Elizabeth, Simon Robb, and Jane Kenway. 2004. 'Creative destruction': Knowledge economy policy and the future of the arts and humanities in the academy. *Journal of Education Policy* 19(1): 3–22.
Canaan, Joyce E., and Wesley Shumar. 2008. *Structure and agency in the neoliberal university*. London: Routledge.
Card, Stuart K., Thomas P. Moran, and Allen Newell. 1983. *The Psychology of Human-Computer Interaction*. Erlbaum: Hillsdale.
Cham, Karen. 2007. Reconstruction theory, designing the space of possibility in complex media. In *Performance play: Technologies of presence in performance*,

gaming and experience design. ed Lizbeth Goodman, Deverill, Esther MacCallum-Stewart and Alec Robertson. Special issue, *International Journal of Performance Arts and Digital Media*, 2 & 3(3): 253–267.

Cham, Karen. 2008. Reality jamming: Beyond complex causality in mediated systems. ISEA 08, Singapore. http://www.isea2008singapore.org/abstract/i-1/p338.html

Cham, Karen. 2011. Architecture of the image. Electronic visualisation in the arts, EVA conferences international, British Computer Society, London. http://ewic.bcs.org/content/ConWebDoc/40614

Cham, Karen. 2014. Virtually an alternative? The medium, the message and the user experience: Collective agency in digital spaces and embodied social change. Fifth LAEMOS Colloquium on organization studies constructing alternatives: How can we organize for alternative social, economic, and ecological balance?, Havana, Cuba. http://laemos.com

Cham, Karen, and Jeffrey Johnson. 2007. Complexity theory: A science of cultural systems? *M/C Journal*, 10(3): 21–34.

Charon, Rita. 2001. Narrative medicine: A model for empathy, reflection, profession, and trust. *Jama* 286(15): 1897–1902.

Charon, Rita. 2006. *Narrative medicine: Honouring the stories of illness*. Oxford: Oxford University Press.

Chatterton, Paul, and John Goddard. 2000. The response of higher education institutions to regional needs. *European Journal of Education* 35(4): 475–496.

Christie, Ian. 1981. Ruiz dossier. *Afterimage* 10: 112–113.

Clifton, Nick, Roberta Comunian, and Caroline Chapain. 2015. Creative regions in Europe: Challenges and opportunities for policy. *European Planning Studies* 23(12): 2331–2335.

Comunian, Roberta. 2012. Exploring the role of networks in the creative economy of North East England: Economic and cultural dynamics. In *Encounters and engagements between economic and cultural geography*, ed. Barney Warf, 143–157. Dordrecht: Springer.

Comunian, Roberta, and B. Conor. 2017. Making cultural work visible in cultural policy. In *The Routledge companion to cultural policy*, ed. Victoria Durrer, Toby Miller, and Dave O'Brien. London: Routledge.

Comunian, Roberta, and Alessandra Faggian. 2011. Higher Education and the creative city. In *Handbook on cities and creativity*, ed. David Emanuel Andersson, Åke E. Andersson, and Charlotta Mellander, 187–207. London: Edward Elgar.

Comunian, Roberta, and Alessandra Faggian. 2014. Creative graduates and creative cities: Exploring the geography of creative education in the UK. *International Journal of Cultural and Creative Industries* 1(2): 19–34.

Comunian, Roberta, and Abigail Gilmore. 2015. Beyond the creative campus: Reflections on the evolving relationship between Higher Education and the creative economy. King's College London. www.creative-campus.org.uk

Comunian, Roberta, and Oliver Mould. 2014. The weakest link: Creative industries, flagship cultural projects and regeneration. *City, Culture and Society* 5(2): 65–74.

Comunian, Roberta, Calvin Taylor, and David N. Smith. 2013. The role of universities in the regional creative economies of the UK: Hidden protagonists and the challenge of knowledge transfer. *European Planning Studies* 22(12): 2456–2476.

Comunian, Roberta, Caroline Chapain, and Nick Clifton. 2014a. Creative industries and creative policies: A European perspective? *City, Culture and Society* 5(2): 51–53.

Comunian, Roberta, Alessandra Faggian, and Sarah Jewell. 2014b. Embedding arts and humanities in the creative economy: The role of graduates in the UK. *Environment and Planning C: Government and Policy* 32(3): 426–450.

Comunian, Roberta, Abigail Gilmore, and Silvie Jacobi. 2015. Higher Education and the creative economy: Creative graduates, knowledge transfer and regional impact debates. *Geography Compass* 9(7): 371–383.

Cornet, Maarten, Björn Vroomen, and Marc van der Steeg. 2006. Do innovation vouchers help SMEs to cross the bridge towards science? CPB discussion paper no. 58, CPB Netherlands Bureau for Economic Policy Analysis. http://www.cpb.nl/sites/default/files/publicaties/download/do-innovation-vouchers-help-smes-cross-bridge-towards-science.pdf

Creativeworks London: A Knowledge Exchange Hub for the Creative Economy, 2012-2016. 2016. London: Creativeworks London.

Crewe, Louise. 1996. Material culture: Embedded firms, organizational networks and the local economic development of a fashion quarter. *Regional Studies: The Journal of the Regional Studies Association* 30(3): 257–272.

Cross, Anita. 1983. The educational background to the Bauhaus. *Design Studies* 4(1): 43–52.

Crossick, Geoffrey. 2006. Knowledge transfer without widgets: The challenge of the creative economy. Lecture, Royal Society of Arts, Goldsmiths University of London, http://www.london.ac.uk/fileadmin/documents/about/vicechancellor/Knowledge_transfer_without_widgets.pdf

Cuba, an African Odyssey. 2007. Directed by Jihan El-Tahari. Paris: Temps Noir. Film, 118min.

Dawson, Jane, and Abigail Gilmore. 2009. Shared interest: Developing collaboration, partnerships and research relationships between higher education, Museums, galleries and visual arts organisations in the North West. Joint Consultancy Research Project commissioned by Renaissance North West, Arts Council England North West and the North West Universities Association.

Deleuze, Gilles, and Félix Guattari. 2009. *Anti-Oedipus: Capitalism and Schizophrenia.* Trans. Robert Hurley, Mark Seem, and Helen R. Lane. New York: Penguin.

Delle Monache, Stefano, and Rocchesso Davide. 2014. Bauhaus legacy in research through design: The case of basic Sonic Interaction Design. *International Journal of Design* 8(3): 139–154.

Department for Culture, Media and Sport. 2004. *Government and the value of culture*. London: Department for Culture, Media and Sport.

Department for Culture, Media and Sport. 2005. *Understanding the future: Museums and 21st-century life*. London: Department for Culture, Media and Sport.

Drassinower, Abraham. 2003. A rights based view of the idea/expression dichotomy in copyright law. *Canadian Journal of Law and Jurisprudence* 16(1): 3–21.

Eagleton, Terry. 2015. The slow death of the university. *Chronicle of Higher Education*, 6 April 2015.

Edwards, Elizabeth. 2012. *The camera as historian*. Durham: Duke University Press.

Feld, Steven. 2000. A Sweet Lullaby for world music. *Public Culture* 12(1): 145–171.

Finnegan, Ruth (ed.). 2005. *Participating in the knowledge economy: Researchers beyond the walls*. Basingstoke: Palgrave Macmillan.

Fuller-Love, Nerys. 2009. Formal and informal networks in small businesses in the media industry. *International Entrepreneurship and Management Journal* 5(3): 271–284.

Garner, Cathy, Jasmina Bolfek-Radovani, Helen Fogg, Jana Riedel, Phil Ternouth, Gerard Briscoe, Mariza Dima, Morag Shiach, Tarek Virani, and London Creative and Digital Fusion Team. 2014. London creative and digital fusion. London Fusion. http://www.creativeworkslondon.org.uk/wp-content/uploads/2015/04/Fusion_digital_Edition_V4.pdf

Gembris, Heiner. 2004. A new approach to pursuing the professional development of recent graduates from German music academies: The alumni project. In *The music practitioner: Research for the music performer, teacher and listener*, ed. J.W. Davidson, 309–318. Aldershot: Ashgate.

Gittelman, Michelle, and Bruce Kogut. 2003. Does good science lead to valuable knowledge? Biotechnology firms and the evolutionary logic of citation patterns. *Management Science* 49(4): 366–382.

Givanni, GianMaria. 2016. JGPACA spatial strategy. June Givanni Pan African Cinema Archive, document, January.

Goddard, John, and Paul Vallance. 2013. *The university and the city*. London: Routledge.

Gollmitzer, Mirjam, and Catherine Murray. 2008. From economy to ecology: A policy framework for creative labour. Report for the Canadian Conference of the Arts. http://www.sfu.ca/cmns/faculty/murray_c/assets/documents/From-economy-to-ecology.pdf

Hall, Stuart. 2011. The neo-liberal revolution. *Cultural Studies* 25(6): 705–728.

Hassenzahl, Marc, Kai Eckoldt, Sarah Diefenbach, Matthias Laschke, Eva Len, and Joonhwan Kim. 2013. Designing moments of meaning and pleasure: Experience design and happiness. *International Journal of Design* 7(3): 21–31.
Henton, Doug, and Jessie Oettinger. 2015. Innovation brokers. In *The Oxford handbook to local competitiveness*, ed. David B. Audretsch, Albert N. Link, and Mary Lindenstein Walshok, 306–319. Oxford: Oxford University Press.
Hesmondhalgh, David, Kate Oakley, David Lee, and Melissa Nisbett. 2015. New labour, culture and creativity. In *Culture, economy and politics: The case of new labour*, ed. David Hesmondhalgh, Kate Oakley, David Lee, and Melissa Nisbett, 36–69. Basingstoke: Palgrave Macmillan.
Hewison, Robert. 2014. *Cultural capital: The rise and fall of creative Britain*. London: Verso.
Housing Problems. 1935. Directed by Arthur Elton and Edgar Anstey. London: British Commercial Gas Association. Film, 13min.
Humphrey, Christopher, Miller Peter, and Robert W. Scapens. 1993. Accountability and accountable management in the UK public sector. *Accounting, Auditing & Accountability Journal* 6(3): 7–29.
Humphreys, Laura, ed. 2015. *Research on display: A guide to collaborative exhibitions for academics*. London: Queen Mary University of London. http://www.geog.qmul.ac.uk/docs/staff/147183.pdf
Immel, Andrea, and Michael Whitmore (eds.). 2006. *Childhood and children's books in early modern Europe, 1550–1800*. Abingdon: Routledge.
Innes, Judith E., and David E. Booher. 2010. *Planning with complexity: An introduction to collaborative rationality for public policy*. London: Routledge.
Jones, Max. 2007. What should historians do with heroes? *History Compass* 5(2): 439–454.
Kandinsky, Vasilii. 1980. *The life of Vasilii Kandinsky in Russian art: A study of "on the spiritual in art"*, ed. John E. Bowlt. Trans. Rose-Carol Washton Long. Newtonville: Oriental Research Partners.
Katan, Simon, Mick Grierson, and Rebecca Fiebrink. 2015. Using interactive machine learning to support interface development through workshops with disabled people. In *CHI '15: Proceedings of the 33rd annual ACM conference on human factors in computing systems*, 251–254. New York: ACM.
Kellett, Mary. 2009. Children and young people's voice. In *Children and young people's worlds: Developing frameworks for integrated practice*, ed. Heather Montgomery and Mary Kellett, 239–241. Bristol: The Policy Press.
Landes, William M. 2000. Copyright, borrowed images, and appropriation art: An economic approach. *George Mason Law Review* 9(1): 1–24.
Laurel, Brenda. 1991. *Computers as theatre*, 2nd ed. Boston: Addison-Wesley Educational Publishers.
Leach, James, and Lee Wilson. 2014. *Subversion, conversion, development: Cross-cultural knowledge exchange and the politics of design (infrastructures)*. Boston: MIT Press.

Lee, Grieveson, and Colin MacCabe (eds.). 2011a. *Empire and film*. London: Palgrave Macmillan on behalf of the British Film Institute.
Lee, Grieveson, and Colin MacCabe (eds.). 2011b. *Film and the end of empire*. Basingstoke: Palgrave Macmillan.
Liarou, Eleni. "World in a cube—Project report." 2013. http://www.creativeworkslondon.org.uk/wp-content/uploads/2013/11/NMN-Creative-Voucher-Final-Report.pdf
Lin, Jianhua. 1991. Divergence measures Based on the Shannon entropy. *IEEE Transactions on Information Theory* 37(1): 145–151.
Lipman, Caron. 2010. *Geffrye museum and Queen Mary University of London partnership: Feasibility study, final report*. London: Queen Mary University of London.
Locke, John. 1960. Two treatises of government, ed. Peter Laslett. Cambridge: Cambridge University Press.
Loiperdinger, Martin. 1999. *Stollwercks Geschäfte mit lebenden Bildern*. Frankfurt am Main: Stroemfeld/Roter Stern.
Löwgren, Jonas, and Erik Stolterman. 2004. *Thoughtful interaction design: A design perspective on information technology*. Cambridge: MIT Press.
MacLeod, Gordon. 2000. The learning region in an age of austerity: Capitalizing on knowledge, entrepreneurialism, and reflexive capitalism. *Geoforum* 31(2): 219–236.
Matheson-Pollock, Helen. 2016. *Creativeworks London: A knowledge exchange hub for the creative economy 2012–2016*. London: CWL. http://www.creativeworkslondon.org.uk/cw-news/creativeworks-london-evaluation-report-a-knowledge-exchange-hub-for-the-creative-economy/
Mayall, Berry. 2002. *Towards a sociology of childhood: Thinking from children's lives*. Buckingham: Open University Press.
McCann, Anthony. 2001. All that is not given is lost: Irish traditional music, copyright, and common property. *Ethnomusicology* 45(1): 89–106.
McIntyre, Alice. 2008. *Participatory action research*. London: SAGE.
McRobbie, Angela. 2016. *Be creative: Making a living in the new culture industries*. Cambridge: Polity Press.
Melville, Caspar. 2005. Building knowledge through debate: Open democracy on the Internet. In *Participating in the knowledge society*, ed. RH Finnegan, 198–212. Basingstoke: Palgrave Macmillan.
Mercer, Kobena. 1995. Art of Africa. *Artists' Newsletter*, December, 28–30.
Merchant, Guy, and Julia Davies. 2009. *Web 2.0 for schools: Learning and social participation*. New York: Peter Lang.
Miles, Ian, and Paul Cunningham. 2006. *Smart innovation: Supporting the monitoring and evaluation of innovation programmes*. Brussels: European Commission.
Miller, Henry K. 2014. Sleeve notes. *The soviet example: From Turksib to night mail*, directed by Victor Turin. London: British Film Institute. DVD.

Mitra, Jay, and John Edmondson. 2015. *Entrepreneurship and knowledge exchange.* London: Routledge.
Moran, Joe. 2010. *Interdisciplinarity: The new critical idiom*, 2nd ed. London: Routledge.
Moravec, John W. (ed.). 2013. *Knowmad society.* Minneapolis: Education Futures.
"Movements: Selections from the June Givanni Pan-African Cinema Archive." Chelsea College of Arts and Birkbeck Institute of the Moving Image, exhibition catalogue, 16–27 October 2014. http://www.creativeworkslondon.org.uk/wp-content/uploads/2014/10/Movements-programme-web.pdf
NESTA. 2011. *A Guide to Creative Credits.* London.
Norman, Donald A. 2002. *The design of everyday things.* New York: Basic Books.
O'Conner, Justin, and Kate Oakley. 2015. The cultural industries: An introduction. In *The Routledge companion to the cultural industries*, ed. Justin O'Conner and Kate Oakley, 1–33. London: Routledge.
OECD Innovation Policy Platform. 2010. Innovation vouchers. http://www.oecd.org/innovation/policyplatform/48135973.pdf
Oswell, David. 2013. *The agency of children: From family to global human rights.* Cambridge: Cambridge University Press.
Palfrey, John, and Urs Gasser. 2013. *Born digital: Understanding the first generation of digital natives*, 2nd ed. New York: Basic Books.
Pascoe, Carla. 2008. Putting away the things of childhood: Museum representations of children's cultural heritage. In *Designing modern childhoods: History, space, and the material culture of children*, ed. Marta Gutman and Ning de Coninck-Smith, 209–221. New Brunswick: Rutgers University Press.
Penny, S. 1996. From A to D and back again: The emerging aesthetics of interactive art. *Leonardo Electronic Almanac* 4(4). http://www.leoalmanac.org/wp-content/uploads/2012/07/LEA-v4-n4.pdf
Pérez-Quiñones, Manuel A., and John L. Sibert. 1996. A collaborative model of feedback in human-computer interaction. Proceedings of the SIGCHI conference on Human Factors in Computing Systems, ACM.
Posner, Richard A. 2005. Intellectual property: The law and economics approach. *Journal of Economic Perspectives* 19(2): 57–73.
Potts, Jason, S. Cunningham, John Hartley, and P. Ormerod. 2008. Social network markets: A new definition of the creative industries. *Journal of Cultural Economics* 32(3): 167–185.
Pratt, Andy C. 2010. Creative cities: Tensions within and between social, cultural and economic development. A critical reading of the UK experience. *City, Culture and Society* 1(1): 13–20.
Pratt, Andy C. 2015a. Do economists make innovation; do artists make creativity? The case for an alternative perspective on innovation and creativity. *Journal of Business Anthropology* 4(2): 235–244.
Pratt, Andy C. 2015b. Resilience, locality and the cultural economy. *City, Culture and Society* 6(3): 61–67.

Pratt, Andy C. in press. Innovation: From transfer to translation. Illuminating the cultural economy. In *The Elgar companion to innovation and knowledge creation: A multi-disciplinary approach*, ed. H. Bathelt, P. Cohendet, S. Henn, and L. Simon. Cheltenham: Edward Elgar.
Pratt, Andy C., and Paul Jeffcutt (eds.). 2009. *Creativity, innovation and the cultural economy*. London: Routledge.
Preece, Jenny, Yvonne Rogers, and Helen Sharp. 2002. *Interaction design, beyond HCI*. New York: Wiley.
Price, John. 2008. *Postman's park: G. F. Watts's memorial to heroic self-sacrifice*. Compton: Watts Gallery.
Price, John. 2014. *Everyday heroism: Victorian constructions of the heroic civilian*. London: Bloomsbury.
Price, John. 2015. *Heroes of postman's park: Heroic self-sacrifice in Victorian London*. Stroud: The History Press.
Prout, Alan. 2005. *The future of childhood: Towards an interdisciplinary study of children*. Abingdon: Routledge.
Quality Assurance Agency. 2014. Subject Benchmark statement, history. The Quality Assurance Agency for Higher Education. http://www.qaa.ac.uk/en/Publications/Documents/SBS-consultation-history.pdf
Ramsey, Phil, and Andrew White. 2015. Art for art's sake? A critique of the instrumentalist turn in the teaching of media and communications in UK Universities. *International Journal of Cultural Policy* 21(1): 78–96.
"Realising the Full Potential of Innovation Voucher Programs: The Riga Declaration." 2010. European Commission Enterprise and Industry. http://hytetra.eu/d/news/Riga_declaration.pdf
Robinson, Ken. 2006. How schools kill creativity. *TED Talks*. http://www.ted.com/talks/ken_robinson_says_schools_kill_creativity
Ross, Andrew. 2010. *Nice work if you can get it: Life and labor in precarious time*. New York: New York University Press.
Russell, Patrick, and James Taylor (eds.). 2010. *Shadows of progress: Documentary film in Post-War Britain*. Basingstoke: Palgrave Macmillan.
Sapsed, Jonathan, and Paul Nightingale. 2013. The Brighton Fuse. http://www.brightonfuse.com/wp-content/uploads/2013/10/The-Brighton-Fuse-Final-Report.pdf
Sargeant, Jonathon, and Deborah Harcourt. 2012. *Doing ethical research with children*. Maidenhead: Open University Press.
Schaffer, Eric. 2009. Beyond usability: Designing web sites for persuasion, emotion, and trust. *UX Matters*. http://www.uxmatters.com/mt/archives/2009/01/beyond-usability-designing-web-sites-for-persuasion-emotion-and-trust.php
Scott, Allen J. 2004. Cultural-products industries and urban economic development: Prospects for growth and market contestation in global context. *Urban Affairs Review* 39(4): 461–490.

"Screen Griots: The Art and Imagination of African Cinema." 1995. British Film Institute programme, August–December.
Seeger, Anthony. 1992. "Ethnomusicology and music law." In "Music and the public interest." Special issue. *Ethnomusicology* 36(3): 345–359.
Seton, Rosemary E. 1984. *The preservation and administration of private archives. A RAMP study.* Paris: Record and Archives Management Programme and UNESCO.
Shiach, Morag, Jana Riedel, and Jasmina Bolfek-Radovani. 2014. Fusing and creating: A comparative analysis of the knowledge exchange methodologies underpinning Creativeworks London's Creative Vouchers and London creative and digital fusion's collaborative awards. Creativeworks London working paper no. 25, Creativeworks London/Queen Mary, University of London. https://qmro.qmul.ac.uk/xmlui/bitstream/handle/123456789/11413/Shiach%20Fusing%20and%20Creating%202014%20Published.pdf?sequence=1
Simunye—The Third Mill. Directed by Peter Grossett. London: Tate & Lyle in partnership with the Royal Swaziland Sugar Corporation, early 1980s. Film, 33min.
Solimano, Andrés. 2006. The international mobility of talent and its impact on global development: An overview. Discussion paper no. 2006/08, UNU World Institute for Development Economics Research (UNU-WIDER), Helsinki. https://www.wider.unu.edu/sites/default/files/dp2006-08.pdf
Sussex, Elizabeth. 1976. *The rise and fall of British documentary: The story of the film movement founded by John Grierson.* Berkeley: University of California Press.
Swann, Paul. 2008. *The British documentary film movement, 1926–1946.* Cambridge: Cambridge University Press.
Taylor, J. 2005. Unweaving the rainbow: Research, innovation and risk in a creative economy. AHRC discussion paper. London: Arts and Humanities Research Council.
Thaler, Richard H., and Cass R. Sunstein. 2008. *Nudge: Improving decisions about health, wealth and happiness.* New Haven: Yale University Press.
Thursby, Jerry G., Richard Jensen, and Marie C. Thursby. 2001. Objectives, characteristics and outcomes of University licensing: A survey of major U.S. Universities. *Journal of Technology Transfer* 26(26): 59–72.
Ulrich, Roger S. 1979. *Landscape research: Visual landscapes and psychological well-being.* London: Taylor & Francis.
Van Heur, Bas. 2009. The clustering of creative networks: Between myth and reality. *Urban Studies* 46(8): 1531–1552.
Van Leyden, Nancy. 1996. Africa95: A critical assessment of the exhibition at the royal academy. *Cahiers d'Études Africaines* 36(141): 237–241.
Virani, Tarek E. 2014. Mechanisms of collaboration between creative small, medium and micro-sized enterprises and Higher Education Institutions:

Reflections on the Creativeworks London Creative Voucher Scheme." Creativeworks London working paper no. 4, Creativeworks London/Queen Mary, University of London. https://qmro.qmul.ac.uk/xmlui/bitstream/handle/123456789/6542/PWK-Working-Paper-4-SEO.pdf?sequence=2

Virani, Tarek E. 2015. Do voucher schemes matter in the long run? A brief comparison of Nesta's creative credits and Creativeworks London's Creative Voucher schemes. Creativeworks London working paper no. 10. Creativeworks London/Queen Mary, University of London. https://qmro.qmul.ac.uk/xmlui/bitstream/handle/123456789/6693/Working%20Paper%2010.pdf?sequence=2

Virani, Tarek E., and Andy C. Pratt. 2016. Intermediaries and the knowledge exchange process. In *Higher education and the creative economy: Beyond the campus*, ed. Roberta Comunian and Abigail Gilmore, 41–58. Abingdon: Routledge.

Vorley, Tim, Oli Mould, and Richard Courtney. 2012. My networking is not working! Conceptualizing the latent and dysfunctional dimensions of the network paradigm. *Economic Geography* 88(1): 77–96.

Webster, Frank. 2005. Research, Universities and the knowledge society. In *Participating in the knowledge society*, ed. RH Finnegan, 245–263. Basingstoke: Palgrave Macmillan

Wheeler, Steve. 2015. *Learning with 'E's: Educational theory and practice in the digital age*. Bancyfelin: Crown House.

Wood, Elizabeth, and Kiersten F. Latham. 2014. *The objects of experience: Transforming visitor-object encounters in museums*. Walnut Creek: Left Coast Press.

Zhu, Hong. 2005. *Software design methodology: From principles to architectural styles*. Oxford: A Butterworth-Heinemann.

INDEX

A
Academic Report and Recommendations, 173
accessibility, 36, 63, 64, 73, 78, 89, 157, 165, 168, 203, 210, 232, 235–6
access to market, 235
accountability, 19, 67, 233
ACE Digital R&D fund, 84
acquisition mechanics, 63
"action research" approach, 9
adaptation, 35, 111, 142
Adi, H., 168
advertising
  films, 47–8
  reverse advertising, 100
advocacy, 233, 239
affective communication, 104
affordances, 62, 73–4
Africa 95, 164
African, 54, 56, 163–78, 184, 185
agile development cycle, 71, 73, 77
Aimé Césaire: Une Parole pour le XXième siècle/ A Voice for the 21st Century, 168

AIR, 190
Akomfrah, J., 164, 168
Al Mubarak, L., 205
American, 164, 185
Application Programming Interface (API), 38
appropriation art, 134, 135
archives, 3, 9, 11, 49, 57–8, 106, 112, 157, 199, 212
  June Givanni Pan African cinema, 163–78, 227
archiving, 52, 155, 168, 172
art(s)
  appropriation, 134, 135
  commissioning, 189, 193, 195
  education, 40–1, 219, 237–9
  and health, 117–19
  and science, 85, 87, 94, 218
  and society, 68, 232
artistic practices, 103–4, 108
Arts and Humanities Research Council (AHRC), 1, 18, 84, 88, 152, 153, 164, 171, 173, 218, 222, 239

Note: Page numbers with "n" denote notes.

© The Author(s) 2017
M. Shiach, Tarek Virani (eds.), *Cultural Policy, Innovation and the Creative Economy*, DOI 10.1057/978-1-349-95112-3

Arts and Humanities Research
    Council (*cont.*)
  Creative Economy Showcase event, 39
  cultural value project, 87
Arts Council England, 238
Association of Art and Industry
    (Chicago), 69
"At Home with Japan: Beyond the
    Minimal House", 149
Attitudes (T&L documentary), 51–4
audio, 32, 136, 139, 165, 167, 175, 198
Audiovisual and Design Industries
    Innovation Scheme, 20
augmented reality, 39, 65
Auguiste, R., 168
Austin, P., 115
avant-garde filmmakers, 48, 57, 60n21
"The Aylesbury Estate as Home",
    157–8

B
Bailey, D. A., 166, 172
Bakari, I., 164, 166, 168
Bakhshi, H., 3
Barts Health NHS Trust, 116
Bauhaus, 68–70
Baxter, R., 157
Beale, K., 206
BeatWoven, 10–11, 133–45, 227
Becker, H., 182
Bell, D., 219
benefits, 209–12, 219
benevolence, 55, 56
Berners Lee, T., 73
biometrics, 71, 73
Biriotti, M., 111
Birkbeck, 9, 11, 12, 46, 49, 164–72,
    175, 189, 194
  Birkbeck Institute of the Moving
    Image (BIMI), 165
Bishops, D., 67
Black Artists and Modernism, 171
Black British, 164

Black Film Bulletin, 166
Black World, 366
Blockbuster, 64
blogs, 41, 222, 223
Blunt, A., 147–61
BOOST, 11, 169, 171, 172, 175, 176
bought, owned and earned media, 67
Bowman, S., 67
Boyce, S., 166, 167
Boyd, J., 183
brand, 10, 63–5, 67, 72, 73, 75, 77,
    90, 110, 235, 237
brand awareness remix app, 90
Brickwood, C., 7
Brighton Fuse, 27
British, 36, 52–6, 58, 68, 164, 182
  filmmaking, 46–50
British Refined (T&L documentary),
    50, 52–3, 55, 56
brokerage. *See* knowledge
    intermediary
BuMDA, 185
business, 1, 3, 100, 111–12, 181,
    183–6, 190, 191, 221, 226, 227,
    235, 237
  commercial, 174
  creative, 18, 23–4, 86, 108, 221,
    223–5
  design thinking, 69
  digital marketing, 85
  impacts of Creative Voucher scheme
    on, 6
  and innovation vouchers, 13, 20
  June Givanni Pan African Cinema
    Archive as, 169–70, 175, 176
  model, 2, 6, 11, 65, 74, 75, 109,
    143, 144
  and technology, 93
  and user experience, 78

C
capacitive sensing, 205
Caribbean, 52, 53, 164

Carthage Music, 11, 181–2
Central Saint Martins, 10, 115, 128, 130, 169, 171, 172
Centre for Studies of Home, 147–53, 157
challenges, meeting, 212–14
Cham, K., 9, 61–81
Cheeseburger Man project, 90
Chelsea College of Art, 166, 167, 169, 171
childhood friendship, 12, 202–4, 209, 211, 215
children, 12, 148, 201–5, 207–8, 209, 212, 215, 227
Chisenhale, 190
Christie, I., 9, 45–60, 166
cinema, 11, 46, 48
  advertising films, 47–8
  June Givanni Pan African cinema archive, 163–78, 227
  new wave, 48
circuits, 185, 204, 205
citizen science, 42
Cockburn, L., 207
co-creation, 1, 2, 8–10, 13, 18, 20, 186, 189
Codasign, 12, 201–5, 202–14, 207–14
code, 87, 110, 128, 139
co-design, 63–4, 68, 75, 76
co-evolution, 62, 68, 72, 73
cognitive engagement, 73
collaboration, 7, 9, 17–44, 147–61, 189–215
  creative, 231–44
  in practice, 204–9
Collaborative Doctoral Awards, 153–5
collection, 185, 208, 209
  film, 46–50, 57, 58
  Geffrye museum, 157, 160
  June Givanni Pan African Cinema Archive, 164, 165, 168–72, 174, 175
collections management, 155

collective action, 104, 107, 112
Commercial Gas Association, 57–8
Commercial User Experience Design, 65
community, 52, 100, 104, 105, 108, 112, 171, 194, 198, 212, 224, 238, 239
  academic, 39, 86–9
  dialysis, 115–31
  engagement, 13, 129, 154
  focus group, 54–6
  Stockwell Community Centre, 174
complex systems, 68, 72
Computers as Theatre (1991), 65
computing, 66, 67, 71, 86, 94, 203
Comunian, R., 8, 13, 231–44
constructivist approach to design, 69
contemporary art, 192
conversations, 32, 121, 126, 130, 165, 176, 189–93, 196–9, 204, 208, 215
conversion rates, 71
cookery, 10, 123–6, 129–30
Cookhouse Gallery, 167
Coombes, A., 166, 168
co-production, 158, 159, 203
copyright, 10–11, 11–12, 133–43, 144n8, 170, 173, 181–5
Copyright, Designs and Patent Act 1988 (CDPA), 138, 140
craft, 48, 84
Cranfield, B., 171
creative
  businesses, 24
  coding, 87
  collaborations (*see* creative collaborations)
  industries, 3–5, 18, 33, 34, 42, 63, 68, 84–5, 86, 105, 180, 182, 186, 220, 221, 234
  programmer, 90
  voucher, 2–6, 10–12, 19, 39, 97–114, 116, 217–18, 220,

creative (*cont.*)
  221, 223, 227, 228 (*see also* Creative Voucher scheme)
creative collaborations
  higher education institutions, role of, 237–9
  margins, 231–4
  networks, role of, 234–6
  policy, role of, 237–9
  power relations, 236–7
Creative Credits, 3, 18–19, 23–6, 220
  long-term effects of, 26
creative economy (CE), 1–3, 7, 9–10, 12, 13, 21, 23, 27, 84–5, 179, 190, 191, 199, 218, 221, 222, 226–8, 231–44
  lexicon, 182–3
  research and innovation in, 83–95
Creative Gallery, 24
Creative Hubs voucher program, 220
Creative Publics, 111
creative repurposing, 46
Creative Technology, 84–6, 89–92, 203–5, 209, 215
  research, incentivising, 86–8
Creative Voucher scheme, 2, 3, 8, 12, 17, 19, 21, 24, 32, 33, 217–29
  approaches to evaluation, 225–7
  idea, unpicking and interpreting, 219–21
  long-term effects of, 26
  reflections on, 228
  stages of, 6
  vouchers, making, 221–5
Creativeworks London (CWL), 1–3, 5–7, 11–13, 17–19, 21, 24–6, 32–3, 36, 38–40, 46, 62, 84, 88, 90, 93, 98, 111, 112, 115–16, 148, 156–7, 159, 164, 166, 168, 169, 172, 175, 189, 190, 210, 217, 218, 220, 222, 223, 225, 228, 229n7, 229n9
creativity, 7, 14, 94, 98, 103, 111, 113, 135, 234, 237–9
  managing, 106
critical thinking, 239
crowdfunding campaign, 86–7
cultural capital, 63, 64, 233, 236
cultural debate, 232
cultural exchange and learning, 112, 151, 152
cultural policy, 18–21, 23, 25, 27, 232
cultural production, 102
culture, 87, 98, 101, 148, 168, 184, 219, 232
curation, 3, 103, 105–7, 205, 213, 224

D
data linking, 38
Davies, J., 41
Deleuze, G., 73
demonstrating value, 5, 12, 233
Denton, N., 168
Department for Business, Innovation and Skills (BIS), 27
Department for Culture, Media and Sport (DCMS), 150
design, 6, 9, 18, 23, 74–8, 116, 122, 136–8, 141–3, 158, 197, 203, 208, 213, 214, 227
  co-design, 63–4, 68, 75, 76
Copyright, Designs and Patent Act 1988 (CDPA), 138, 140
  of Creative Credits scheme, 26
  of creative vouchers, 3
Digital Transformation Design, 61–81

experience-based design approach, 116, 131n2
generalised accessible design, 89–90
human-focused design, 67
participatory design, 75
Point, Line & Plane approach to design, 69
textile, 133, 136–8, 141
"trickle up" design research, 89
user centred design, 67
user experience design, 65–7, 78
user interaction design, 66
visual communication design, 71
design lead, 61, 64, 70
The Design of Everyday Things, 66–7
design space, 69
"Design Thinking" movement, 69–70
dialysis community, 10, 115–31
  learning about ward, 117
  narrative medicine, 117–18
  observing ward, 119–20
  outdoor visual environments, 126–8
  patient and staff interviews, 120–1
  patient complaints, 118
  patient forum, 128–9
  project ideas, developing, 122–4
  project ideas, piloting, 124–6
  taking stock, 121–2
Dialysis Cookbook, 124–6, 128–30
diaspora, 164, 168
Dibosa, D., 167
diffusion, 219, 220
digital, 9, 21, 33, 35, 49, 85, 174, 182, 205
Digital R&D, 89
disruption, 61, 63–4, 67–8, 70
Dix, A., 86
Docherty, D., 27
documentary, 46–9
domestic interiors, 148
Dowling, D. A., 87

Drucker, P., 219
Druiff, E., 12, 189–200
Dubber, A., 187n1
Duran, L., 179, 181

E
Eagleton, T., 180
Earle, W., 45–60, 166
early career researchers, 155, 159
East London, 10, 48–9, 50, 54, 147–9, 158, 212
eBay, 63
Economic and Social Research Council (ESRC), 18, 148
economic crisis 2007–2008, 232
economy, 8, 13, 18, 19, 68, 85, 87–8, 109, 111, 171, 191, 218
ecosystems, 13, 61, 64, 67, 72, 183, 221, 225
Edmondson, J., 3
education, 10, 27, 52, 75, 159, 169, 180, 194, 203, 222, 223, 227
  arts, 40–1, 219, 237–9
  higher, 10, 13, 27, 190, 219, 231–9
  learning and education programmes, 151, 153, 154
  and policy, 231–3, 237, 238
  and technology, 41
EEG, 73
electronics, 12, 139, 201, 203, 210, 215
emotional capital, 62, 73
emotional engagement, 62, 63, 73, 100
Emotional Touchpoints, 116, 131n3
emotion recognition technologies, 64
Empire Marketing Board, 47
e-textiles, 203, 204, 210
ethnomusicology, 184
European Commission, 88
European Regional Development Fund (ERDF), 21, 222

evaluation, 12, 24–5, 89, 92–3, 98, 110, 112–13, 117, 218, 220, 225–7, 228
  of technology projects, 6
Everyday Heroes of Postman's Park mobile app, 39
exclusivity, 63, 68
exhibitions, 9, 149, 151, 154–5, 157–9, 165–8, 170, 171, 176
exoticism of tropical labour, 56
experience-based design approach, 116, 131n2
Experience Questionnaire, 116
Experiences in Visual Thinking (1973), 69
eye tracking, 62, 71, 73

F
fabric, 58, 135–41, 231
faceless workforce, 53
"factory gate" filming, 46
A Family Affair (T&L documentary), 51
Faste, R., 69
feasibility study, 148
feature creep, 91
film, 9, 45–6, 45–58, 158, 164–8, 170–3, 175, 227
Finnegan, R., 186
The Fish Police (band), 10, 90
focus group
  community, 54–6
  history, 52
forum, 12, 128–9, 151, 201, 205–14
found footage, 57, 60n21
friendship, 207–9
  childhood, 202–4
The Friends of the Watts Memorial, 42
Frith, S., 179
funding, 11, 17, 19–21, 62, 148, 180, 189–91, 198, 199, 217, 222, 225, 226, 235, 237–9
  applications for, 33
  Centre for Studies of Home, 150, 152–5, 157, 159–60
  Creative Technology, 86–90
  Creativeworks London, 1, 2
  crowdfunding campaign, 86–7
  cuts, 194, 232, 233, 237, 239
  for digital collaboration, 38, 40
  higher education, 27, 30n26
  leveraged, 226
  long-term, 170
  "Making Friends" project, 210–14
  Platform 7, 108–10
  private sector, 109
  public, 13, 84, 89, 93, 110, 171, 173, 175
  pump-prime, 83
  short-term, 108
  software services, 86–7
  and sustainability, 110
  of technology projects, 93–4
  World in a Cube project, 46, 49
Fusion Collaborative Awards (FCA) scheme, 20–1
Future Cemetery Project, 33

G
gallery, 24, 102, 157, 160, 166–8, 172, 209
Galloway, A., 7–8
Garcia, D., 7
Gasser, U., 40
Geffrye Museum of the Home, 11, 147–60
General Post Office, 47
Gibbs, D., 116
Gilbert, J., 187n1
Giles, E., 12, 201–15
Givanni, J., 11, 163–78, 227
global city, 149
"Globe", 158

Goldsmiths Digital, 9–10, 83–95, 111, 174, 189
Goodwin, P., 166, 167
Gould, G., 166
governance, 238
government policy, 180, 219
Granger, A., 117, 118
Great Events and Ordinary People (1979), 56
Gregson, G., 32–9
Grierson, J., 48
Grierson, M., 9, 83–95
griots, 181
Gropius, W., 69
Grundkurs, 69
Guattari, F., 73
guest curators, 63

H
hardware, 10, 84
Harvard Graduate School of Design, 69
Heart n Soul, 10, 89–94
Heritage Lottery Fund (HLF), 160, 173
 Start-Up Grant, 173
 Young Roots and Transitional Grants, 173
Heroes of Postman's Park: Victorian Self-Sacrifice in Victorian London, 39
heroism, 34, 37, 38
higher education, 10, 13, 190, 219, 231–9
 funding, policy for, 27
Higher Education Funding Council of England (HEFCE), 27, 30n26
Higher Education Innovation Fund (HEIF), 169
higher education institutions (HEIs), 194, 199

role in creative collaborations, 237–9
Hinder, H.
 Money No Object, 227
historical research, 8–9, 31–44
history, 34, 39, 41–2, 51, 55, 58, 71, 78, 158
 filmmaking, 48, 49
 focus group, 52
 post-colonial, 53
 visual, 57
History of the World in 100 Objects (BBC), 41
HMV, 64
home, 147–61
"Home and the Housing Crisis", 158
"Homes of the Homeless: Seeking Shelter in Victorian London", 149
Hope, S., 12, 189–200
hospital, 10, 115–17, 120–2, 128
hospitality industry, 67
housing crisis, 158
Housing Problems (documentary), 58, 60n23
Hulme, S., 75
human centred, 61, 64, 69, 71, 111
Human-Computer Interaction (HCI), 62, 66, 67, 71
human-focused design, 67

I
Ideas Pools, 3–6
IDEO, 69, 70
image recognition technology, 32, 34
Immel, A., 203
impact, 112, 169, 180
 of austerity politics, 191
 of change in sociopolitical environment, 190
 of Creative Credits scheme, 25, 26
 of Creative Technology, 85, 87–9

impact (*cont.*)
  of Creative Voucher scheme, 6, 12, 17, 226–7
  of economic crises, 232
  of feature creep, 91
  of innovation, 83
  of innovation voucher schemes, 2, 3, 13, 18
  of networks, 234
  non-quantifiable, 109
  of P7, 107–9, 111
  of peer-to-peer news network, 67
  of power, 236
  research, 142–4, 150
  of Watts Memorial app project, 40, 42
implicit response testing, 73
incentivization techniques, 71
industrial relations, 54
infringement, 138, 140, 142, 144, 145n15
Innovate UK, 20, 86–8
innovation, 2, 13, 18–21, 23, 25, 27, 40, 68, 78, 98, 100, 111, 182, 186, 218–20, 234
  in creative economy, 9–10, 83–95
  reductive, 61
innovation broker. *See* knowledge intermediary
innovation voucher scheme, 2, 3, 8, 12, 13, 17–24, 182, 220. *See also* Creative Voucher scheme
  mechanisms, 20
  types, 22–3
  variability of, 26
instrumental value, 232–3
intellectual property (IP), 27, 134, 182
  rights, 134
interaction design, 66
Interaction Design, Beyond HCI, 66
interactivity, digital, 66, 72
interdisciplinarity, 34–5, 38
Itten, J., 69

J

Jeavons, C., 164
John, E., 147–61, 151
June Givanni Pan African Cinema Archive (JGPACA), 11, 163–78, 227

K

Kelley, D. M., 69
Kenyon, J., 46, 58n2
Kesimoglu, A., 99
kidney disease, 117, 120, 121
Kingston University, 74, 75
Kneepens, S., 115
knowledge
  connecting and disconnecting, 234–6
  narrative, 117–18
  and power relations, 236–7
  providers, 19, 20
  society, 219
  support, 235
  trading, 110
  transfer, 18, 19, 24, 98, 160, 171, 185, 218–20, 228
knowledge exchange, 2, 3, 8, 10, 12, 17–30, 97, 98, 106, 107, 113, 151, 152, 218–20, 222, 223, 225, 227, 228, 233
knowledge intermediary, 25–6
Knowledge Transfer Partnerships, 21
Knowmads, 40–1
Kodak, 64

L

labour markets-network interaction, 234–5
Laing, D., 179
Laurel, B., 65

law, 11, 133–5, 137–40, 142, 143, 184
Leach, J., 3
learning and education programmes (museums), 151, 153, 154
leveraged funding, 226
Liarou, E., 45–60
Lipman, C., 148
literature, 3, 20, 25, 106, 219, 234
localism, 174, 186, 190, 234, 235, 237–9
Loiperdinger, M., 59n7
London Creative and Digital Fusion programme, 20–1, 84
London Fusion, 88
London small scale art organisations, 191
Louis, R., 10, 115–31
Löwgren, J., 66, 71

M
Mady, K., 183
maker movement, 87
"Making Friends", 12, 201–15, 227
  childhood friendship, 202–4
  collaboration in practice, 204–9
  complex challenges together, meeting, 212–14
  powerful resourcing, benefits of, 211–12
  shared ethos, benefits of, 209–11
marble telephone answering machine, 67
Markel, K., 45
Markham, J., 75
Massiah, L., 168
Matheson-Pollock, H., 12, 217–29
Mattocks, K., 99
McKiernan, J., 10, 97–114
McKim, R., 69
meaning, 63, 72, 85, 112, 113, 193, 218, 225

media, 40, 62, 64–7, 72, 74, 102, 106, 109, 128, 157, 169, 180, 205
Melville, C., 179–88
Merchant, G., 41
Mériau, N., 157
Merkel, K., 45–60
methodology, 18–21, 49, 64, 67, 68, 72, 78, 89, 100, 112, 113, 182, 195, 198, 201, 205, 208–10, 212, 226, 227
  of Creative Voucher scheme, 26
  FCAs, 21
  film research, 46
  in historical research, 42
  research, 2, 52
micro-enterprises, 107
micro-locality, 10
middle class, 148–9, 154
migration, 52, 56, 62, 149, 158
Mills, C. W., 182
Mitchell, S., 46, 58n2
Mitra, J., 3
mobile applications, 31–44
mobile culture, 8, 9, 31–44
modernism, 69
Mogaji, A., 45–60
Moholy-Nagy, L., 69
Money No Object, 227
mood boards, 136, 145n10
Moran, T., 66
Moravec, J., 40
Morris, G., 183, 184
Movements: Selections from the June Givanni Pan-African Cinema Archive, 167, 168, 171
Mulvey, L., 165, 166, 168
museums, 11, 31, 45, 55, 171, 175, 178n17, 208, 209, 227
museum-university partnership, 147–61

music, 11, 85, 89–90, 133, 135–43, 145n15, 145n20, 145n21, 179–85
 ethnomusicology, 184
 promotion, 48
 publishing, 182

N
narrative knowledge, 117–18
Narrative Medicine, 117–19
National Co-ordinating Centre for Public Engagement, 39
Engage Competition, 39
National Endowment for Science Technology and the Arts. *See* NESTA
National Research Ethics Service (NRES), 116
natural right theories, 135
needlework, 122
Négritude and the Archive, 168
neoliberalism, 150, 180, 185, 220
NESTA, 27–8n4, 84, 88
 Creative Credits scheme, 3, 18–19, 23–6, 220
Netflix, 63
networks, 12, 13
 of artists, 106
 interaction with labour markets, 234–5
 role in creative collaborations, 234–6
neuromarketing, 73
Newell, A., 66
New Media Networks, 9, 45–6
NHS, 116–17, 128, 131n2
Norman, D., 65, 66
nudging, 28n6
Nurse, P., 87
nutrition, 126, 129

O
Ocran, N., 165
Olleson, M., 32–9
One Sixth of the World (1926), 48
ontologies, 38
oral history, 53
Oswell, D., 202
outdoor visual environments, 126–8
outreach, 173, 174, 205, 224
Owens, A., 11, 147–61

P
Palcy, E., 166, 168
Palfrey, J., 40
Pan-African, 164–6, 168, 169, 175, 176
Pan-African Cinema, 168
participation, 9, 13, 72, 75, 99, 102–4, 205–8, 211, 213
Participatory Action Research (PAR), 99, 112
participatory design, 75
partnerships, 1, 9, 13, 24–6, 41, 42, 46, 55, 190, 196, 199, 223, 225, 229n7, 233, 237, 238
 within academics, 37
 Creative Voucher scheme, 2
 Knowledge Transfer Partnerships, 21
 museum-university, 11, 147–61
Pascoe, C., 203–4
paternalism, 55, 56
Paterson, R., 166
patient interviews, 120–1
patronage, 166, 231
Peckham Platform, 190, 191, 194
Peck, R., 166
peer-to-peer news network, 67
period rooms, 148, 149, 156, 157

persuasion, emotion and trust (PET), 71, 72
Pervasive Intelligence Ltd, 33
PhD students, 151–3, 155, 159
photography, 154
physical computing, 203
physical infrastructure, 237–8
physical labour, 56
place-based activities, 104
Platform 7, 10, 97–114
Platun, J., 158
Point, Line & Plane approach to design, 69
Polding, R., 166
policy, 10, 12, 13, 93, 98, 113, 128, 136, 148, 180, 218, 219, 231–44
 cultural, 2, 3, 8, 17–30, 232, 233
 economic, 233, 238
 higher education, 231–3, 237, 238
 innovation instruments, 19, 221 (*see also* innovation voucher scheme)
 neoliberal imperatives, 150
 New Labour, 232
 public sphere, 233
 role in creative collaborations, 237–9
Postman's Park, 8, 31–44
poststructuralism, 72
powerful resourcing, benefits of, 211–12
power relations, 233–4, 236–7
practice-based research, 62, 158, 195
Pratt, A., 10, 12, 97–114, 217–29
predictive analytics, 71
Preece, J., 66
Price, J., 8, 31–44
Private Finance Initiative (PFI), 128
problem definition, 70, 71
process as outcome, 183–5
process flow diagram, 75, 76

professional development, 235
Prophet Mohammed, 67
Prossimo Ventures, 32, 39, 40
pro-sumption, 108
prototype product customization, 62
prototyping, 89, 90, 92
public engagement, 9, 33, 49, 150, 151, 222
 with films, 52
public realm, 102
pump-prime funding, 83

Q
Quality Assurance Agency, 41
Queen Mary University of London (QMUL), 11, 201, 202, 208, 212, 213

R
rapid development frameworks, 92–3
RAPID-MIX, 88, 93
RDF ontology, 38
recipe, 124–7, 129
reflection, 101
relational value, 232, 233
Remembrance Day, 104
remix competition, 57
renal. *See* dialysis community
reproduction, 139–41
research
 in creative economy, 83–95
 and design, 69
 grants, 86–8, 87, 159, 211
 historical, 8–9, 31–44
 impact, 142–4, 150
 methodologies, 2
 practice-based, 62, 158, 195
Research Excellence Framework (REF), 85, 86, 150
"Research in Progress Day", 151

RESTful API, 38
The Retirement of Mr Strauss (T&L documentary), 51, 53, 55
reverse advertising, 100
Reynolds, S., 187n1
Ricketts, N., 143
Riga Declaration, 20
Roberts, M., 166
Rodney, D., 10, 90
Rogers, Y., 66
Ross, A., 180
Royal Commonwealth Society, 49
Ruiz, R., 56
Russell, P., 59n10
Rutherford, A., 157

S
Sandon, E., 11, 163–78
science, 113
 and arts, 85, 87, 94, 218
 citizen science, 42
 and higher education, 238
 parks, 219
The Sciences of the Artificial (1969), 69
Scottish Health Council, 131n3
Screen Griots, 164
secondary school, 190
semantics, 72–3
Shaffer, E., 71
Shakiry, R., 73
shared ethos, benefits of, 209–11
Sharp, H., 66
shedding of empire, 55
Shemtov, N., 10–11, 133–45
Shiach, M., 1–15, 17–30
Shonibare, Y., 58
Shoreditch, 148, 157
The Showroom, 190
Silent Cacophony (SC) event, 10, 98–9, 101–2
Simon, H. A., 69

Simunye—The Third Mill (T&L documentary), 51, 53
sketchbooks, 136
small and medium size enterprises (SMEs), 1–3, 5, 7, 13, 17–20, 23–7, 33–5, 37, 86–7, 93, 165, 172, 181, 182, 184–5, 194, 199, 211, 221, 226–7
SOAS, 181–2
Social Art Map (SAM), 12, 189–200
social art practice, 189, 191, 192, 199
social capital, 233, 236
social change, 52–3, 195
social networks, 181
soft infrastructure, 238
software, 37, 84
Soundlab Framework, 89–90
specifications, in technology projects, 91–2
Spotify, 63
Sprint0, 70, 73
staff interviews, 120–1
Steinmann, C., 181, 183
stereotypes, 56
stock, taking, 121–2
Stockwell Community Centre, 174
Stoke Newington School, 201, 204, 207, 212, 213
Stolterman, E., 66, 71
storytelling, 73
"Studies of Home", 151
Sullivan, L. H., 69
superdiversity, 149
sustainability, 109–10
system two cognition, 62, 73

T
Tate & Lyle Sugars, 9, 45–60
technology, 12, 32–4, 61, 64–5, 67–8, 70, 78, 93, 133, 135–6
 Creative Technology, 84–92, 203–5, 209, 215

INDEX 269

digital, 3, 40, 42, 157
  and education, 41
  emotion recognition, 64
  image recognition, 32, 34
  "Making Friends" project, 201–15
  projects, 6, 91–4
  and young people, 40–1
television advertising, 48
Terracciano, A., 175
textile, 10–11, 133–45
  design, 133, 136–8, 141
  e-textiles, 203, 204, 210
The Culture Capital Exchange (TCCE), 2, 3, 221, 222
Thoughtful Interaction Design: A Design Perspective on Information Technology, 66
The Tights Ball: in the tights project, 114n3
time-based activities, 104
transatlantic slave trade, 53
transformation, 8, 11, 32–3, 46
  Digital Transformation Design, 9, 61–81
  of micro-locality, 10
  use as creative expression, 133–5, 142
translation, defined, 137
"trickle up" design research, 89
Trindade, L., 166
Trip Advisor, 67
Turin, V., 48
TurkSib (1929), 48, 59n8

U
Uber, 65
UK Copyright Act, 138–40
universities, 1–2, 180, 186, 190–1, 219, 222, 231, 236, 238
  as anchor institutions, 18, 27, 30n26
  networks developed with, 235

university-museum partnership, 11, 147–61
University of Lancaster, 20–1
University of Roehampton, 39
University of Surrey, 33
University of the Arts, London, 166–7, 168, 171, 172, 175
"Unlocking the Geffrye", 160
Urheberrechtsgesetz (UrhG), 142
use-inspired research, 83
user centred design (UCD), 67
user completion model, 63, 64, 75, 76
user experience, 35, 61, 62, 64, 66, 67, 71–3
  definition of, 65
user experience design (UXD), 65–7, 78
User Experience Realisation (USR), 32, 35
user generate content (UGC), 9, 62–3, 67, 68, 72
user interaction design (UID), 66
US Patent and Trademark Office, 70

V
value chain, 68
value mechanics, 62, 63, 73
Vertov, D., 48
Virani, T. E., 1–15, 17–30, 217–29
virtual connectivity, 107
Visit-AR, 33
visual communication design, 71
visual history, 57
visualisation, 157
Vital Arts, 10, 115, 119, 128, 130, 227
Vorkurs, 69
Vormittag, L., 10, 115
voucher experience, 10, 97, 112
voucher scheme. *See* Creative Voucher scheme; innovation voucher scheme

W

Ward, S., 75
Watts, G. F., 31, 42
Watts Memorial, 8, 31–2, 33, 35, 37–9, 42
Web 2.0, 67
WEB Dubois: A Biography in Four Voices, 168
Web Services Description Language (WSDL), 38
Webster, F., 186
Welford Road Cemetery app, 33
"West Indian Front Room: Memories and Impressions of Black British Homes", 149
Wheeler, K., 172
Wheeler, S., 41
Whitehouse, T., 12, 201–15
"Widening the Register", 222, 223
Willcocks, J., 171
Willis, C., 67
Wilson, L., 3
Window to the Outside World, 126–30
Wood, J., 111
Worden, P., 58n2
workshop, 6, 33, 152, 164, 166, 182, 223
  creative technology, 203–5, 209–14
  Idea Forum, 12, 201
World in a Cube project, 45–60
Wright, F. L., 69

Y

young people, 54, 159, 203–8, 211
  and digital technologies, 40–1